Mary,
the First Disciple

Mary,
the First Disciple

A Guide for Transforming
Today's Church

Marie Azzarello CND

NOVALIS

© 2004 Novalis, Saint Paul University, Ottawa, Canada

Cover design: Caroline Gagnon
Cover image: Photodisc
Layout: Christiane Lemire and Francine Petitclerc

Business Office:
Novalis
49 Front Street East
Toronto, Ontario, Canada
M5E 1B3

Phone: 1-877-702-7773 or (416) 363-3303
Fax: 1-877-702-7775 or (416) 363-9409
E-mail: cservice@novalis.ca
www.novalis.ca

Library and Archives Canada Cataloguing in Publication

Azzarello, Marie
         Mary, the first disciple : a guide for transforming today's
church / Marie Azzarello.

Includes bibliographical references.
ISBN 2-89507-521-2

         1. Mary, Blessed Virgin, Saint. I. Title.

BT603.A99 2004   232.91   C2004-904289-0

Printed in Canada.

The Scripture quotations contained herein are from the New Revised Standard Version Bible, copyright © 1989 by the Division of Christian Education of the National Council of Churches of Christ in the United States of America. Used by permission.

We acknowledge the financial support of the Government of Canada through the Book Publishing Industry Development Program (BPIDP) for our publishing activities.

5 4 3 2 1   08 07 06 05 04

NOVALIS

Table of Contents

Acknowledgments

Countless persons have accompanied me on the journey of writing this book. I am deeply grateful to my Congregation of Notre Dame Sisters and Associates, among whom I continue to discover that the strength and depth of Marguerite Bourgeoys' vision of education lie in two pivotal moments of Mary's life: the Visitation and Pentecost. Both moments call us to presence and collaboration with others in building a Church and a world where justice and equality for all persons are possible.

I would particularly like to thank Fr. Johann Roten, S.M., director of the International Marian Research Institute, Dayton, Ohio, with whom I first shared my desire to write this book. His continued interest and inquiry into its progress has been a source of encouragement. I am very indebted to Fr. Bertrand Buby, S.M., a professor at the Institute, who, despite his heavy schedule, has carefully read this book at each stage of its development, offering suggestions, friendship, and encouragement. I very much appreciate the staff of the Institute, especially Br. Bill Fackovec, S.M., Librarian, whose hospitality made research a pleasure.

I am especially grateful to Rosemary Brosseau, Maura McGrath, Anne McNally, Elaine O'Grady, Patricia Landry, Kathryn Quigley, members of my Congregation and companions on the journey, for their continuous support and encouragement throughout these years. I am deeply thankful for my family's continued support and encouragement at all times and their interest in the progress of this book. I am also grateful to Barbara and Harold Thuringer for their friendship and encouragement to stay the course. Patricia Coon – wife, mother, friend,

Associate of my Congregation – has read this book chapter by chapter and raised questions that led me to further reflection and clarification of the text, and I am very appreciative of her help. I am indebted as well to Dr. Daniel Cere, Director, Newman Centre, McGill University, Montreal, for his assistance along the way and the many conversations we have shared about Cardinal Newman's perception of the priestly character of Christian men and women engaged in the world.

Abbreviations

CL   *Christifideles Laici* (Lay Members of Christ's Faithful), John Paul II, 1990, Pauline Books and Media.

DeV   *Dominum et Vivificantem* (Encyclical Letter on the Holy Spirit in the Life of the Church and the World), John Paul II, 1986, Pauline Books and Media.

DV   *Dei Verbum* (Dogmatic Constitution on Divine Revelation) in Austin Flannery, *The Conciliar and Post Conciliar Documents*, Vol. 1.

EN   *Evangelii Nuntiandi* (Evangelization in the Modern World), Paul VI, 1975, Pauline Books and Media.

GS   *Gaudium et Spes* (Pastoral Constitution on the Church in the Modern World), in Austin Flannery, Vol. 1.

LE   *Litterae Encyclicae* (Letter to All Consecrated Persons Belonging to Religious Communities and Secular Institutes on the Occasion of the Marian Year), John Paul II, *L'Osservatore Romano* (22 May 1988).

LG   *Lumen Gentium* (Dogmatic Constitution on the Church), in Austin Flannery, Vol. 1.

MC   *Marialis Cultis* (For the Right Ordering and Development of Devotion to the Blessed Virgin), Paul VI, 1974, Pauline Books and Media.

MD   *Mulieris Dignitatem* (Apostolic Letter on the Dignity and Vocation of Women), John Paul II, 1988, *Origins* (October 6, 1988).

MR   *Redemptoris Mater* (Mother of the Redeemer), John Paul II, 1987, Pauline Books and Media.

RH   *Redemptor Hominis* (Redeemer of Man), John Paul II, 1987, Publication of the Canadian Conference of Catholic Bishops.

RM   *Redemptoris Missio* (The Mission of the Redeemer), John Paul II, 1990, Pauline Books and Media.

Introduction

This is a book about Christian discipleship that presents Mary, the mother of Jesus, as a guide to a renewed image of discipleship and the transformation of the Church in today's world.

In the Acts of the Apostles, Luke provides the last image of Mary in the scriptures. Mary is in the Upper Room – united in prayer with the apostles, with certain women, and with Jesus' brothers – waiting to receive the Holy Spirit, as Jesus had promised. She is also there at the joy-filled moment when the Spirit comes upon the group gathered at Pentecost.

Through the centuries, Christians have held these texts sacred. As the memory of Pentecost celebrates the foundational moment of the Church year after year, they remind us of the central place of prayer in the life of the Christian community, and emphasize that Mary and other women were present at Pentecost.

Part I examines first the impact that scriptural silence about the presence of and active role these women played in the early Christian community has had on the life of the Church. We also become aware of the limitations that arise from Mary being presented as the model of Christian discipleship based solely on her "Yes" to God at the Annunciation. This perception of Mary limits her influence as a disciple of Jesus to the realm of private spirituality – a Christian's personal relationship with God. This image of Mary and the silence about the women disciples have helped maintain patriarchal structures in the Church, limiting women's participation in its life. A way out of this dilemma is a renewed image of discipleship that can speak to the reality of women and men trying to live their commitment as disciples of Jesus in today's continually evolving, complex world.

Part II proposes that this renewed image of discipleship can be found in the biblical memory of Mary, especially in reconnecting Luke's narratives of the Annunciation and the Visitation. In so doing, we see how Mary emerges as the archetype of Christian discipleship for women and men. She shows us that after hearing the word of God and allowing it to take shape in our hearts, we must share it with others – not simply by repeating it, but by interpreting it so that Jesus can be good news for others.

But Mary's story does not stop here. Scriptural references to Mary, read in the light of her vocation and Israel's perception that God's visitation is found in life experience, shed light on her growth as a disciple of Jesus, her faith journey – a journey which led her to and beyond Jesus' death and resurrection to Pentecost, the birth of the Church. Connections are made to every Christian's call as a disciple of Jesus, their faith journey.

We see how holding this memory of Mary offers Christian men and women a distinctive "journey spirituality" in keeping with the emphasis on life as journey, found in modern psychology and spirituality. Like Mary, Christians are called to carry Jesus with them wherever they go, to live in an attitude of visitation with all they meet.

Turning to the Christian disciple's call into community, Part III, drawing on the parallel structure of Luke and Acts, unfolds the connections between Mary as the archetype of Christian discipleship and the story of Pentecost. Step by step, we see that these narratives share the same motif of being sent in Jesus' name.

Finally, Part IV, connecting Pentecost, life in the primitive Christian community and the Church today, shows how Mary, the archetype of Christian discipleship, becomes a guide for the transformation of the Church into a community of equal disciples. Within this discussion, discipleship rooted in Jesus, modelled on Mary, becomes the operative identity of the community. As such, this Church becomes a church of participation, a church of solidarity, a church of communion, a servant church on fire with its priestly, prophetic, royal mission in Jesus' name.

It is my hope that these reflections on the scriptural memory of Mary will provide a prophetic, active, dynamic image of discipleship rooted in baptismal identity that speaks to the reality of Christian life in our complex, evolving world. Even though our times and social context are very different from those of Galilee and the Jerusalem that she knew, may Mary be the guide for the transformation of today's Church into a community of equal disciples.

Note: The traditional terms "Old Testament" and "New Testament" are problematic. "Old Testament" can mean "old" or "out of date" for some people. Out of respect for our Jewish brothers and sisters, the people of God of the First Covenant, I have chosen to use the terms "First Testament" and "Second Testament" in this book to designate the two main divisions of the Bible.

To designate historical periods, I use the abbreviations BCE ("Before the Common Era") and CE ("Common Era"), which cover the same periods as BC ("Before Christ") and AD ("Anno Domini" = "The Year of the Lord") respectively. The terms BCE and CE are more commonly used by biblical scholars than are BC and AD.

Part 1: Seeing with New Eyes

1

Setting the Stage: Luke and Acts

The opening verses of the Acts of the Apostles recount the appearances of the risen Jesus: his final teachings to the eleven, his instruction to them to wait in Jerusalem for their baptism in the Holy Spirit, and his Ascension (Acts 1:1-11). The eleven apostles, whom Luke (whom scholars agree also wrote Acts) has positioned alone at Jesus' Ascension, return from the Mount of Olives to Jerusalem, where they immediately go to the Upper Room. Luke even names them: Peter and John, James and Andrew, Philip and Thomas, Bartholomew and Matthew, James son of Alphaeus, Simon the Zealot, and Judas son of James. He notes that "all these were constantly devoting themselves to prayer, together with certain women, including Mary the mother of Jesus, as well as his brothers" (Acts 1:14). We learn that the group of women and men gathered together numbered about 120 (Acts 1:15). We gain some insight into the inner group of the community awaiting the fulfillment of Jesus' promise of the Holy Spirit (Acts 1:14). The text conveys a mood of expectancy.

Beyond prayer, we find the group, led by Peter, addressing the problem that the number of apostles has been reduced to eleven because of Judas Iscariot's death. Restoring the group of chosen apostles to twelve seems to require immediate attention. Peter makes it clear that Judas' replacement will join them as witnesses to Jesus' resurrection. For this to happen, he must be chosen from among the men who, along with them, have been with Jesus from the baptism of John until Jesus' ascension (Acts 1:21-22). Peter takes the lead, and the entire community, women and men, gathers to pray and cast lots to find Judas' replacement.

They choose Matthias. Following his election, we encounter the group all together in one place on the Jewish feast of Pentecost (Acts 2:1).

Pentecost, which took place 50 days after Passover, was one of the three pilgrimage festivals.[1] Jews were expected to celebrate the feast in Jerusalem, the Mother City (Lev 23). Known as the Feast of Weeks, Pentecost was a joyful celebration, a sacred assembly, a time for prayer and thanksgiving to God for the fruits of the spring harvest. No work was allowed on this day (Lev 23:21). The seven weeks from Passover to Pentecost link the two holidays.

It's hard to know what went on during this time. From the end of the sixth century BCE, this feast celebrated not only the first fruits of the harvest, but also God's covenant with Noah (Gen 9:15); in many scholars' view, by Jesus' time this feast was identified with the appearance of God to the Israelites at Mount Sinai in the desert (Exod 19). It also celebrated the anniversary of God's giving of the Torah (the first five books of the Bible) to the Israelites. This covenant between God and Israel, which enumerated the commandments, was the most important aspect of these celebrations.[2] Additionally, some ancient Jewish sources teach that Pentecost is the conclusion of Passover, claiming that the liberation from slavery commemorated at Passover is incomplete without God's revelation to the Israelites at Mount Sinai.[3]

During these days, Jerusalem would have been bustling with activity; the markets would have been filled with people selling and buying corn, fruit, vegetables, livestock, and wool, and also auctioning slaves. The money-changers would have been in great demand to give pilgrims exchange for their foreign currency; the pilgrims would also have paid their annual dues to the Temple treasury.[4]

Because this was an important Jewish feast, it is not surprising that Mary and Jesus' disciples were in Jerusalem to celebrate it.[5] Luke's description of the outpouring of the Spirit on the disciples using imagery of the God of the storm and of the fire descending on Mount Sinai (Exod 19:16, 18) is no doubt influenced by the Pentecost connection to the Sinai covenant, as well as by the imagery of the wind as the Spirit of God moving over the face of the waters at the creation (Gen 1:2). Jerusalem now replaces Sinai as the site of a renewed covenant with God that will touch all peoples: "And suddenly from heaven there came a sound like the rush of a violent wind, and it filled the entire house where they were sitting. Divided tongues, as of fire, appeared among them, and a tongue rested on each of them, filling with the Holy Spirit those who are to proclaim this renewed covenant" (Acts 2:14-17).[6]

In the text that follows, readers become aware that Mary, the other women, and the disciples, empowered by the Spirit, move out of the security of the Upper Room and into the streets. When they spoke their message, the Spirit allowed the people visiting Jerusalem to hear the message in their own native languages (Acts 2:2-11). Reactions varied. Some received what they saw and heard as mighty works of God (Acts 2:12); others scoffed at them and claimed they had been drinking (Acts 2:13).

Luke does not equate the disciples' ability to speak in different languages with glossolalia (speaking in tongues), which Paul refers to elsewhere (1 Cor 14:2); this gift requires the presence of an interpreter to help others understand what is being said. At Pentecost, however, the crowd did not need interpreters. The people gathered understood immediately what was being said to them (Acts 2:5-13).[7]

Peter, emerging as spokesperson for the group, recalls a First Testament prophesy of Joel: "In the last days it will be, God declares, that I will pour out my Spirit on all flesh, and your sons and your daughters shall prophesy.... Even upon my slaves, both men and women, in those days I will pour out my Spirit; and they shall prophecy" (Acts 2:17-18). Peter announces to the crowd that what they see and hear indicates that the prophesy is being fulfilled. He goes on to say that although Jesus had died, God raised him up (Acts 2:22-24).

Acts tells us that 3,000 Jewish pilgrims had assembled in Jerusalem for Pentecost. After their hearts are touched by Peter's speech about Jesus, many accept his invitation to "Repent, and be baptized every one of you in the name of Jesus Christ so that your sins may be forgiven; and you will receive the gift of the Holy Spirit" (Acts 2:38).[8] Peter extends this promise not only to them and their children, but to all who are far away – to all whom God calls (Acts 2:39).

For the Israelites, Passover, which commemorates the liberation of the Israelites from Egypt, was completed at Pentecost by the revelation of Sinai (Exod 19:16, 18). Now, "Jesus' liberating action for all humankind brought about through his death on the cross at Passover is completed by the revelation through the power of the Spirit given to the disciples at Pentecost that 'God had made Jesus both Lord and Messiah' (Acts 2:36)."[9]

Luke concludes chapters 1 and 2 of Acts with a description of this fledgling community, along with the first converts, devoting themselves to the apostles' teaching and fellowship, to the breaking of bread, and to prayers. All who believed, he says, were together, sharing all things in common, going daily to the temple, breaking bread at home, and praising God. Those who didn't join the group held them in high esteem (Acts 2:42-47).

For Luke, Pentecost began a new era in salvation history – a time when the main characteristic of the Church would be life in the Spirit. Peter's use of Joel's words supports the fact that the entire group gathered at Pentecost, not just the Twelve, received the power of the Spirit and the gift (charism) of prophecy equally, enabling them to become courageous missionaries in Jesus' name. The remainder of Peter's speech underlines Luke's perception that the reception of the Spirit was a gift for all.

The remaining chapters of Acts highlight the Spirit's role in the missionary activity that followed Pentecost, leading to the inclusion of Gentiles in the community of believers and to the awareness that Jesus was not only the Jewish Messiah but also the Saviour of the world.

These opening chapters of Acts raise a serious question: How might the early Christian community for which Acts was written have received these opening chapters?

Acts 1 and 2 and Luke's Christian Community

Such a dramatic story about the Spirit's entrance into the lives of these first disciples of Jesus must have provided this early Christian community with a sense of its roots. The first two chapters of Acts not only provided present and future believers with a memorable story of the Spirit's presence and guidance in the lives of Jesus' first followers, but also affirmed their continuity with Jesus. This was likely a source of encouragement and inspiration for Christians as they looked to the future in the hopes of inviting others to faith in Jesus.

The story of the Spirit's entry would likely have appealed to a Hellenistic audience, which would have seen wind and fire as signs of divine presence. The description of each person hearing in their own language (Acts 2:6) would have been credible in a society where divinely inspired speech was often discussed and described in works of pagan antiquity.[10]

Some Jewish listeners would have recalled that the values noted (Acts 2:42-47; cf. 4:32) as the glue of communal life in Jerusalem were also found in the descriptions of the Essenes' communal life.[11] Those coming from a Greco-Roman culture would have been familiar with the fact that sharing common property (Acts 2:44) had a long history in Greek and Latin literature.[12] The resolution of conflicts in the remainder of Acts suggests that these values were probably received as guidelines for how the Christian community was to live and work together. It is not surprising that the ideals describing communal life in the Jerusalem community have been presented since the beginning of the Church as worthy of emulation and as criteria by which to assess the quality of life within any group gathered in Jesus' name. How, though, would Luke's community, which lived in a Greco-Roman stratified society in and around Antioch, have heard, read, and interpreted Acts 1 and 2? These scriptures place Mary and certain other women alongside men, receiving the Spirit equally with them and moving together to found the Jerusalem community, which eventually becomes known as the Church.

A wide range of opinions around this question has surfaced in our time. For some, Mary's presence in the Upper Room establishes that Jesus was a historical figure. Mary provides the link between Jesus' birth and life and the birth and life of the Church. One commentary says that "the listing of the group in the Upper Room represents continuity with the Gospel. The apostles could bear witness to the public ministry of Jesus and the risen Jesus. The women could bear witness to the burial and the empty tomb (Lk 23:55–24:10) and Mary to events of Jesus' birth and youth (Lk 1–2)."[13] These observations on Acts 1:14, while significant, overlook the women's presence and involvement with Jesus during his ministry (Lk 8:1-3). They also do not emphasize that Luke saw Mary as a disciple of Jesus from the Annunciation onwards.

Luke's acknowledgment of her presence in the Upper Room (Acts 1:12-14) more likely expresses the Christian community's sacred memory of her. Mary, the woman who said "Yes" at the Annunciation, was now with her son's followers, united with them in prayer, open to a new call of the Spirit, and open to a new "Yes," this time with the community gathered.

Others suggest that Mary and the women's being in the Upper Room would have been perceived as playing a supportive role, in keeping with the way women were expected to act in a Greco-Roman society. Another assumption often heard in Christian circles is that Judaism's treatment of women was inferior to that of Christianity, even to the surrounding Greco-Roman world,[14] the presence of Mary and the women at Pentecost would have assured Luke's audience that Christianity offered a Spirit-centred community, where women and men were equal and free from the religious and cultural restraints of Judaism or of Greco-Roman society. And yet, if this were true, the scarcity of references in the remaining chapters of Acts to women's involvement or leadership in the expansion of Christianity is puzzling. Such contradictions have led some commentators to conclude that Luke attempted to present Christianity as non-threatening to the hierarchical, patriarchal structure of Greco-Roman society, where women were second-class citizens and only men held public leadership roles. To do this, Luke altered his sources to downplay women's active participation in prophecy, mission, and leadership in the early Church.[15] If this assessment of Luke's motive is accurate, Mary and the women would have had to drop out of sight after Pentecost.

Within this discussion, some biblical scholars use historical criticism to emphasize that Acts is not a chronological outline of historical events, although it is plausible that a small group of Jesus' followers – including Mary and certain women – were in Jerusalem for Pentecost. Rather, Luke, who arrived on the scene late in the first century, is attempting here to use historical facts from oral and written sources to describe the beginnings and the expansion of the first Christian community, the emerging Church, from a theological perspective.

Strictly speaking, after Pentecost Acts paints in broad strokes a picture of how the Church spreads the gospel. Through the power of the Spirit, the gospel spreads beyond Jerusalem and Judea (Acts 1–7), Samaria, and surrounding areas (Acts 8–12) to the broader Greco-Roman world, particularly Rome (Acts 13–28). It concludes with Paul in Rome, "proclaiming the kingdom of God and teaching about the Lord Jesus Christ with all boldness and without hindrance" (Acts 28:30), leaving the door open for the ongoing proclamation and witness of the gospel.

This view of Acts suggests that women's place in the patriarchal and hierarchical structure of the Greco-Roman society, their lack of credibility as witnesses, and their inability to travel unaccompanied required that Luke place the men in the forefront as apostles and missionaries to explain the rapid expansion of the Jesus movement and its credibility. "Luke's narrative, focusing primarily on Peter and Paul as the two chief figures in early church history, is seen to arise out of a concern to present a unified picture of how the word of God advanced into the Roman empire," says Raymond Brown.[16] This analysis suggests that Mary and the women of Pentecost disappeared from Luke's story, as did most of the apostles, because they were not needed for Luke's purpose.[17]

Recent studies of Mediterranean culture, Judaism, and Christians living in a Greco-Roman society show conflicting views on women's place in this society. Women's ability to participate in the public forum, and in leadership roles outside the home, seems to vary by region; it is influenced not only by religion but also by economic factors and social customs. This makes generalizing on women's expected behaviour in this historical period difficult.[18]

One of the earliest homilies on Pentecost, given by St. John Chrysostom (354–407 CE), shows that a first-century tradition existed affirming the women's reception of the Spirit at Pentecost and their missionary activity:

> Was it upon the twelve that 'the Spirit' came? Not so; but upon the one hundred and twenty or Peter wouldn't have quoted 'the prophet' Joel.... And 'the Holy Spirit' sat upon each of them. Observe now that there is no longer any occasion for that person to grieve, who was not elected as was Matthias. And they were all filled, not merely received the grace of the Spirit, but were filled. And began to speak with other tongues, as the Spirit gave them utterance.[19]

Chrysostom concludes that if the Holy Spirit had descended on the Twelve alone, there would have been more reason to name them here, as they were named in the first chapter (Acts 1:13).[20]

In this same homily, Chrysostom invites the listener to see that no distinctions were present in this group, "neither male nor female." He confirms that women, in the beginning of the Church, travelled with the apostles as missionaries and preached the gospel, but indicates that this was possible because of the "angelic condition" that existed.[21] "See the dignity of the church," he says, "the angelic condition. I would that the Churches were such now."[22] To grasp his concern, one must go to his homily on Matthew 23:14, where he laments that flirtatious behaviour in the Temple of God has brought about the separation of men and women in the churches. He reminded his audience that this separation, according to the elders, did not exist in the beginning days.[23] Chrysostom, elaborating further on women as missionaries, says that evil reports never circulated about these women who travelled into far countries, because they were completely centred on spreading the word of God.[24] We may interpret Chrysostom's motives behind this homily and the reasons he gave for the present state of affairs in the Church of his day in different ways. However, the fact that he acknowledged that women and men together were empowered by the Holy Spirit at Pentecost and acclaimed these women as apostles, witnesses to Jesus as Risen Lord, cannot and must not be overlooked. As for Luke, whatever his motives were, in my opinion, his omission of the involvement of Mary and the women in the Jerusalem community after Pentecost and his minimal references to women in Acts impoverish the story of our Christian origins, as we can see when we consider the discrepancies between Luke and Acts.

Discrepancies Between Luke and Acts

In Luke's gospel, the risen Jesus eats his final meal with the broader circle of men and women disciples, "the eleven and their companions gathered together" (Lk 24:33). Within this context, Jesus explains to them the meaning of his suffering and gives his final instructions, telling them that they are to be witnesses of his death and resurrection and are to wait to be clothed with the power of the Spirit. This larger group of Easter witnesses is found in Acts 1:13 and 2:1. Since there is no suggestion that the eleven were alone with him at his departure (Lk 24:36-53), what led to Luke's emphasis in Acts on the eleven as the key witnesses of Jesus' final instructions (Acts 1:2)? Women were the first to see the empty tomb, to receive the angel's news of Jesus' resurrection, and to announce it to the eleven and the other disciples (Lk 24:5-10). Jesus appeared to the whole group (Lk 24:36). So how did the men become known as the sole witnesses of Jesus' resurrection (Acts 1:22), especially when the gospel relates the women's response to the angel's announcement of the resurrection?

Luke notes that the angel reminded the women that, when they were in Galilee, Jesus had told them that he would be crucified and rise again on the third day. According to Luke, the women remembered what Jesus had told them (Lk 24:1-9), which implies that the women had been in Jesus' company when he gave this teaching (Lk 9:18-22). And yet in Acts, they are not among those who can officially witness to the resurrection of Jesus (Acts 1:21-22). Why? By the time Acts was written, "only the men were empowered to speak and act and bear responsibility within the movement."[25]

These discrepancies between the accounts are unsettling, especially since Luke opens his gospel by saying that he is writing an "orderly account" of events (Lk 1:1). Also, since Luke's gospel closes with Jesus' ascension, and Luke opens Acts by referring to his earlier work and giving greater detail on the Ascension, the reader might suppose that an orderly account of events will follow in Acts. But while the eleven are named in Acts 1:13-14, the women are not. This enables the men to stand out as individuals while the women, apart from Mary, are given the impersonal designation of "certain women,"[26] which downplays their importance.

The fact that Mary and the women are acknowledged to be among the first of Jesus' followers in the founding moments of the Church cannot be ignored. Carla Ricci, in her book *Mary Magdalene and Many Others*, considers all the women named in the gospels. In doing so, she concludes that there were likely twelve women who had fairly close dealings with Jesus. In all accounts that refer to the women followers of Jesus, Mary Magdalene is mentioned first. Ricci maintains that had a first-century compiler set out to show (not invent) the special part played by twelve women close to Jesus, he would not have had difficulty doing so.[27] This might be difficult to determine beyond any doubt. However, a reader of Acts 1 and 2 can justifiably ask how this tradition was lost. In Luke's gospel, these women followers of Jesus are identified as the women from Galilee[28] who were witnesses of his death and resurrection and recipients of his final instructions. How could Mary, portrayed in Luke's gospel as the disciple par excellence, and the women present in the circle of disciples that received the Spirit of prophecy to bear witness to Jesus, be ignored in the beginning days of the Church?[29]

Luke and Acts contain many references to women and their involvement in the Church. Luke mentions that Philip had four daughters who prophesied, even though they are not named (Acts 21:9). Priscilla and Aquila, a married couple, took Apollos aside to explain "the way of God to him more accurately" (Acts 18:26).[30] Tabitha was hailed as a disciple (Acts 9:36). Mention is made of Mary, the mother of John Mark, in whose home many had gathered and were praying (Acts 12:12), and Lydia, who was likely head of the house church in her home (Acts 16:11-40). These references suggest that women were more prominent in the ministry than Luke and Acts lead us to believe.[31]

In the description of the first persecution in Jerusalem following Stephen's death, Acts notes that Saul (later Paul) tried to destroy the growing community of believers. He entered house after house, dragging out men and women believers and throwing them into prison (Acts 8:3). Believers who escaped from Jerusalem were said to go "from place to place, proclaiming the word" (Acts 8:4). Not only is the presence and witness of women validated, it is considered as threatening as that of the men believers. Saul's continued pursuit of the women and men followers of the Way before his conversion is confirmed in the account of his conversion (Acts 9:2; 22:4-5).

A reading of Paul's letters reveals also that he considered himself to be as much an apostle as the Twelve. Others bear this title of apostle as well. In his letter to the Romans, Paul mentions Andronicus and Junia as persons who are "prominent among the apostles" (Rom 16:7). He also indicates that there is a group of apostles distinct from the Twelve (1 Cor 15:5, 7), which suggests a "broad understanding of the term, quite in contrast to its later canonical use," according to Elizabeth Schüssler Fiorenza.[32]

A look back at the election of Matthias as one of the Twelve (Acts 1:15 ff.) points out that the selection process used, despite the focus on a male successor to Judas, involved women and men equally in decision-making. As early as the fourth century, St. John Chrysostom, in a homily, pointed out that Peter did not act in a highhanded fashion. Rather, he sought the group's consensus in the choosing of Matthias "in order that the one chosen would be accepted and respected."[33] Participation in decision-making was not linked to gender (Acts 4:23-31; 15:13-21; 17:6-12).

Mary and the other women's active involvement in the growth of the Church in those founding years has been lost from the Church's memory. Consequently, throughout the centuries, iconography and art, liturgy, church documents, and church practice have largely ignored or downplayed that the Spirit at Pentecost was given to the community of women and men gathered, not to the Twelve alone.

Acts 1 and 2 in Iconography and Art Through the Centuries

Eventually, images of the Ascension and Pentecost inspired by Acts 1 and 2 began to appear in icons. The earliest depictions date from the Rabbula Gospels, a sixth-century Syrian manuscript. In the icon of the Ascension, Mary holds the central position, with six apostles on each side. By placing Mary at the Ascension, and including twelve apostles, thereby replacing Judas, the artist has taken the liberty of going beyond the scriptural text. Mary, with her hands raised in the liturgical prayer gesture and standing below her Son ascending to heaven, is the most prominent figure in the painting. Interpretations of this icon present Mary as the personification of the Church. "Her posture suggests the continued prayer of the faithful Church, however unfaithful its individual members might be."[34]

In the Rabbula Gospels' icon of Pentecost, Mary again is central. The dove directly above her, representing the Holy Spirit, sends tongues of fire over her head and the heads of the apostles. In this Pentecost scene, Mary is acclaimed as a symbol of the Church. It is presumed that the artist was influenced as much by Jesus' words on the cross to his mother and the beloved disciple (John 19:27) as he was by Luke's account of the Ascension and Pentecost in Acts 1:6-11 and 2:1-4. Her presence in both the Ascension and the Pentecost icons is often seen to be symbolic of her role as centre of unity and mother of the Church.

"For nearly one thousand years the visual tradition of the Pentecost [and one might say of the Ascension], intentionally or unintentionally had reinforced the priestly aspect of the Apostles and the founding of the Church by limiting the recipients of the Holy Spirit to the Twelve and, by association, Mary," says one author.[35] Other depictions of the Ascension and Pentecost in this period include neither Mary nor the women.

By the Middle Ages, a more inclusive reading of Pentecost emerged. Paintings of the event included three women around Mary, who retained her central position, in addition to the twelve apostles.

In the latter half of the sixteenth century, Pope Gregory XIII promoted a new image of Pentecost that included the addition of a large crowd of disciples. This broader version of Pentecost reflected his perception of the missionary expansion of the Church through the grace of the Holy Spirit and his desire "to unify and enlarge the Universal Church."[36] Preaching at this time also supported this expanded view of Pentecost, underlining that the crowd who received the Holy Spirit on Pentecost day consisted of both women and men and numbered as many as one hundred and twenty.[37]

Both the art and the preaching of this time emphasized the inclusive character of Pentecost and the generous and continuous gifts of the Spirit to the entire body of the Church. Care, however, was taken to ensure that priestly functions were preserved for the apostles and their successors. One preacher pointed out that the apostles had previously received certain gifts of the Spirit. On Pentecost they "received a superabundance of grace and wisdom that enabled them alone to go out into Jerusalem to preach through the gift of tongues. This same plenitude of grace gave them the right to administer the sacraments and forgive sins."[38]

In the seventeenth century, Jean Jacques Olier asked Charles LeBrun to paint a picture of Pentecost to hang behind the main altar in the seminary chapel of Saint Sulpice in Paris. The artist, drawing on a popular perception of Jewish worship and custom, depicted Mary on an elevation with the holy women but separated from the men. Mary is shown in the centre, receiving the fullness of the Holy Spirit, which then divides itself in proportion on the apostles and the rest of the assembly.[39] For Olier, Mary's presence in the Upper Room was:

> to receive the Spirit and apostolic grace, (that is to say, the spirit of zeal for the glory of God and the salvation of humanity); learning from this that the Church will never be renewed except in the company of Mary and through participation in her spirit.[40]

While Olier may have with this comment given Mary a more universal role in the Church, he also was clear that the purpose of the painting was to depict "Mary as the Queen of the Clergy, the channel of grace to all ministers."[41] While this painting clearly denotes an expanded group of persons receiving the Spirit, including several women along with Mary and the apostles, efforts are made to ensure that the priestly character of the apostles is upheld. No reference to the women is made.

In the eighteenth century, Adriaen van der Werff, born at the end of the Golden Age of Dutch painting, used Roman costumes, deep emotion, and dramatic gestures in his painting entitled *The Pentecost.* Mary holds the central place in a large group of disciples, many of whom are shadow images. Van der Werff uses points of light to depict the Spirit coming upon the group. Seven points of light have fallen upon Mary and a few disciples, as eight more float down through the dusky haze, leaving the viewer with the impression there are more to come. In spite of the action apparent in the scene, it is strangely silent. The gift of tongues has not yet reached the disciples.[42]

Icons and religious art depicting the Ascension and Pentecost, transmitted through the centuries, have greatly influenced people's perception of these events. More often than not, these important moments in the foundation of our Church have presented images of the apostles alone. Scanning the centuries, one is left with the impression that those in ecclesial authority, pious groups such as the Order of Santo Spirito in sixteenth-century Rome, and patrons of the arts who had the financial resources to engage painters manipulated the Pentecost scene for their own purposes. Mary and, more often, the women were painted in or out of the picture according to the purpose the painting was to serve. Even to this day, a large number of Christians perceive that the apostles were alone with Jesus at the Ascension, and that the Twelve, after the election of Matthias, were the sole recipients of the Holy Spirit at Pentecost. The manner in which readings from Acts 1 and 2 are used in the liturgy, especially on the feasts of the Ascension and Pentecost, reinforces this perception.

Acts 1 and 2 in the Liturgy of the Word Today

The first reading of the Liturgy of the Word for the feast of the Ascension in the three-year liturgical cycle (Years A, B, C) unfolds Jesus' final instructions to the eleven, and his ascension in their presence (Acts 1:1-11). Christians who are less familiar with the scriptures will not perceive that a discrepancy exists between the closing of Luke's gospel and his first verses in Acts. In Luke's gospel, Jesus gives his final instructions to the larger group of disciples (Lk 24:33ff). There is no indication that the eleven are alone with Jesus at the time of his ascension. The gospel for the Ascension (Year A) relates Jesus' prayer for his disciples (Jn 17:1-11a); Years B and C present Mark's and Luke's description of the Ascension and Jesus' missioning of the disciples to go out to the whole world (Mk 16:15-20; Lk 24: 46-53).

On Pentecost Sunday, the Liturgy of the Word opens with Acts 2:1-11 announcing the coming of the Holy Spirit on the group gathered. The opening line from Acts notes simply that on the day of Pentecost they were "all together in one place." The gospels for Years A, B, and C recall Jesus' appearances to his disciples and their reception of the Spirit (Jn 20:14-23; Jn 15:26, 27; 16:12-15; Jn 14:15, 16; 23b-26).

The word "all" in the text of Acts 2:1-11 is vague concerning who received the Spirit, unless a connection is made to what has transpired in the preceding verses. Such vagueness tends to reinforce the message in the minds of the faithful that the Twelve alone were the privileged recipients of the Holy Spirit at Pentecost, causing them to bypass the point that Mary the mother of Jesus, certain women, Jesus' brothers, and a larger group of disciples (Acts 1:15-26) all received the Spirit at Pentecost and became Jesus' witnesses.

With the exception of the election of Matthias (Acts 1:15-26), read on the seventh Sunday of Easter (in Year B), the remaining verses of Acts are divided over several Sundays of Easter. Acts 1:12-14 identifies a larger group of disciples prayerfully waiting for the promised Spirit. Peter's sermon (Acts 2:14, 22b-28) and its conclusion (Acts 2:36b-41) highlight an extraordinary number of conversions on Pentecost day. These scriptures are the first reading of the seventh, third and fourth Sundays of Easter, respectively. The summary statement about life in the Jerusalem community (Acts 2:42-47) appears on the second Sunday of Easter.[43]

The manner in which readings from Acts 1 and 2 are presented, especially on the feasts of the Ascension and Pentecost, tends to convey a one-sided picture of the foundation of the Church. People leave the Sunday liturgy during the Easter season unaware that a group of women and men were present at Pentecost and equally empowered by the Spirit. Mary and the women, excluded from the Church's memory of events in the Liturgy of the Word, are out of sight and out of mind.

Studying the use of Acts 1 and 2 in the Liturgy of the Word during the Easter season highlights the omission of the verses of Peter's speech where the prophesy of Joel is used to explain to the crowd what has happened to them (Acts 2:17-18; Joel 2:28-32).[44] These verses are not included in the Liturgy of the Word on Sundays or on weekdays of Ordinary Time.

Unquestionably, liturgy sustains the memory of past events, making them present for believers today. The only scripture texts many hear are those proclaimed on Sunday. The texts that are chosen by the Church for the lectionary, which churches use for the Liturgy of the Word, have significant ramifications for the community. After all, our attitudes are shaped by what we hear. We are faced with several questions: Why were these verses of Peter's speech excluded from the lectionary? What could including these verses mean for our Church? An attempt to answer these questions must consider Joel's prophecy and how Luke inserts it into Peter's speech.

Acts 2:17-18 and the Prophecy of Joel

The prophecy of Joel grew out of his perception, in keeping with the thought of his day, that any natural disaster could be considered a Day of the Lord. The locust plague, which ravaged the land in his time, had profound implications for the people. Joel responded by turning the crisis into an occasion for reform and penance, summoning the people to return to the Lord with all their hearts, with fasting, weeping, and mourning: "Rend your hearts and not your clothing. Return to the Lord" (Joel 2:13). This call to conversion focused on their hearts because the heart was seen as the centre from which decisions were made.[45] Joel's prophecy included God's concern for both the people and the land, and a promise of future abundance so the people would know that God was in the midst of Israel (Joel 2:18-27). This assurance of

God's blessing on the land is followed by an oracle foreseeing a miraculous outpouring of the spirit of God on the people at the end time:

> Then afterward I will pour out my spirit on all flesh; your sons and your daughters shall prophesy, your old men shall dream dreams, and your young men shall see visions. Even on the male and female slaves, in those days, I will pour out my spirit. (Joel 2:28-29)

Scripture commentaries note that in Joel, the Spirit will be distributed to all Israelites, regardless of sex, age, or social rank. Joel's prophecy was said to predict the fulfillment of Moses' desire for a nationwide influence of God's Spirit, uttered in opposition to Joshua, who sought to limit the prophecy to certain groups (Num 11:29).[46]

Joel's prophecy echoes God's word through Ezekiel,

> A new heart I will give you, and a new spirit I will put within you; and I will remove from your body the heart of stone and give you a heart of flesh. I will put my spirit within you, and make you follow my statutes, and be careful to observe my ordinances.... you shall be my people and I will be your God. (Ezek 36:26-28)

The Israelites were familiar with the power of God's Spirit at creation. Throughout the centuries, each generation had seen God's Spirit inspiring their leaders and prophets and summoning people to courage and fidelity to God's covenant. The age of the Messiah would differ.

In those times "no longer would Israel lean upon an occasional hero or prophet, but the whole nation possessed by God's Spirit would emerge as an ideal community."[47] This universality of the outpouring of the Spirit is evident in Joel's prophecy, and in Luke's use of the text, as spoken by Peter. Peter, however, offers this universal gift of the Spirit to all who come to believe in Jesus and accept him as the Messiah. They will form the ideal community.

A closer look at Joel's prophecy spoken by Peter highlights other significant changes in the text.

JOEL	PETER
Then afterward I will pour out my spirit upon all flesh. Your sons and your daughters shall prophesy, your old men shall dream dreams, your young men shall see visions; even on the male and female slaves, in those days, I will pour out my spirit. (Joel 2:28-29)	In the last days it will be, God declares, that I will pour out my Spirit upon all flesh, and your sons and your daughters shall prophesy and your young men shall see visions, and your old men shall dream dreams. Even upon my slaves, both men and women, in those days I will pour out my Spirit; and they shall prophesy. (Acts 2:17-18)

Joel refers to those days as an end time in an indefinite future. For Luke, the last days refer to what is taking place in an expanded sense – the time of the church, the final age of salvation history[48] (Joel 2:18; Acts 2:14). Luke plays down the idea that the end of the world is near. A significant difference in Luke's text is found where "the male and female slaves" in Joel (v. 18) is changed to read "my male and female slaves" in Peter's speech (Acts 2:18). In making this change, Luke indicates that Mary and the disciples were God's slaves. Christians today cringe before such language as an expression of a person's relationship with God, but that society did not find it problematic.

Joel uses the word "servant" to indicate social status, and foresees the Spirit being given to all regardless of sex, gender, or class; even the slaves of the Jews will receive the Spirit. "The promise in Joel of the outpouring of God's Spirit is a promise of life, deliverance, leadership, and prophecy. It is a fulfillment of God's fidelity to the covenant," says one writer.[49] All class distinctions would be broken down.

In Acts, the outpouring of the Spirit is the fulfillment of Jesus' promise to his disciples – the beginning of the new covenant established with him. As the Spirit guided Jesus through his ministry, the Spirit will guide the disciples.

In those days, the prophetic Spirit – the inspirer of speech – was to be the privilege of all, not the prerogative of a few (Acts 2:14-18, 38). Prophecy as a missionary function belonged to all the "new people of God."[50]

The members of this fledgling community came to see that "the new gift of the Spirit was not only for the Israelites but also for the Gentiles (Acts 10:44-48; 11:11-18)."[51] This gift was the power to witness to Jesus and his resurrection – the ultimate sign that good, not evil, and life, not death, will prevail.

Peter's first sermon likely reflected what Luke saw happening around him. Luke reminds us "that the Church by virtue of its reception of the Pentecost gift, is a prophetic community empowered for a missionary task. The Spirit is the power which enables Christians to go public with the good news of Jesus Christ."[52]

Omitting Acts 2:17-18 (the announcement that the Spirit was given to men and women equally) from the lectionary encourages people today to interpret the Pentecost event as the gift of the Spirit to the Twelve apostles alone. Even when the presence of Mary and the women at Pentecost is acknowledged, many authors are quick to distinguish between the prophetic roles of women and men. At Pentecost, the male disciples alone received the prophetic role to proclaim and interpret the good news about Jesus. The woman received no such mission. Consequently, the prophetic role of women is defined by their femininity. Drawing on bridal imagery, women's role is to witness to the inner life of believers – to the union with Christ, to which each person is called by virtue of their baptism, and to the Church, which is called to be the bride of Christ.[53] Such gender distinctions ensure that patriarchal structures in the Church remain in place. Above all, Mary's mission – her call to carry to others the Word of God, Jesus, conceived at the Annunciation and expressed in the Visitation – is overlooked (Lk 1:26-58).

Omitting these two verses also downplays the presence of the Holy Spirit in the lives of Christians, who are called in baptism to participate in Christ's prophetic office and to share with others the good news about Jesus.

Because the events of the Ascension and Pentecost described in Acts 1 and 2 have been interpreted in iconography and in art in a certain way, and because the lectionary omits the Joel prophesy included in Peter's first speech (Acts 2:17ff.), we need to consider their place in recent church memory.

Acts 1 and 2 in Church Memory Since Vatican II

Chapter VIII of *Lumen Gentium*, (the Dogmatic Constitution on the Church) outlines Mary's role in relation to Christ, in the economy of salvation, and in the Church. She is described as devoting herself totally to the person and work of her son; her journey of faith from the conception of Jesus to his death unfolds within this context. The focus then shifts to the apostles who, before Pentecost, are seen "constantly devoting themselves to prayer, together with women, including Mary the mother of Jesus, as well as his brothers" (Acts 1:14). Mary is described as prayerfully asking for the gift of the Spirit, who had already overshadowed her in the Annunciation. No mention is made of the women or of the Pentecost event.[54]

Following Vatican II, Pope Paul VI issued *Marialis Cultis*, an encyclical that dealt with the place of devotion to Mary in the Church. There, he stressed the importance of Mary's prayer under the title "The Virgin in Prayer."

For Paul VI, Mary's presence in the Upper Room (Acts 1:14) represents her "prayerful presence in the early Church.... Mary's prayer continues in heaven through her mission of intercession."[55] He sees Mary's prayer as a model of the Church in divine worship – an example for Christians, in their turn, to make their lives an offering to God. "The faithful," he says, "are called upon to imitate her by making their lives an act of worship of God and making their worship a commitment of their lives."[56]

Pope John Paul II, in his encyclical *Redemptoris Mater* (Mother of the Redeemer), traces Mary's pilgrimage of faith and acknowledges her prayerful presence in the Upper Room, where all present receive the Holy Spirit and the gift of tongues (Acts 1:14, 2:1-4). He points out that Mary's pilgrimage of faith preceded Pentecost and joins with the Church's pilgrimage of faith from that moment as it unfolds in individuals and peoples. He also emphasizes Jesus' mandate to the apostles, whose mission began the moment they left the Upper Room. The Church is born and then grows through the testimony that Peter and the apostles bear to the crucified and risen Christ. While this first group knew that Mary was a unique witness to the mystery of Jesus, she did not directly receive an apostolic mission to teach.[57]

While looking only at the ways in which Acts 1:12-14 and 2:1-4 are included in recent church documents focuses on one small piece of all that is said in these documents about Mary and her role in relation to Jesus, his saving mission, and our Church, it does help us to see that the Church's memory of Mary, which is based on these texts, never claims an active role for her in the foundation and evolution of the Jerusalem church.

While church documents are rarely read by the average Catholic, those who attend Sunday and other Eucharists and hear the scriptures proclaimed are exposed to patriarchal attitudes that continue to be strong forces in the Church today. Consequently, the laity, especially women, often feel like second-class citizens. If the Church, in its celebration of Pentecost, included the memory of Mary and the women receiving the power of the Spirit equally, enabling them to become missionaries in Jesus' name, it would be taking a giant step forward. This approach would correct the imbalance in the present lectionary as it communicates women's and men's experience of Jesus and the Spirit. Women today who listen to the readings must largely interpret their experience from stories that present the salvation event happening to men only, and usually interpreted by men only.

Claiming Our Future

For years, feminist scholars have attempted to address the problem of our male-focused scriptures. In searching the scriptures, they have made and continue to make heroic efforts to uncover women's presence, leadership, and active participation as missionaries and apostles in the early Church. Research into early Christianity has recovered Mary Magdalene in her Second Testament role as "chief female disciple, first witness of the resurrection, apostle to the apostles."[58]

Although Mary Magdalene fulfilled the criteria to be an apostle, both witnessing the empty tomb and proclaiming the news to the other disciples, history has claimed that she took the news no further.

In the West, as early as Ambrose in the fourth century, confusion began to set in concerning Mary Magdalene, the woman who wept over Jesus' feet and whom Jesus forgave her many sins because of her great love (Lk 7:36-50), and the woman taken in adultery (John 7:53–8:11). With Gregory the Great's homily delivered at the basilica of St. Clement in Rome around 591, Mary Magdalene's identity as a prostitute was settled. Her conversion was offered as an example to the people of Rome to turn from their own sins.[59] By the 17th century, she would be the model for cloistered women who lived a life of austerity and penance.[60] This perception of Mary Magdalene as a prostitute and converted sinner has persisted in the West to this day, in spite of the fact that many biblical scholars in recent years have pointed out that she should not be identified with the woman in Luke who bathed Jesus' feet and received his forgiveness.

A close look at the scriptures gives no indication that Mary Magdalene was either a prostitute or a sinner. The earliest mention of her connection with Jesus is in Luke 8:2, which asserts that seven demons had gone out of her. In the Bible, seven is a symbolic number for fullness or completeness. "The ancients, not having the benefit of modern medical knowledge, attributed many illnesses to demonic possession. What Luke states is that Mary Magdalene had been very ill and that she was healed."[61] The fact that she is named in the scriptures as Mary Magdalene (that is, Mary of Magdala), and not identified in relation to a husband or father, suggests that she might have been a prominent businesswoman in Migdal, a well-known fish-processing village near Capernaum.

For the Church to revalue Mary Magdalene's role would make a major contribution towards acknowledging women's presence and active involvement as disciples of Jesus, missionaries in the early days of the Church.[62] The loss of first- and second-century manuscripts is a huge obstacle. Were the scanty memory of women in the First Testament included in the Liturgy of the Word, the story of Jesus could never be proclaimed without weaving in the stories of the circle of "his own" women as well as men.[63] This would include remembering and celebrating that Mary his mother, and the women were empowered by the Spirit, along with the male disciples, to give birth to the Church.[64] But even if this were to happen, we would still face a major hurdle. The scriptural silence in Acts about Mary and the other women's involvement in the early days, months, and years of the Church continues to support the patriarchal church structures and limit women's involvement. One way out of this dilemma is to provide a renewed image of discipleship that can speak to the reality of Christian men and women trying to live their commitment as disciples of Jesus in today's continually evolving and complex world.

Reassessing Mary, the First Disciple

Pope Paul VI, in his apostolic letter *Marialis Cultis*, written ten years after the Council, noted that the Church proposes Mary to the faithful as an example to be imitated:

Not precisely in the type of life she led, much less for the socio-cultural background in which she lived and which today hardly exists anywhere. Rather, she is held up as an example for the way in which, in her own particular life, she fully and responsibly accepted God's will (Lk.1:38), because she heard the word of God and acted on it, and because charity and a spirit of service were the driving force of her actions. She is worthy of imitation because she was the first and most perfect of Christ's disciples.[65]

Some theologians, "because no historical evidence exists about Mary having followed Jesus during his ministry, or about her preaching or teaching in the first Christian community, have turned to other women mentioned in the Second Testament, particularly Mary Magdalene, as much more potent models of female discipleship."[66] Their reasoning is based on the fact that the gospels place Mary Magdalene among the women who followed Jesus, witnessed his death and burial, and were the first witnesses of the empty tomb. Mary Magdalene became the first apostle of the resurrection (Jn 20:11-18).[67]

Mary Magdalene's presence is historic. Since "most of women's early Christian heritage is probably lost and must be extracted from androcentric early Christian records,"[68] to propose that Mary Magdalene replace Mary as a model of female discipleship would be unjust to both women and to their relationship to Jesus and to his ministry.

There is no question that Mary, the mother of Jesus, as the model of perfect discipleship has been an unattractive, unattainable model for many Christians, especially women. Traditionally, the Church, based on her "Yes" to God at the Annunciation (Lk 1:38), has limited her influence as a disciple of Jesus to the realm of private spirituality – the Christian's personal relationship with God. None of this does justice to the biblical Mary. I propose that a renewed image of discipleship for men and women can be found in the biblical memory of Mary, especially in reconnecting Luke's Annunciation and Visitation narratives (Lk 1:26-55). In so doing, we uncover a fundamental principle of discipleship in the rich dialogue between Mary and Elizabeth. The Word of God, conceived in our hearts, must be shared, interpreted, and communicated in language that enables it to be good news for others. Drawing on Luke's parallels between these infancy narratives and Pentecost (Acts 2:1-4ff.), we discover that what the Spirit did for Mary at the

Annunciation, the Spirit did also for the community of the Church born at Pentecost.

By unlocking this biblical memory of Mary we meet a woman with her own history, her own growth as a disciple of Jesus as his mother, and her own faith journey. I believe that uncovering this image of Mary will provide Christians with a much-needed prophetic, active, and dynamic image of discipleship rooted in their baptismal identity that speaks to the reality of their lives in this complex world. This image of discipleship, not constrained by titles or clerical office, would also facilitate the transformation of the Church into a community of equal disciples. But we must begin at the beginning. Our journey of discovery begins with a reflection on Mary in the Annunciation–Visitation narratives in Luke's gospel.

Part II: Shaping a New Story

2

The Annunciation–Visitation:
Mary's Vocation Is Revealed

The Story Begins

The Annunciation in Luke's gospel is, first, an announcement about Jesus. In identifying Jesus as the Son of God, the Messiah, from his conception, Luke represents the perception of Jesus' identity that evolved in the believing communities after his resurrection. As the early Christians grew in their understanding of who Jesus was, they concluded that he had been the Messiah from the beginning of his life, even though he wasn't initially perceived as such.[1] Our understanding of Jesus as the Son of God, the Saviour of the world, on the other hand, develops over time.

If the Annunciation is not read in the context of Luke's entire gospel, we risk assigning to Mary full knowledge of her Son's identity from his conception. While Luke presents Mary as the perfect disciple because of her "Yes" to God at the Annunciation, his gospel shows that her awareness of her son's identity evolved over time, as do her understanding of discipleship and her faith journey.[2]

Luke's opening of the Annuciation with the phrase "In the sixth month" places Gabriel's visit to Mary in a specific time frame. Luke invites the reader to keep in mind that this event occurs several months after Gabriel's announcement to Zechariah that his wife, Elizabeth, who is now past normal child-bearing age, would conceive a son (Lk 1:13). Luke's indirect reminder of this event foreshadows Gabriel's announcement to Mary of her cousin Elizabeth's extraordinary pregnancy, which is an assurance of God's power. These words prompt Mary to set out to visit Elizabeth right away.

God's choice of Mary as the mother of the Messiah is at the heart of the Annunciation narrative. Right from the beginning, Luke's text presents Mary as a woman who has "found favour with God" (1:30). As the narrative unfolds, we learn that Mary will become the mother of the Son of God through the power of the Holy Spirit (Lk 1:35). The narrative reaches its climax when Mary consents to be God's servant; this is her response to God's love for her and to God's invitation (1:38). We can more fully appreciate the Annunciation and Mary's free consent to become Jesus' mother if we see them in the light of the religious climate of Israel, and within the social context of her day.

Mary and Her People, Israel

Mary, a young Jewish woman, was formed in the religion of her people, Israel, which was rooted in the Hebrew scriptures and in the traditions that made their faith concrete in everyday life. Central to Israel's faith was their belief that God – the God of Abraham and Sarah, Rachel and Isaac, Rebecca and Jacob – was one God. Israel's basic obligation was to be faithful to God, which meant being dedicated to the fulfillment of God's will as expressed in the Ten Commandments (Exod 19, 20; Deut 6:4-5). Their commitment was summed up by two commandments: You shall love the Lord your God with all your heart, with all your soul, with all your mind, with all your strength; and You shall love your neighbour as yourself (Deut 6:5; Lev 19:18). For the Israelite, love of God was rooted in humility – an awareness that all life, including one's own, came from God – and grounded in fear of God expressed in reverence, piety, and hatred for sin. To the Israelite, life and work had value and meaning only in relationship to God. God called them into life and into service.

The Israelite was called to stand before God in sorrow, joy, misfortune, and happiness.[3] This stance called for confidence, hope, and trust in God, even amidst the harsh and seemingly contradictory realities of life.

The covenant was also a call to show compassion for others where tolerance, forgiveness, mercy, and understanding – along with help and support for those in need – guided interpersonal relationships. To love your neighbour as yourself meant neither hardening your heart nor hating your neighbour.[4] For the Israelite, living according to the commandments meant choosing life (Deut 30:11-20).

At this time, Judaism was influenced by the Pharisees, a religious lay reform group within Judaism. While they strictly observed the Torah, the Law, the Pharisees held that the commandments had to be carefully rethought as people's needs changed. Within this context, the Pharisees emphasized that all creation was sacred. They viewed themselves as a priestly people and saw every ordinary human action as sacred – an act of worship. The views of the Pharisees influenced the rituals that the Jewish people carried out in their synagogues and homes.

The priests, on the other hand, stressed that sacrifice at the Jerusalem Temple was the primary means of relating to God and becoming holy.[5] Interestingly, Zechariah receives the announcement that Elizabeth will conceive a son as he carries out his duties in the Temple (Lk 1:8-9). The Annunciation to Mary about the conception of Jesus takes place outside the Temple – apparently in her home (Lk 1:26). In this way, Luke shows that both the home and the Temple can be places of God's visitation and connected to the holy.

For Mary, as for Israel, "everything begins with a free choice – a call that comes from God's love and initiative. Both are called to the same willingness to listen to God's voice, and to carry out what God asks," says Marcel Dubois.[6] In fact, the Hebrew scriptures, over and over again, tell stories about the covenant with God being broken and renewed. Each story confirms God's love, fidelity, and continual calls for individuals and the nation to have a relationship with God.

Mary was steeped in the religion of her people and surrounded by a community of faith at home and in her village. She would have shared in her people's hope in God's promise, announced through the prophets, that a Messiah would soon come who would show them the way of true freedom – a way of justice and peace. Mary held this expectation in her heart.

Mary's life was marked, too, by the reality that strangers from Rome ruled her nation and imposed their ways on her and her people. The Romans did not suppress the Israelites' religion, but they watched religious worship and celebrations closely, afraid that they might become the rallying points for an uprising against Roman authority. The hope for a Messiah must have been a source of courage for Mary and her people as they faced the oppressive structures that pervaded their lives.

Painting the religious and social climate of any society in broad strokes leads to the danger of missing the emotions of actual people and the reality of their lives. What is known of this Mediterranean world suggests that patriarchy was the normal structure of religion and society; women's status was defined in relation to their fathers or their husbands, who more or less owned them and made choices for their lives. Since the male alone was seen as the creator of new life,[7] women were valued for their ability to bear children.

Luke's gospel was written for Jews, Gentile Christians, and those who lived in a Greco-Roman society who were coming to faith in Jesus, and is set within this Mediterranean world. A close reading of the Gospel and the Acts of the Apostles reveals that, more often than not, Luke legitimized women's silence and subservience.[8] For Luke to allow Mary to speak for herself at the Annunciation is important for us today as we consider the significance of the Annunciation and the Visitation for our lives as disciples.

When we encounter Mary for the first time in Luke's account of the Annunciation, we must remember that Mary is prefigured within the vocation of her people, Israel. She follows a long line of women who played a significant role in Israel's salvation history, including Sarah, Hagar, Rachel, Rebecca, Miriam, Deborah, Naomi, Hannah, Judith, Esther, and Elizabeth, as well as the women named in the genealogy of Jesus: Tamar, Rahab, Ruth, Bathsheba.

Luke introduces us to Mary by announcing that she is engaged to Joseph, which according to Raymond Brown is

> the first of two formal steps in first-century Jewish marriages. This entails an official exchange of promises before witnesses, and payment of the dowry. From this stage on the groom has legal rights over his woman. Any infringement on her chastity was considered a challenge to his honor. Only at the second stage does the husband take his wife into his home.[9]

In addition to the social and religious context of Mary's life and the society for which Luke wrote his gospel, we must keep in mind her humanity: a teenage woman engaged to be married and carrying hope-filled dreams for her future. This image of Mary helps us to understand this young woman who receives and accepts an invitation that will alter her life forever.

The Annunciation — Mary's Vocation Story

Introduction: God specifically enters a human life.	In the sixth month the angel Gabriel was sent by God to a town of Galilee called Nazareth, to a virgin engaged to a man whose name was Joseph, of the house of David. The virgin's name was Mary.
The Angel's Greeting.	And he came to her and said, *"Greetings, favoured one! The Lord is with you."*
Person's fear, questioning.	But she was much *perplexed* by his words and *pondered what sort of greeting this might be.*
Reassurance given.	The angel said to her, *"Do not be afraid, Mary, for you have found favour with God.*
God presents a mission (calling).	And now, you will conceive in your womb and bear a son, and you will name him Jesus. He will be great and will be called the Son of the Most High, and the Lord God will give to him the throne of his ancestor David. He will reign over the house of Jacob forever, and of his kingdom there will be no end."
Person presents obstacle to call.	Mary said to the angel, *"How can this be, since I am a virgin?"*
Reassurance (which involves a sign).	The angel said to her, *"The holy Spirit will come upon you, and the power of the Most High will overshadow you;* therefore the child to be born will be holy; he will be called Son of God. And now, your relative Elizabeth in her old age has also conceived a son; and this is the sixth month for her who was said to be barren. For nothing will be impossible with God."
Person free to say "Yes" or "No."[10]	Then Mary said, *"Here am I, the servant of the Lord; let it be with me according to your word."* Then the angel departed from her.

In presenting Mary's call to become the mother of Jesus, Luke chooses two literary forms used in the Hebrew Scriptures. In the literary birth pattern, God's intervention through an angelic messenger announces the birth of sons who will play a significant role in Israel's history.[11] The biblical vocation pattern is used to call prophets and leaders from among the people of Israel.[12]

Luke has melded these two literary forms to announce the birth of Jesus and the vocation of Mary, with emphasis on the latter. With this knowledge in mind, we can observe the interaction between Mary and the messenger of God. Only at the end of Jesus' life will she realize that her "Yes" at the Annunciation made her the bridge between God's covenant with her people at Sinai and God's desire for a new covenant with all people. This role came in and through the child she conceived, birthed, nurtured, taught, and raised to adulthood. In the conception and birth of Jesus, Mary helped to affirm that all humankind was sacred.

When we look closely at the dynamic intervention of God in Mary's life, we see that this turning point in Mary's life also had significant ramifications for her future husband, her family and friends, all Israel, and people for countless generations to come. Initially perplexed and frightened by this message, she opens herself to listen and enters into dialogue with Gabriel, God's messenger.

The text of the Annunciation does not say that Mary had a vision of an angel, despite artistic depictions of this event through the centuries. Rather, the text focuses on the message she hears and her response to it. How the angel's assurance that she would experience the creative power of the Spirit entered her consciousness, we do not know. What we do know is that Mary's "Yes" to conceive Jesus – to be a vehicle for God's great love for all humankind and the whole of creation – was a free, unconditional response given in faith. God initiates the encounter and Mary touches deeply God's love for her. Love received calls for love to be given in return.

In analyses of the Annunciation, this final step is usually designated as consent. Mary did consent, and we treasure her response, but it is important to note that she *freely* gave her consent. Otherwise, we see her only as a passive, docile, obedient woman rather than a strong and courageous woman of faith – a risk-taker.

Mary's initial hesitancy is a normal response, one that most of us feel when we must face calls that stretch us beyond our comfort level –

whether these calls are from the depths of our being or from family, friends, work, or another external force. Our own decision-making is not usually as linear as this account of the Annunciation indicates. Unless the decisions we must make are very clear, there is usually more back-and-forth dialogue and gathering of information for clarification. Like Mary's decision at the Annunciation, our decisions – whether they relate to a choice of career; a change of lifestyle; a choice of a marriage partner; a choice to co-habit, live singly, undertake church service as a lifelong commitment, or live in community – affect others as well as ourselves. Any serious decision involving life choices is a leap into the unknown, a leap of faith. Once the decision is made, other factors enter into the equation, affecting our ability to control its direction. Our "yes" to any commitment is lived in the present moment only.

As the Gospel unfolds, we see that the same was true for Mary. Her pilgrimage of faith and growth as a disciple emerged through her relationship with Jesus and through his ministry and the events surrounding their lives. Her vocation was not static.

The Annunciation pattern provides a framework for our personal life choices and major decisions. Going through the dialogue between Mary and God's messenger can help us identify steps in our own decision-making processes.

The first words Mary hears are "Greetings, favoured one!" (Lk 1:28). The Greek word we translate as "greetings" actually means "rejoice." In the tradition of the Greek Church Fathers and the Byzantine liturgy, this opening has been universally understood as "an invitation to joy."[13]

In the West, our traditional introduction – "Hail, Mary" – does not communicate this sense of joy. The Greek word, when used in passages related to Israel, always expresses Israel's need to rejoice in the salvation that God offers (Zeph 3:14-15). Joy is a major theme in Luke's infancy narratives. Zechariah is told that not only will he have joy, but that many others would rejoice in the birth of his child (Lk 1:14). As soon as Elizabeth hears Mary's greeting, her child leaps in her womb for joy (Lk 1:44ff.). Mary rejoices in God her Saviour, who has done great things for her (Lk 1:46). Later, when the shepherds are told of Jesus' birth, it is good news of great joy (Lk 2:10).

During his ministry, Jesus will call those who suffer in his name to rejoice and to leap for joy (Lk 6:23). The 70 disciples, whom Jesus sent out two by two in his name, return with joy. Jesus rejoices in the Holy

Spirit at what they had done (Lk 10:17, 21). Later, Jesus reminds his listeners that God rejoices when one lost sheep is found and that heaven will rejoice when one sinner repents (Lk 15:5, 7). Zacchaeus, disliked and considered a sinner by his community for excessive taxation and his connection to Roman authorities, welcomes Jesus with great joy and repents (Lk 19:6). At Jesus' triumphant entry into Jerusalem, the whole multitude of disciples praise God with joy for all the mighty works they had seen Jesus do (Lk 19:37). After Jesus' resurrection, the disciples are filled with joy when he appears among them (Lk 24:41). Following his ascension, the disciples are reported to have returned to Jerusalem with great joy (Lk 24:52).

It is not surprising, then, that Paul calls joy the second fruit of the Spirit and places it between love and peace (Gal 5:22). Joy is difficult to describe. While it can be manifested by an outward expression of happiness, it is more often interior – a deep sense of well-being. All of us can probably name a person who, while struggling with suffering, adversity, and pain, has also experienced profound inner joy and peace. For Mary and for others in the scriptures, as for us, inner joy does not depend on a life free of contradictions or pain. Rather, joy is a fruit of the Spirit rising out of the awareness that we are loved and cherished by God at all times and in all circumstances. Consequently, the joy to which Mary is called cannot be separated from her being named "favoured one" and being told that the Lord is with her (Lk 1:28).

Mary's initial reaction to the greeting is fear, not joy. She is perplexed and ponders the meaning of the greeting for her. All biblical stories of vocation show fear as a natural response to God's call to perform a special task for Israel. Earlier vocation stories are about men: Noah (Gen 6–8), Abraham (Gen 12–25), Moses (Exod 33:12-17), Gideon (Judg 6:17), and Samuel (1 Sam 2:26). In the Annunciation, a patriarchal society hears that "a woman is graced by God and will be the vehicle for salvation to God's people. God's messenger speaks directly to her; the message is not mediated through her father or her intended husband."[14]

God's reassurance lies at the heart of every vocation story. Gabriel assures Mary that she does not need to be afraid, because she has found favour with God (Lk 1:30). Perhaps Mary remembers that, beginning with Abraham and Sarah, God has always told those whom he called that they need not fear, because God was with them. Gabriel continues to speak, unfolding God's wish for her. When Gabriel finishes, Mary expresses a need for clarification. She asks how this could be, since she is a virgin (Lk 1:34). Gabriel responds that the Holy Spirit will come upon her and the power of the Most High will overshadow her (Lk 1:35). He concludes with the startling news that Elizabeth, her elderly cousin who was barren, is six months' pregnant, for "nothing will be impossible with God" (Lk 1:37). In the face of God's assurance, Mary must make a decision. She answers, "Here I am, the servant of the Lord; let it be with me according to your word" (Lk 1:38).

The Annunciation reveals the courage of this woman as she steps out of traditional behaviour and makes her own decision without first consulting her father or intended husband. As wonderful as this call was, Mary had to realize that it would alter her plans for life with Joseph. She had to wonder if she would be believed. Would her family or Joseph reject her? What would happen to her? That must have been frightening. Moving out of the status quo always is.

Filled with the inner sense of God's life in her, Mary hastened to take her news to her cousin Elizabeth, rather than to her parents or her intended husband.

Gabriel's opening words to Mary claim her as favoured and assure her that the Lord is with her (Lk 1:28). For centuries, this identification as "favoured one" has been understood to indicate Mary's holiness. The only other time this Greek verb form for favoured is used in the Second Testament is in Ephesians 1:6, where Paul speaks about our being transformed by this wonderful grace of God freely bestowed on us through Christ. In the Annunciation text, the Greek verb suggests that a change has already been brought about in her. Addressing Mary as "favoured one" indicates that she has been transformed by God's grace. We are not told how that has happened,[15] but some commentators suggest that her transformation has taken place in view of her impending motherhood. But is there a connection between what is said of Mary and what Paul says in Ephesians about our own transformation?

In the First Testament, "Lord" is more than a title for God – it is God's name. We read in Exodus that God told Moses to tell the people that "the Lord, the God of your ancestors, the God of Abraham, the God of Isaac, the God of Jacob, has sent me to you" (Exod 3:15). The title "Lord" identifies God as being present at all times. Mary, favoured with God's grace, is assured that God is with her. While not forgetting

Mary's unique calling, could we say that what has happened to her has taken place in us also? This seems to be confirmed by Paul, who says that "God chose us in Christ before the foundation of the world" (Eph 1:4) – a fact that we claim of Mary. Baptism ought to bring home to us the wonderful free gift of God's love and grace offered to every person from birth.

"Greetings, favoured one" and "the Lord is with you" – the first words addressed to Mary at the Annunciation – reveal the depths of communion with God offered to all of us. While we respect Mary's unique vocation as Jesus' mother, at the same time it is important to cherish our own unique call.

The Annunciation to Mary becomes every Christian's story. Knowing this invites us to insert our name in place of Mary's when we read the Annunciation narrative, and listen deeply as we are addressed as God's favoured one in whom God is present. What happens to us when we do this? What is our experience of being personally loved and favoured by God? How do we name that love? How do we experience God's presence in us? What impact does this have on our lives?

Equally important to our understanding of the Annunciation as every Christian disciple's story are Mary's virginity, her being overshadowed by the Holy Spirit, and her response: "Here am I, the servant of the Lord; let it be done with me according to your word" (Lk 1:38).

To appreciate Mary's questioning how she could conceive Jesus because she was a virgin, it is helpful to remember that in Judaism, a woman's virginity was an essential condition for marriage.

The status of a virgin was dealt with legally. Remaining a virgin had no spiritual significance;[16] women, through marriage and motherhood, ensured the existence of future generations and built up the community of the people of God. This gave them their worth, recognition, and status. In presenting Mary as a virgin, Luke is not making a statement about her morality, he is simply saying that she is an engaged woman who has not had a sexual relationship with a man. This negates any pious interpretations that Mary had made a vow of virginity.[17]

At the Annunciation, Luke is presenting Mary within the story of biblical history. Throughout the Hebrew Scriptures, from the time of Abraham and Sarah, barrenness emerges in God's relationship with Israel and God's intervention to alleviate this condition. For Israel, barrenness and fertility closely linked women with the land. Land that produced crops abundantly and women who bore children were considered to have God's love and protection and were assured continuity of life. So the opening pages of Luke's gospel deal with Elizabeth's barrenness, the resulting shame of being childless, and God's intervention on her behalf. (Until recently, only the woman was thought to be responsible for childlessness; the possibility that a man could be infertile was not considered.)

While Mary is childless and Elizabeth is barren, both women experience God's mysterious action in their lives. A closer look at the Annunciation shows that the virginal conception of Jesus in Luke's gospel (as in Matthew's) is not a comment on human sexuality – neither an endorsement of virginity nor a disparagement of marriage. Rather, says Donald Senior,

> it is a comment on the paradoxical way of God's salvation. Mary takes her place in a long line of biblical characters, and indeed with the people of Israel as a whole. She shares in the poverty and barrenness of Israel. Without the power of God her being is empty and sterile. With that power, incredible life bursts into the world. Mary, like the great saints of Israel, opened her empty arms to God and was willing to be filled with God's Spirit. This is the lesson the Gospels want to draw.[18]

By the second or third century, the Church Fathers had given Mary the title of "faithful virgin." They understood virginity as faith (fidelity) and hope in union with charity. At the heart of this image was the understanding that fruitfulness comes from the true gift of self to others. Fruitfulness, often used to describe success in the Gospel, evokes an image Jesus used in relation to his own death: "Unless a grain of wheat falls into the earth and dies, it remains just a single grain; but if it dies, it bears much fruit" (Jn 12:24). Mary is a person whose heart is open and free. She is ready to hear and conceive God's word and to let it grow in her and be born.

At the Annunciation, Mary is an image of the good soil in whom the seed, the word of God, flourishes. We might ponder the parable of the sower (Lk 8:11-15). What kind of soil are we? Are we fertile ground for something truly new to happen? Do we have the humility to see that ordinary life is holy ground filled with possibilities if we are not locked into always doing things the same way? Fixed attitudes limit us and stifle the spirit. Faith, on the other hand, allows us to live with ambiguity.

More often than we realize, we have annunciations – moments when we are "pregnant with a new form of life that we should trust and accept."[19] These often call us to enter into our own darkness, to discover God's presence there – God's light shaping and transforming us.

From a spiritual and psychological point of view, these ideas imply an internal grounding that carries the potential for the new to happen, for openness to life and its mystery. Taking time to grow as persons – touching our deepest self in relation to God and solidarity with our neighbour each day – has to affect our commitments, choices, and values.

Mary's Annunciation and commitment to live under the guidance of the Spirit invite us to ask ourselves some important questions: What do we conceive in our hearts? To what do we give birth each day? What are the guiding forces in our relationships at home, at work, in our church, in our neighbourhoods, and in our politics: compassion, nurturing, and non-violence, or aggression, control, and dominance? How does what we hold in our hearts affect our relationship with God and our neighbour?

Mary's response shows her faith in a personal God who will be faithful to her and whom she can trust. Reflecting on her virginal heart invites us to consider our own inner space – what helps or hinders the freedom of our own hearts to hear, receive, and be changed by God's word? The heart is the very centre of conversion.

Pregnancy provides a wonderful image for this process. It suggests that after God's word is heard, a time of gestation, or patience, is needed for it to come to full life in us and be ready for birth, or actualization, in our daily behaviour. Our Christian call, whether we are women or men, is to give birth to Christ again and again.

Mary's virginal heart paves the way for the power of the Spirit to bring about the conception of Jesus. In recent times, some have compared Mary's conception of Jesus and divine–human intercourse described in Greek mythology. The people in the late first century believed in divine conceptions, such as that of Augustus. In Luke's

The Annunciation—Visitation

community, as in Matthew's, believers most likely did not see the Holy Spirit as the male partner in the conception process.

The Greek word used for "overshadow" in the Annunciation text is the same word used in Genesis to describe the spirit hovering over the waters of creation (Gen 1:2). Inherent in the term is a sense of protection and empowerment. It has no sexual connotations.[20]

The scriptures abound with images of the Spirit as the life force. From the beginning of creation, the Hebrew scriptures portray the Spirit at work, bringing forth life and renewal for each generation. The Spirit led the prophets to speak, and guided women and men throughout Israel's history to act on behalf of their people. The creative power of the same Spirit is at the origin of Mary's life. When Mary co-operates with the Spirit, new life – Jesus – is conceived. Her "Yes," born of a discerning heart, opens her life to the Spirit's guidance.[21]

The Annunciation shows God's respect for human freedom and God's dependence on personal responses. We must keep in mind that Mary had the choice to say yes or no. That she answered yes speaks of her ability to trust herself – a strong indicator of ability to trust God and neighbour.

Mary, who describes herself as the Servant of the Lord, is in Luke's eyes a woman who from the moment of Jesus' conception fulfills the gospel description of a true disciple – one who hears the word of God and acts on it (Lk 8:21). For Luke she is the first disciple.

The idea of Mary as a Servant of the Lord who was obedient to God's word is a stumbling block for many people today. Unfortunately, through the centuries she has been portrayed as docile, passive, and submissive to God's will. Consequently, she was used as a role model for women in relation to their husbands, to authority within religious congregations, and to the Church as represented by clergy and the hierarchy. To adopt the Annunciation—Visitation motif as a renewal of our identity as disciples of Jesus and of the Church as a community of disciples in the world, we must understand the meaning of the term "Servant of the Lord."

It is based on a First Testament meaning of "servant," which "exemplifies a love-relationship in which the human person has been chosen, called and formed in the love of God, only to answer with the affection of total dedication."[22] Mary, as Servant of the Lord, shows us the depths of a love relationship with God that is possible when we say yes to God's call. In Chapter 4, we will see that her formation as a disciple of Jesus and her faith journey reveal a life in which love "is service patterned on the mission of Jesus, the Servant of God himself."[23] This is the call to every disciple "to let the same mind be in you that was in Christ Jesus" (Phil 2:5; Eph 3:14-21).

Being a Servant of the Lord connects to the first Beatitude: "Blessed are the poor in spirit." In biblical theology, to be poor is to be with God, to make one's heart available, and to be passionately attentive to the presence of God within us, in our neighbour, and in all creation – the only images of God we see. We are required to live in an attitude of obedience that calls for an open, listening, and receptive heart – not a passive obedience to authority, domination of our lives by any person, or emotional passivity to the daily events that touch us, but the inner freedom to hear, to listen attentively, and to be receptive to others as we search for directions for our lives.

In the Annunciation, Mary stands as a woman whose fidelity to the Spirit led her to move out of the security of her tradition and cross the threshold into an unknown future. Her example invites Christians to seek continually the Spirit's guidance, assured that God always respects our human freedom.

Mary shows us also that "receptiveness, openness, attentive listening are characteristics of a humane and above all a believing attitude."[24] These characteristics summon us to live life in love – a love that overflows more and more with knowledge and full insight so that we can determine the best choice for the moment (Phil 1:8-10).

Mary's openness to the Spirit led to Jesus' conception. It also led her to accept the extraordinary message of her cousin Elizabeth's pregnancy as a final assurance of God's power.

For Elizabeth to conceive in those days, considering her age, would undoubtedly have surprised her and all who knew her. In today's age of reproductive technology, when women can conceive beyond the normal child-bearing age, the story of Elizabeth and Zechariah may lose some of its ability to amaze us, and we may ignore God's presence and interaction with humankind in the very heart of their relationships. Elizabeth's surprising pregnancy is a reminder of that other moment in an earlier time in Israel's history when Sarah, Abraham's wife, conceived in her old age (Gen 21:2). Then, as now, the message is the same: "nothing will be impossible with God" (Lk 1:37).

Mary, as Servant of the Lord and influenced by the Spirit, hastens to visit Elizabeth. Luke is showing that God's visitation to Mary and God's word planted within her womb are experiences to be communicated and shared with another person. The Visitation brings Mary and Elizabeth, two pregnant women, together.

The Visitation: Women of Faith, Hope, and Vision Meet

Luke does not tell us what Mary says as she enters her cousin's house. He focuses on Elizabeth and her reaction to the sound of Mary's voice. Elizabeth, touching her experiences of the joy-filled movement of the child in her own womb,[25] cries out to Mary, "Blessed are you among women" (Lk 1:42).

In the Hebrew scriptures, blessing comes from God; it began with God's blessing at creation, when men and women become co-creators with God (Gen 1:27-28), that they might fulfill

all the potential that was theirs as persons from the very creation.... The normal response to God's blessing is to bless God.... While blessing God, we also invite all of the creation to join us in the blessing. Finally, as co-creators, human beings can also bless others, that they might fulfill all the potential that is theirs as human beings from their creation and birth.[26]

Mary is not the first woman to be described as "blessed" in the scriptures. Deborah, the prophetess, speaking about Jael, who had murdered a leader of Israel's enemy, says, "Most blessed of women be Jael" (Judg 5:24). Uzziah acclaims Judith for a similar action on behalf of her people, saying to her: "O daughter, you are blessed by the Most High God above all other women on earth; and blessed be the Lord God, who created the heavens and the earth, who has guided you to cut off the head of the leader of our enemies" (Jud 13:18). It is not surprising that Uzziah prays that praise for Judith will remain in the hearts of those who remember the power of God, and become a perpetual honour for her. He also asks God to reward her with blessings because she risked her own life when their nation was brought low, and she averted their ruin, walking in a straight path before God (Jud 13:20). Jael and Judith, like women before and after them, showed courage and creativity in risking their lives for their people.

The Israelites believed that Jael and Judith were guided by God's power (Jud 13:20). Their belief is a sign that God works in and through the messiness of everyday life, bringing about liberation and transformation on a personal and collective level.

In the New Testament, the word "blessed," as used in the Beatitudes, is an adjective, conveying an existing state of happiness or blessing. In the Visitation narrative, the verb form used to describe Mary is properly addressed to God who is to be blessed by human beings. When it is extended to men and women, such a blessing is a wish; it asks that the one being blessed be granted divine favours; but here the Holy Spirit enables Elizabeth to recognize that the blessing "on Mary" has already been granted by God.[27]

For Elizabeth to name Mary "blessed" affirms and deepens Gabriel's addressing Mary as "favoured" – already transformed by God's grace. Mary has been filled with grace for a new mission – the bringing forth of new life. Elizabeth first blesses Mary as a woman and then her child. Later, Jesus acknowledges that his mother is blessed because she heard God's word and acted upon it (Lk 11:29).

Elizabeth, in recognizing Mary as blessed among women, not only acknowledges her role as God-bearer but also recalls valiant women of the Hebrew scriptures. Elizabeth then acknowledges that the child in Mary's womb is also blessed.

Elizabeth is the first person to call Jesus "Lord" – a title previously used only for God. Luke puts a post-resurrection understanding of Jesus on Elizabeth's lips, showing that she recognizes who Jesus is from his conception. Elizabeth's words to Mary echo Mary's Magnificat. She affirms Mary as the ideal disciple, calling her blessed because she believed that what the Lord told her would be fulfilled.

The climax of the Visitation is Mary's song of praise, the Magnificat, which expresses "the inversion of earthly values and circumstances, the beginning of a new order of reality, the revolution of love and liberation in the name of love."[28]

The Magnificat – Song of Freedom

Mary's Magnificat, modelled on the classical biblical hymn of praise,[29] opens with Mary praising God and recognizing what God has done for her. The central part of the hymn deals with God's action on behalf of the community. The hymn closes with the assurance that God has been faithful in the past, is with the people now, and will be present for future generations. The Magnificat foreshadows Jesus' teaching in the Beatitudes where the poor and those who suffer are promised many blessings (Lk 6:20-26).[30]

The Magnificat is one of four canticles in the Infancy narratives.[31] (The canticles were likely early Christian hymns that Luke adapted.) Without the first three verses of the Magnificat, this hymn would make perfect sense for a Jewish community that had accepted Jesus. It has been suggested that this community had characteristics of those known as the *Anawim*, the Poor Ones. Scripture scholar Raymond Brown explains,

> While the term originally designated those who were physically poor (and frequently still included them), it came to refer more widely to those who could not trust in their own strength but had to rely in utter confidence upon God: the lowly, the poor, the sick, the downtrodden, the widows and the orphans. The opposite of the Anawim were not just the rich but the proud and self-sufficient who had no need for God nor God's help.[32]

The Anawim may have been among the first Jewish people to believe in Jesus, so it is not unreasonable to think that they saw in him – the one who blessed the poor, the hungry, the afflicted, the downtrodden, and the persecuted (Lk 6:20-22) – "the fulfilment of their messianic expectations and used hymns to hail what God had accomplished in Jesus."[33] Among them was Mary, who was "deeply imbued with the spirit of the 'poor of Yahweh' who in the prayer of the Psalms awaited their salvation from God; placing all their trust in God (Ps 25; 31; 35; 55)."[34] As a member of the Jerusalem community, Mary was a fitting spokesperson for them.

The Magnificat can be read on many levels. First, it expresses Mary's joy and sense of wonder at being chosen to become Jesus' mother, and reflects God's goodness in the meeting of the human and the divine in her. She acknowledges herself as being favoured by God because of her lowliness. She points out that in a society where women's status was dependent on their fathers and their husbands, true worth emanates from one's relationship with God. For Mary, being in partnership with God transcends all else.

Second, this hymn not only celebrates Mary's freedom, her ability to risk, but also expresses her capacity for interiority and intimacy with God. She identifies that the first call of a disciple is to enter deeply into self to listen to God's word and be attentive to the Spirit's guidance.

Third, here Mary announces the first reversal – that she freely made herself available for God's service. In the Israel of her time, a young woman could not act independently. Mary reverses the social value of a person based on gender, which emphasized male superiority, age, and economic background. For Luke, Mary represents the community of God's people whose fundamental status is grounded in their relationship with God.[35]

Finally, in the Magnificat, Mary looks back to the God who remembers and whose love endures from age to age, and anticipates Jesus' ministry and founding community, of which she, a faith-filled woman and model disciple, will be a member.

Luke was also concerned with critiquing the socially stratified Greco-Roman society. The Magnificat pits opposites against each other: the rulers against the lowly, and the hungry who are filled against the rich who are poor and empty. God is praised for being faithful to those who fear God, whose identity comes from their relationship with God and is rooted in the values of God's kingdom: mutuality, respect, and equality. These are set in contrast to the rich, the arrogant, and the proud of heart, who have no need of God and evaluate their worth in terms of wealth, power, and prestige. The less fortunate have no place among them.

The stratified society that was Luke's community had to have been affected by this prayer. These words must have threatened the wealthy and powerful. Mary's Magnificat announces God's justice and liberation for the poor. In fact, Luke's entire Gospel can be read in terms of the reversals that Jesus inspired by his behaviour and through this teaching: the greatest among you must serve (Lk 22:24-27). Luke's narrative of the Visitation makes this gospel mandate concrete in the two prophetic women he has brought together, Mary and Elizabeth, who rejoice in God's wonderful works.

The Visitation – Model of Genuine Encounter

Beyond Luke's use of the narrative for his own theological purposes, the meeting of Mary and Elizabeth points out the importance of genuine human encounter. It is not difficult to imagine Mary's need to be near someone who is also pregnant and understands the changes she has begun to experience. Her unique pregnancy placed her in a precarious situation – open to suspicion and accusation by the people around her. It would be natural for Mary to turn for understanding to Elizabeth, who likely had known years of shame and disgrace because of her inability to conceive. Elizabeth would also have needed Mary for support during this time.

Mary and Elizabeth witness to us that "God is able to bring holiness and good from even the most apparently shameful situations.... The incarnational God is to be found in the midst of the messiness of painful human plights."[36] Mary's visit to Elizabeth presents these two women as persons in their own right, valued for who they are – women of faith, hope, and vision.

According to the scriptures, Mary stayed with Elizabeth for three months. Using our imaginations, we can visualize both women in ordinary daily activities – washing, cleaning, cooking, fetching water at the well, conversing with the people in the village, and talking about the children growing in their wombs. What difference would these children make in their lives? We see these pregnant woman – attentive to life stirring within – encouraging each other, questioning what will happen, sharing the incomprehensibility of these events, and returning often to the call to trust that "nothing will be impossible with God" (Lk 1:37). Two pregnant women – open, attentive, and receptive to the Spirit's action in their lives – recognize that God has visited both of them.

Earlier, we looked at the interrelationship of virginity and barrenness. The Visitation, whether or not we have physically conceived and given birth to a child, allows us to ponder moments in our lives when we have felt inwardly barren. We can contrast those moments with other experiences when, in conversation with another, we have felt life stir deep within us because two people, in truly meeting one another, have called forth all that is good in each other. This is the heart of Visitation – encounters of freedom between two persons, where each walks away conscious of the unique mystery within.

True visitation comes from the inside out. For this to happen we must first appreciate our own uniqueness. Secure in ourselves we can then "forget ourselves, to allow another to approach us, to let their distinctive personality unfold, even though it can frighten or repel us."[37] In the meeting of Mary and Elizabeth, and the meeting of the two children in their wombs, we find the true meaning of mutuality: people recognizing and valuing the other, and acknowledging the unique call of each person and the important contribution each person can make. Elizabeth and Mary helped each other to see and to stand in the mystery of God pervading their beings. When a spirit of mutuality prevails, people work together, focused on the task to be accomplished. No one tries to outdo the other. In such a climate, interdependence and reciprocity – which the gospel defines as giving without expecting anything in return – can flourish.

The Annunciation–Visitation Motif

Luke, in presenting Mary at the Annunciation, paints a portrait of a woman who, according to Ramond Brown, "became the first disciple of Jesus by hearing and accepting the good news of Jesus' identity as Messiah and God's Son. In the Visitation he portrays her hastening to share this gospel word with others. In the Magnificat we have her interpretation of that word."[38] She emerges from the Annunciation– Visitation narratives as the archetype of Christian discipleship, and shows us that we, too, after hearing the word of God and accepting it, must share it with others, "not simply by repeating it but by interpreting it so that they can truly see it as good news."[39]

The Visitation unites Mary's vocation and her mission – intimacy with God and service of others – into one call.[40] It is a strong statement that integrates the interior and exterior parts of her life: contemplation and action go hand in hand.

Elizabeth, the one who is visited, also visits Mary. The encounter between these women calls us to be mindful that every moment carries the potential of God's visit and of God's word being spoken to us. To live in visitation is to be open at all times to the mystery of God's all-pervading presence.

The Visitation establishes Mary as a disciple and apostle – a woman on a journey of mission for the gospel. Her vocation as the mother of Jesus, and the meaning of discipleship for her as his mother, will unfold as his life does. For this reason, it is important to consider what other scriptural references to Mary reveal about her growth as a disciple – her faith journey.

3

Mary, Woman of Visitation

A God Who Visits

Down through the centuries, the word "Visitation" has identified the encounter between Mary and Elizabeth (Lk 1:39-56), even though neither "visit" nor "visitation" appears in this text. What makes it a visit is Mary and Elizabeth's recognition and acknowledgment of God's presence in recent events in their lives and in the moment they are experiencing together. They celebrate and share the good news of God's visit to them with joy. In contemporary language, they evangelize each other.[1]

Both Mary and Elizabeth were shaped by the Hebrew scriptures. People of that time saw God's presence and God's visitation to them in various life events. God's visitation was interpreted in several ways: a great gift; a feast; or a time of liberation, new life, and salvation for the person and for Israel. For the Israelites, living in an attitude of visitation meant being mindful that God was with them and had a word to speak to them at all times.[2]

Each scriptural reference to Mary can be read as God's visitation to her in other significant events in her life, and in her relationship with Jesus and the people she meets along the way. In fact, her vocation to be a disciple of Jesus, as his mother, unfolds throughout her life, which she lived in visitation – attentive to God and to God's word.

The Birth of Jesus

Luke concludes the Visitation narrative with a simple sentence: "Mary remained with Elizabeth about three months and returned to her home" (Lk 1:56). Luke, unlike Matthew, gives no indication of what happened when Joseph learned that Mary was pregnant. After the birth of John the Baptist, Luke paints a detailed picture of the historical circumstances that, in his view, led to Jesus' birth in Bethlehem (Lk 2:1-7).[3] Mary reappears, engaged to Joseph, beside him on the road to Bethlehem as he obeys an edict to register for the census in his ancestral town. This enables Jesus to be born in the town of David, underlining that Jesus receives his Davidic heritage through Joseph, not Mary. Joseph gives legitimacy to Jesus in this patriarchal society.

These minute details shield the human and divine drama that is unfolding. To grasp the wonder of it, we need to use our creative, historical imagination to visualize the human journey of Mary and Joseph to Bethlehem.

Our modern eyes readily see the difficulty of a woman travelling in her final stages of pregnancy. Yet it is not that unusual: many pregnant women today must flee oppressive regimes and give birth on foreign soil, far from the comfort of family and friends. In this sense, many women can identify with Mary's journey to Bethlehem.

The opening lines of Jesus' birth story allow us to look back to the moment Mary returned home from visiting Elizabeth. We can imagine her experiencing the changes in her body, feeling the life within her as her child stirred – a woman in visitation with the child she carries in her womb. Women are known to have mixed feelings during their pregnancy. It is not difficult to picture Mary's joy, the dreams she harboured for her child, and her anxieties about his future. Carrying a child requires courage and patience.

The journey to Bethlehem enables us to look forward. Luke's minimal detail allows us to imagine the journey from Nazareth to Bethlehem, approximately 120 km (75 miles) through occupied territory. Christmas cards tend to romanticize this journey, but it must have been a difficult one.

This is a good moment to enter into dialogue with Mary. How did she feel bumping along the dusty roads on a donkey? Although Joseph was by her side, did she feel alone, longing for Elizabeth's womanly understanding as well as her own parents' support? Was she lost within herself, recalling all that had happened to her and holding on to the Annunciation experience, her visit with Elizabeth, and God's promise? Was she speaking to her unborn child, telling him that though she really wanted to be his mother, she was at times afraid?

And what about Joseph? Here is a man co-operating, ready to claim and give legitimacy to a child that wasn't his. Was he concerned that he couldn't offer them all he would want for the woman he was to marry and the child he would raise as his own?

Luke's narrative lets us imagine Mary's experience as she gives birth, swaddles her son to keep him warm, and lays him in a manger (Lk 2:7),[4] gazes upon her newborn, nurses him, and contemplates the mystery of this child. This visitation between mother and son would be repeated often as Mary responded to his ever-changing needs as he grew up.

Unless we journey with them, the story of Jesus' birth unfolds before us like a movie, moving from scene to scene but not necessarily engaging us. We may scoff briefly at the innkeepers who would turn a labouring woman away. Then we may passively watch the shepherds coming to worship him (Lk 2:8-14), while missing the heart of the Christmas message: God's unimaginable love for us concretely expressed in the birth of Jesus. We may lose the connection between Jesus' birth and his adult life, when he will show us how to live and die as we, too, uncover God's life in us. Mary's "Yes" at the Annunciation, her willingness to make the journey, and her openness to what life offers will also be obscured. This is one message Luke wishes to convey.

Luke delivers a second message by placing Jesus' birth at a time of census in Israel during the reign of Caesar Augustus. Moments of census at other times in Israel's history had caused horrific uprisings among some Jewish groups against their oppressors. In Raymond Brown's words, by highlighting that Jesus' parents obeyed the requirements of the census, Luke points out that "Jesus from his birth was never a party to rebellion against Rome. Instead, the census of Quirinius provided the setting for the birth of a peaceful saviour who would be a revelation to the Gentiles and a glory for the people of Israel (Lk 2:32)."[5]

As soon as Jesus is born, an angelic chorus shares the good news with Jewish shepherds watching their sheep on the hills outside Bethlehem.

Shepherds had hard lives. They stayed with the herd in the hills and outlying areas, watching for thieves or predators. On that life-changing night, they hear the angel's words: "Do not be afraid...to you is born this day in the city of David a Saviour, who is the Messiah, the Lord. This will be a sign for you: you will find a child wrapped in bands of cloth and lying in a manger" (Lk 2:10-14). Urged on by the message, they hurry to Bethlehem.

Scripture tells us that they saw in Bethlehem exactly what the angels had described (Lk 2:20). The wonder of the story lies in the fact that these shepherds, from whom society never expected anything unusual or astonishing, inform Mary and Joseph what they had been told about this child (Lk 2:10, 11). In this visitation, the shepherds echo Gabriel's message of good news. Mary is evangelized as she hears again what had been said to her in the Annunciation and affirmed by Elizabeth: Jesus is Lord and Saviour of the world.

The shepherds are also evangelized as Mary presents her son to them. Jesus is proof that the good news the angels told them is true.

"There is no question that the titles assigned to Jesus that the shepherds heard as those given to him in the Annunciation were born of resurrection-faith and pushed back to the beginning of Jesus' very earthly existence," says scripture scholar Joseph Fitzmeyer. "In the visit of the shepherds Luke concretizes the reversals of the Magnificat, and foreshadows Jesus' announcement of his mission at the beginning of his public ministry that he had come for the poor (Lk 4:18-19)."[6]

Joy can be an immediate response to God's word, but it may not necessarily take root (see Lk 8:13). Mary, however, "treasured all these words and pondered them in her heart" (Lk 2:19). She exemplifies those who, "when they hear the word, hold it fast in an honest and good heart, and bear fruit with patient endurance" (Lk 8:15).[7] In the visit of the shepherds, Luke implicitly affirms Mary, as Elizabeth had done in the Visitation. For Luke, Mary is not only the first believer who heard God's word and followed it. She is the first believer who tries to understand what has happened as a result of Jesus' birth.

At the Annunciation, Mary was perplexed by Gabriel's words (Lk 1:29). Here she is present to God in the mystery of life – a believer who, because she cannot fully comprehend what is happening, takes it on faith.

Faithful to Jewish Law

As the infancy narrative unfolds, Luke portrays Mary and Joseph as faithful Jews. In keeping with Jewish religious customs, Jesus is circumcized and receives his name officially eight days after his birth. With his circumcision, Jesus' identification with the covenant of Abraham is established. From then on, every moment of his life is steeped in the sacred.

Jewish law required that a woman present herself to the priest 33 days after her son's circumcision.[8] From the birth until then, she was allowed to touch nothing that was considered holy or to enter into the sanctuary of the temple (Lev 12:4), as she was considered ritually unclean.

Here, Luke seems to blend two separate religious Jewish rituals: a woman's need for purification after childbirth, and the redemption of a first-born male (Exod 13:2, 12). The former required that a woman offer a year-old lamb as a burnt offering and a turtle dove or young pigeon as expiation for sin. A woman who could not afford a lamb offered instead two turtle doves or two young pigeons. Following this offering, the priest made atonement on the woman's behalf and she was then considered clean (Lev 12:7-8). The redemption ceremony (which did not have to take place in the Temple) required not only that the male child be consecrated to the Lord, but also that the parents should redeem their first-born son through their payment of five shekels to a member of a priestly family. Luke fails to mention this point in his narrative (Num 3:47-48; Lk 2:23, 24). Scripture commentaries suggest that Luke's lack of familiarity with Jewish law led him to confuse these two ceremonies, wrapping them into one event.

In the midst of these two rituals, an extraordinary visitation takes place. At the Temple, Mary and Joseph encounter two prophets: Simeon and Anna.[9]

When Simeon sees Jesus, he takes the child in his arms and begins to praise God. In Simeon's words we hear an echo of Gabriel's message to Mary at the Annunciation: "My eyes have seen your salvation, which you have prepared in the presence of all peoples, a light for revelation to the Gentiles, and for glory to your people Israel" (Lk 2:29-32).[10] Simeon then makes a prophetic announcement about Jesus' future to Mary: "This child," he says, "is destined for the falling and the rising of many in Israel, and to be a sign that will be opposed so that the inner thoughts of many will be revealed – and a sword will pierce your own soul too" (Lk 2:34-35).

Most Christians have traditionally seen Simeon's words to Mary as a metaphor describing her experience of her son's crucifixion and death. Yet Luke, unlike the evangelist John, never mentions Mary's presence at the cross: her presence can only be presumed from the fact that in Acts, Luke places her among the believing disciples waiting for Jesus' promise of the Spirit (Acts 1:14). In the light of Luke's gospel, how are we to interpret Simeon's statement to Mary that a sword of sorrow would also pierce her own heart?

His message is linked to what he says about Jesus causing the rise and fall of many in Israel. Luke draws this image from Ezekiel 14:17, where a sword of discrimination goes through the midst of the people, separating those destined for destruction from those who will receive God's mercy. What Simeon suggests is that Mary, like all disciples, will have difficulty understanding God's word.[11]

This comes as no surprise when we remember that the Annunciation did not give Mary full knowledge and insight about Jesus and his mission, and the message of the shepherds left her pondering the event in her heart (Lk 2:19). Here, Simeon tells Mary that she, like other Israelites, will be faced with choices in relation to Jesus and his mission – a point that we will examine more closely when considering Mary's experience during Jesus' public ministry. For now, we will simply note that Luke, in placing her among the disciples in the Upper Room (Acts 1:14), implies that she has successfully met this demand.[12]

The encounter between Mary and Simeon shows Israel's understanding that God visits in and through life events. In this light, we see that Simeon realizes that God is visiting him in this newborn child, whom he describes as a light for the Gentiles and the glory of Israel.

God also visits Mary and Joseph. Simeon's praise of God and joy at seeing the child must have elicited a joy-filled response in Mary and Joseph. Luke tells us that they were amazed at what was said about Jesus (Lk 2:33). In this time of visitation, did anguish replace joy in Mary's heart as she received Simeon's ominous prophecy – "a sword will pierce your soul"? What fears for herself, for her child rose within? Was she mindful of God's assurance to her at the Annunciation, that "Nothing is impossible with God" (Lk 1:37)?

Traditionally, Simeon has always taken centre stage in our church. Anna, a prophetess whom Luke describes as a widow in her 84th year who worships at the Temple with fasting and prayer night and day (Lk 2:36-38), also delivers an important message to Mary and Joseph.[13]

Anna begins to praise God and to speak about the child to all who were looking for the redemption of Jerusalem (Lk 2:38). While she uttered no canticle that was preserved, we can rejoice at this woman whose intuition allows her to know and acknowledge who is before her and to speak of it to all who will hear.[14]

Luke does not mention Mary and Joseph's response to Anna's presence or her words, yet this encounter again affirms what Mary was told at the Annunciation. Anna's proclamation of Jesus to all who look for the redemption of Jerusalem reminds Mary that her son must be proclaimed to all. Both Anna and Mary are visited, and each is evangelized in the visit.

In describing the offering Mary and Joseph make in the Temple, Luke places them among the poor. This is a strong reminder of the Magnificat, which announced that God's blessing and presence are for those who know who they are before God and who God is before them.

Symbolically, the presentation of Jesus in the Temple would have reminded Jewish believers or those coming to faith in Jesus of Malachi's prophecy: "The Lord whom you seek will suddenly come to his temple" (Mal 3:1). At the time of Jesus' presentation, the temple of God was considered to be bereft of God's presence, because the Ark of the Covenant had been destroyed in the Babylonian captivity and was never rebuilt (Jer 3:16). For Luke, the presentation of Jesus in the Temple signified the Lord's entrance into the empty Holy of Holies. Unlike the Ark, Jesus does not remain in the Temple; in Jesus, God dwells once again among the people. God is housed not in the temple building, but in the temple of our hearts.[15] There God can visit and be visited by us at any time.

Luke concludes this narrative simply, saying that when they had finished everything required by the law of the Lord, they went home to Nazareth, a town in Galilee, and settled down into ordinary daily life. Jesus "grew and became strong, filled with wisdom; and the favour of God was upon him" (Lk 2:40).

Every year, Luke tells us, Jesus' parents went to Jerusalem for the feast of Passover, one of the three pilgrimage feasts.[16] This festival, which he describes in Luke 2:41-52, was significant because Jesus was now twelve years old. Boys of this age were required to present themselves in the Temple before their religious elders, who judged a boy's religious maturity according to his knowledge of the Torah.[17] From this point on, any Jewish boy older than twelve could officiate at religious worship in his home synagogue.

At the end of the festival, his parents, assuming that Jesus is among their relatives and friends, join the group of travellers heading for home. After a day's journey they realize Jesus is not among them. Returning to Jerusalem in search of him, they find him in the Temple, sitting among the teachers, listening to them and asking them questions. All who heard him were amazed at his understanding and his answers. "When his parents saw him they were astonished; and his mother said to him, 'Child, why have you treated us like this? Look, your father and I have been searching for you in great anxiety.' He said to them, 'Why were you searching for me? Did you not know that I must be in my Father's house?' But they did not understand what he said to them" (Lk 2: 48-9).[18] Jesus' first spoken words in Luke's gospel provide us with the image of a twelve-year-old boy acquiring a sense of his own identity independent of his parents. Here, Jesus announces his awareness of his relationship with God, whom he calls "Father," and his mission. His manner of questioning his parents seems to convey disappointment that they haven't grasped his vocation, which for him surpasses family ties and responsibilities. In the end, Jesus goes home with them to Nazareth and is obedient to them. Luke closes by noting that Mary treasured all these things in her heart, as she had done following the shepherds' visit (Lk 2:41-51).

Mary's humanness also shines forth in this encounter with her son. Any parent who has lost a child will identify quickly with the anguish that Mary expresses on behalf of herself and Joseph. Despite Luke's theological purpose, this apparent confrontation between Mary and Jesus echoes the experience of most parents as teenage children become conscious of their own identity and assert their independence.

Read through the lens of visitation, this encounter between Mary and Jesus draws attention to their call to be attentive to God's word spoken through the events in their lives. It also recalls Mary's encounter with Simeon, where his prophetic announcement that a sword of sorrow would pierce her soul, would call her to make choices in relation to her son and his mission. Mary's coming to faith in Jesus and understanding of his mission would unfold with the years.[19]

Mary in Matthew's Infancy Narrative

At the time Matthew's Gospel was written,[20] his community, a strongly Jewish-Christian church, had been joined by an influx of non-Jewish Greek-speaking converts. As the Gentile influence began to be felt, the Jewish members feared they would lose the traditional Jewish beliefs and practices that they had brought to their faith in Jesus. They had an identity crisis. Meanwhile, Judaism, reeling from the destruction of the Jerusalem temple around 70 CE, was trying to be reborn out of the ashes. A renewed Pharisaism, centred in strict observance of the law, had replaced the liturgical role of the Temple. Strict norms for Jewish identity arose, and the village synagogue became the centre of power. A split in the community seemed inevitable. To avert such a calamity, Matthew, beginning with the infancy narratives, builds his Gospel to help both groups.

Beginning with a long genealogy, Matthew sets out to assure both Jewish and Gentile Christians that Jesus' birth is not by chance. He is not only Israel's promised Messiah, but also the Saviour of all people. To help settle internal conflicts in the community over interpretation of the law, he shows that Joseph's troubled response to Mary's pregnancy is righteous in the face of Jewish law. Joseph, open to the message in his dream, later sets aside his fears and chooses Mary's welfare. Matthew points out that all that has taken place fulfills the promise in Isaiah that a virgin shall conceive and bear a son who will be named Emmanuel, God-is-with-us (Mt 1:23). Matthew, as Luke did in his infancy narrative through the visit of the shepherds, assures his audience that God, through Jesus' birth, is on the side of the people.

In portraying Jesus' conception and birth as the fulfillment of Isaiah's prophecy, Matthew shows that from the beginning of Jesus' life, Gentiles come to worship him.[21]

For the Gentile members of this community, the story of the Magi's search for Jesus shows that the good news of salvation is made available to Gentiles as well as Jews. Herod's hatred and fear of the child, on the other hand, shows that not all Jews welcome Jesus' birth. This emphasizes the twofold response of acceptance and rejection,[22] which becomes more evident after the resurrection. The actions of Herod, the chief priests, and the scribes remind us that knowledge of the scriptures alone does not guarantee a faith response.

Matthew concludes his infancy narrative with the warning Joseph receives in a dream to flee to Egypt with Mary and the child because Herod wants to kill Jesus. Once again, Joseph listens to and obeys a message received in a dream. He travels with Mary and Jesus under cover of night to an unfamiliar land where they live out of the reach of Herod's wrath. Herod, enraged at being deceived by the Magi, massacres all children in and around Bethlehem under two years old; the cries of their mothers echoes from the page. Upon Herod's death, Joseph is advised in a third dream to return to Israel. Fear of Herod's son, who is now on the throne, results in a final dream and the family's resettlement in Nazareth in Galilee.

This dramatic story signals that God is protecting Mary's child.

Matthew begins his Gospel with a genealogy, tracing Jesus back to Abraham (Mt 1:1-17), including women who, like Mary, had an unexpected pregnancy, to show that God could work wonders out of even the messiest situations. These facts, along with Joseph's movement away from legalism and the visit of the Magi from the East, suggest that Jesus' coming opened the way for the new to be born. Matthew is like the master who "brings out of his treasure what is new and what is old" (Mt 13:52). God's revelation to both the Israelites and the Gentiles in the visit of the Magi is a reminder to the Jewish community that faith in Jesus requires them to look at their traditions with new eyes.

Matthew's infancy narrative provides some insight into the emotional responses of Joseph, the Magi, Herod, the chief priests, and scribes – and, indirectly, the mothers whose children were massacred. At no time does he write about either Mary's character or her personal thoughts and feelings about these events. Despite the silence surrounding Mary here, strong moments of visitation emerge.

Use of historical imagination helps us break the silence around Mary and enter into the heart of these events. Let us revisit the announcement of Jesus' birth, where we encounter Joseph's awareness and response to the pregnancy of the woman to whom he is engaged (Mt 1:18, 19).

These two verses remind us of Mary's precarious situation. While Mary would have sought comfort and assurance from Elizabeth (Lk 1:39 ff.), she would likely have wanted even more comfort, understanding, and acceptance from Joseph.

According to Jewish law, an engaged woman was considered to be a wife even though she continued to live at home for about a year. Matthew makes it clear that Mary and Joseph are between these two steps (Mt 1:18). Any apparent infidelity on the woman's part was considered adultery and was punishable by stoning (Deut 22:20-21).[23] (To be fair, the man was subject to the same punishment.) Joseph's reaction to Mary's news is understandable. He knows the child is not his. In light of the law, what does he do with Mary?

Joseph's dream, in which he is assured about the truth of Mary's pregnancy, occurs only after he has made a decision to divorce her. Justice, not legalism, guides his decision to divorce her quietly. Implicit in his behaviour is the theme of rejection-acceptance. In visiting Joseph, Mary and the child in her womb are not received as good news at first.

In Luke's infancy narrative, we are left with the image of two women – Mary and Elizabeth – recognizing, embracing, and standing in joy before the mystery and the mission of the children they carry in their wombs. In Matthew, Joseph, unlike Elizabeth, requires time and divine assurance. Through the medium of a dream, his whole person is opened to the truth. As a result of God's annunciation to him, he takes Mary to his home and the legalities of the marriage are completed (Mt 1:25). Joseph shows courage by changing his mind: his honour lies not in being righteous before the law, but in hearing God's word and acting on it.

Joseph, like Mary, was called to set aside his fear. His "Yes" opens him up to an unknown future, as hers does. Now he can stand with Mary within the mystery and mission of the child she carries. Mary is a catalyst for God's annunciation to Joseph. At the same time, she is visited anew, as Joseph's "Yes" – his acceptance of her and her child – reinforces the promise of God's fidelity to her.

Like Joseph's, our openness and receptivity to God's presence is not guaranteed. Like him, we must trust the messages our unconscious communicates to us.

The story of the Magi is also significant for us. Their journey through the darkness invites us to ponder our own movements in the darkness of our lives.

Joseph and the Magi were called to leave the security of what they knew and to venture forth on an uncharted route. The Magi, unlike Herod, do not fear the news of the birth of the Messiah, but embrace it. Like the Magi, we need inner quiet and space to hear God's message above the clamour of other voices.

We need to contemplate the silent exchange of this visitation when they arrive in Bethlehem – Mary showing and sharing her child with these foreign visitors, and the Magi's response: recognition, adoration, and prostration. The Magi's gestures announce the beginning of a new kingdom. Jesus, the good news, is shared and interpreted for this new moment.

The fact that this exchange takes place in a humble setting – not a palace or a temple – cannot be overlooked. Various "houses" are described in the gospels – the home in Bethlehem in Matthew; Mary's home in Nazareth, Elizabeth's in Ain Karim, and the stable in Luke. In the house or stable, class barriers breaks down and hospitality flourishes.[24] These homes foreshadow the future, when "houses will be the setting for gathering a variety of social classes across the Greco-Roman world to remember and to proclaim the birth, the life, the death, and the resurrection of this Jesus whose birth story is told here."[25]

These birth stories, above all, affirm that God is found among people in ordinary life. God is Emmanuel, or God-with-us. The Magi and the shepherds – in visiting Mary, her child, and Joseph – reveal the truth about Jesus' identity. God's revelation to us can come from the most unexpected people, places, or happenings in our lives. God is with us now and always (Mt 1:23; 28:30).

Like ordinary people of Israel throughout history, Jesus must flee from the danger of the country's ruler. In one scholar's view,

> Jesus is identified with and characterized among those in Israel's past and present who were in need of liberation from oppressive rulers and structures. Matthew portrays the danger Jesus faces at the hands of Herod in terms similar to that encountered by the children of Israel who were led north out of the city (Jerusalem) on their way to exile.[26]

Here, as elsewhere, we have to go inside the text to imagine Mary's experience. In Matthew, Mary and Jesus are always together (Mt 1:18, 25; 2:11, 13, 20, 21). From the beginning, Mary faces the fear of rejection with her child; she experiences the fear and the reality of being a refugee on the run from those who will use their power to kill whoever stands in the way of their own ambitions. Along with Jesus and Joseph, she becomes a woman in exile, removed from her family and friends, finding shelter in a foreign land.

The cries of the mothers of the slaughtered innocents "point back to the beginning of the narrative, to its hopes and possibilities."[27] Matthew hides whatever fear Mary felt for her child and any sorrow for so many innocent children and their mothers.[28] Mary seems to escape weeping now. She will not escape it later, when her son is killed – an innocent like the innocents of Bethlehem. Herod's opposition to Jesus and the family's flight to Egypt and eventual return to Nazareth signal for us Jesus' going away in death but coming back to life in the resurrection. In writing about both acceptance and rejection of Jesus in the beginning stages of his life, Matthew makes his infancy narrative, like Luke's, a gospel in miniature.[29]

The Genealogy of Jesus

Matthew's opening genealogy, which includes women – Tamar, Rahab, Ruth, and Bathsheba – among Jesus' ancestors, breaks the primacy of male descendants.

Biblical accounts of these women's stories tell the unusual circumstances leading to their pregnancies (Mt 1:18-25): all of them were saving events in Israel's salvation history. The fact that these women are mentioned, says Elaine Wainwright,

> links Jesus as much with these women descendants, and as
> closely to his mother Mary, of whom he is born, as to Abraham
> and David. As Matthew's infancy narrative unfolds, it becomes
> obvious that Mary's presence in the genealogy, a silent witness
> to her courage, and decisiveness in accepting to conceive Jesus,
> to be his mother, enables this to happen. From this moment,
> Mary, as the women, can never be invisible.[30]

The genealogy notes that Jesus was born of Mary (1:16); his identity is not bestowed by the male head of the house, even if Joseph, in "accepting Mary and naming the child (Mt 1:21) socially legitimizes both mother and son, and becomes Jesus' legal father by adoption."[31]

Mary's presence in this genealogy is her first visitation as the mother of Jesus to Matthew's community. She is a strong witness to God's surprising presence and involvement with women and men of every generation. Jesus receives his identity from his mother. In this visitation, the stage is set for the transformation of a patriarchal society where children and women's identity come from fathers and husbands.

Some scripture commentators see Matthew's genealogy as an echo of the book of Genesis. In this sense, the word "prefaces not only the ancestral origin, birth, and beginnings of Jesus; but it also encompasses a view of the whole story of Jesus as a new creation, even greater than the old," says Raymond Brown.[32] Into this new creation, God visits us in and through Mary who conceives and births Jesus, God's Son and her son, who has been given the task of saving the people from their sins (Mt 1:21), from all the breakdowns in peoples' relationship with God, with one another, with the whole of creation. Elaine Wainwright adds,

> Where liberation from sins – from all the manifestations of the breakdown of the divine–human relationship that mars God's dreaming with humanity that humankind and the universe might live in right order and hence fullness of life – continues, there God continues to be with God's people. Jesus is with us to the close of the age (Mt 1:23; 28:20).[33]

Reading the infancy narratives in light of Israel's understanding that God visits through the ordinariness of life, we can see how Mary's vocation as Jesus' mother unfolded through her life.

With Jesus in Nazareth

Recent archaeological discoveries have uncovered that Nazareth in Jesus' time "was an important village three to five miles from Sepphoris, one of the four major centres of Greco-Roman culture and Roman administration for all of Galilee."[34] To the east, within 32 km (20 miles) of Nazareth, Herod Antipas built the city of Tiberias between 17 and 20 CE, making it the new capital of Galilee. Residents of Nazareth interacted with people en route to these major centres, and thus were exposed to other cultures and religions.

Judaism at this time upheld the belief that men and women were created equally in the image of God (Gen 1:27). They took for granted that "men and women are meant to be different in status, rights, and obligations and to complement rather than equal one another."[35] While the debate about women's status and roles during this time is not over, recent discoveries have provided some insight into women's life in the villages. As Carol L. Myers tells us,

> Daily life centred on what can be called the "family household" which was the basic unit of society. This designation involved not only the people related by marriage and descent who lived together. It also denotes that the family's viability was linked to the building(s) that housed it, its tools and utensils, its livestock, and its fields and outbuildings. Daily life for most Israelite women, men, and children took place within its physical and social boundaries.[36]

Many women worked in the fields growing barley and wheat. Because they were also raising children, a portion of the day was spent near home so they could care for their children and their homes; cook meals; tend the vines, gardens, and fruit; and fetch water at the village well. With their extended families, they built community in the household that likely influenced village life. Several generations would have lived, probably in cramped quarters, in caves on the side of Nazareth's hilly terrain.

Both parents played an authoritarian role in families. Loyalty and bringing honour, not shame, to the family was a controlling factor in Mediterranean life. Within this context, the mother-son bond was the strongest.[37] Knowing this prepares us for the impact that Jesus would have had on displacing the value of kinship and family loyalty ties.

For the Jewish people, the universe was filled with God's Spirit – the Lord was present everywhere. Consequently, every moment of life was religious, at the service of the God of Israel. All shared in this intimate presence of God in nature, religious customs, and the observance of the law. As Albert Nolan tells us, "Israelite men and women spoke and thought of time as a quality, not a blank space to be filled in with constant activity. Given the central religious orientation of their lives, they located themselves in relation to events, places and time such as Creation, Exodus, and their Covenant with God."[38] This made the pilgrimage feasts of Passover, Pentecost, and Tabernacles, which took place in Jerusalem, moments of great celebration.

These celebrations were dominated by strict purity laws for men and women. "Women with a flow of blood were excluded from the Temple altogether. Jewish men entering the inner courts of the Temple had to observe a variety of rules, including abstention from sexual relations with a menstruating woman. The general idea that worship required purity restrictions and abstentions was part and parcel of Jewish religious life," says Amy L. Wordelman.[39]

In the villages, the synagogue was a central gathering place: "Women attended the synagogue not only on Friday eve and the Sabbath but also during the week when prayer and study took place."[40] Not unlike today, men and women were expected to discover ways in which God's word could transform their lives.

Within these broad strokes of Israelite village life, we can picture Mary in Nazareth during the formative years of Jesus' life. She would have worked with the women in her extended family, her neighbours and friends, helping to build community life. Like any mother, she would also have cared for her child, guiding him through childhood and adolescence to adulthood.

Since the early years of education were done by the mother, she would have taught Jesus about the Jewish faith and answered his questions about the traditions and customs of their religious life. She would have helped him see how their faith permeated the very structures of their society and was the heart of community life in family and among their village neighbours. She would have prepared the house and food for the Shabbat (Sabbath); lit the candles for Shabbat prayer on Friday evening; gone to synagogue for prayer and the reading of scripture; and made the annual pilgrimage to Jerusalem for the feasts of Passover, Pentecost, and Tabernacles.

In their encounters and dialogue, surely God's promise about Jesus, which Mary held in the intimacy of her heart, was slowly being shaped by her son. He carried God's desire for the liberation of humankind within himself as he obeyed her and Joseph (Lk 2:51) and grew into an adult.

In the process, Jesus learned how to live and worship God as a Jew, to be a member of his family, to become a carpenter like his father, to be a neighbour, and to live under Roman occupation.

Lack of any mention of Joseph in Jesus' adulthood suggests that he had died by the time Jesus responded to God's call and set out to begin his ministry. We can only imagine the love and care exchanged between Mary and her son as he set out on his mission. Her life lived in visitation called her to be attentive to God's presence, God's word spoken to her in her daily life in Nazareth. Attentive to her vocation as his mother, her growth as Jesus' disciple, her faith journey would be shaped by his teachings and activities during his ministry.

Mary's Encounter with Her Son During His Public Ministry

Mark, Matthew, and Luke (the synoptic gospels) all report one encounter between Mary and her son during his public ministry (Mk 3:31-35; Mt 12:46-50; Lk 8:19-21). Jesus left Nazareth at 30 years of age to begin his ministry of preaching and healing, making his home in Capernaum. In John's gospel, Mary is with Jesus at the wedding at Cana, where Jesus' ministry begins, and at his death on the cross (Jn 2:1-11; 19:25-27).

Let's begin with Mark and see how Mary's life as Jesus' mother, lived in visitation, shaped her understanding of Jesus, his mission, and her relationship with him.

Mark tells numerous stories of Jesus healing people, of the Pharisees' attack on Jesus because his disciples broke the Sabbath law by picking grain, and of Jesus' selection of the Twelve (Mk 1:21–3:13). Back home in Capernaum,[41] the crowd's demand for Jesus is so great that he is prevented from eating. News of this situation reaches his mother and his family in Nazareth. Upset by what they hear, and concerned for the family's reputation, they set out "to restrain him, for people were saying, 'He has gone out of his mind'" (Mk 3:21). While Jesus and his disciples are travelling towards Capernaum, scribes come from Jerusalem to denounce Jesus as being demonic. Jesus refutes their claim by stating clearly the differences between God's kingdom and Satan's (Mk 3:22-30). At this point, Mary arrives with Jesus' brothers and sisters.

> Then his mother and his brothers came; and standing outside, they sent to him and called him. A crowd was sitting around him; and they said to him, "Your mother and your brothers and sisters are outside, asking for you." And he replied, "Who are

my mother and my brothers?" And looking at those who sat around him, he said, "Here are my mother and my brothers! Whoever does the will of God is my brother and sister and mother." (Mark 3:31-35)

This narrative can be read on many levels. The most obvious is the concern of a mother and family for one of their own. The scriptural text shows that they do not understand Jesus or his actions. They may feel that their reputation is at stake.

The contrast between Mary and the family standing outside the circle of Jesus' teaching and the crowd inside his house listening to him is striking. Here we receive the first inkling that Jesus is creating a new family where God comes before human relationships.[42] From this perspective, his family has no special claim on him.

To grasp the significance of this text, we must consider the context in which this gospel was written. The destruction of Jerusalem and the temple had resulted in a crisis of identity for Jews and Christians. Following Jesus and his gospel led to public and domestic persecution. Jesus' teaching about family assured and encouraged his followers that their identity and honour as believers arose from their attachment to him and voluntary solidarity with his family of followers, not from their biological families and the surrounding culture. This story provides a backdrop for the cost of discipleship. Later in Mark's gospel, Jesus says that "there is no one who has left house or brothers or sisters or mother or father or children or fields, for my sake and for the sake of the good news, who will not receive a hundredfold now in this age" (Mk 10:29-30).

Jesus' new family not only transcends biological relationships, but also places men and women on an equal footing in this patriarchal society. This point is suggested by the omission of "father" in Jesus' new family, indicating that God's will replaces the human father's dominant authority in the patriarchal family.

Jesus gives his followers no program to follow, only himself. He is the teacher with authority, the one whose words and actions speak God's will. Taking what he says to heart and reaching out in compassion, forgiveness, mercy, and justice – as he does – is how to do God's will. Such people move within the circle of his followers, and become family. As John Dominic Crossan explains,

Within the social context of Jesus' time, this message of companionship and empowerment had to be very attractive to peasants who had become marginalised, often dispossessed of their lands, the result of expanding urbanization in the Galilean cities of Sepphoris and Tiberias. Urbanization had increased economic and political power in the hands of a few. Then as today, it had a spiralling downward effect. People were often led into poverty, forced to move away from the family centre to find work elsewhere, if possible. This led to the break-up of families that were unable to take care of their own. Those already poor often were reduced to beggar status, or day labourers removing their dignity and security.[43]

Jesus' teaching restored their dignity, and offered them hope and intimacy with him and his followers.

Some scholars suggest that this story proves that Mary never believed in Jesus, and remained outside his intimate circle of followers. While Mary doesn't appear again in this gospel, Mark leaves us with the impression that she must discover what this means for her as Jesus' mother. For Mark, believing in Jesus and following him has a price.

Mary is mentioned a few chapters later, when Mark describes Jesus' rejection in Nazareth, his hometown (Mk 6:1-6). The village people listening to him react with astonishment; after all, he is only the carpenter, the son of Mary.[44] This seemingly offhand remark by the village folk suggests that Jesus' family was like any other family in Nazareth. The heart of this story is Jesus' reaction to their words: "Jesus said to them, 'Prophets are not without honour, except in their hometown, and among their own kin, and in their own house.'... And he was amazed at their unbelief" (6:4, 6a).

Rereading these texts from the point of view of God's visitation in Mary's life shows a different picture. Mary, hastening to visit her son in Capernaum out of concern for him, surprisingly confronts the reality of a radical change in her relationship to her son and to her understanding of family structure as she knew it. She, like everyone else, has to learn how to embrace her son's teaching on this point, to learn to hear the word of God from his lips. Her concern for him is understandable. What Jesus proposed threatened the established religious and social order. Mary had enough experience living under

Roman occupation to know that for Jesus to gather such large groups could incite the wrath of the authorities.

Matthew includes the same story, but omits Mark's observations about the concerns of Mary and the family for Jesus and his activities. To have presented Mary as Mark did would have undermined the character of Mary, whom he had depicted in the infancy narrative as committed to God and to bringing God into the world in Jesus (Mt 1:23). For Matthew, the arrival of Mary and Jesus' brothers on the scene becomes the occasion for Jesus' teaching about the true meaning of discipleship.

> While he was still speaking to the crowds, his mother and his brothers were standing outside, wanting to speak to him. Someone told him, "Look, your mother and your brothers are standing outside, wanting to speak to you." But to the one who had told him this, Jesus replied, "Who is my mother, and who are my brothers?" And pointing to his disciples, said, "Here are my mother and my brothers! For whoever does the will of my Father in heaven is my brother and sister and mother."
> (Mt 12:46-50)

While Matthew later affirms one's duty to honour one's father and mother (Mt 15:4-5; 19:19), here he, like Mark, shows that following Jesus and participating in his mission to "make disciples of all nations" (Mt 28:19) can be costly and can cause conflicts within families and with the pervading culture.

When this gospel was written, choosing to follow Jesus was risky: "As conflict sharpened between the believers-in-Jesus and some Jewish community leaders, the followers of Jesus were alienated from their families and excluded from the assembly of the majority group of Jews."[45] It is the cost of discipleship, as we see in Jesus' words to Peter, who questions what those who have left everything to follow Jesus will get in return. Jesus' answer is straightforward: "Everyone who has left houses or brothers or sisters or father or mother or children or fields, for my name's sake, will receive a hundredfold, and will inherit eternal life" (Mt 19:29).

Only in this context does the radical demand of following Jesus make any sense: "I have not come to bring peace, but a sword.... Whoever loves father or mother more than me is not worthy of me;

and whoever loves son or daughter more than me is not worthy of me; and whoever does not take up the cross and follow me is not worthy of me" (Mt 10:34, 37-38). Jesus certainly does not wish to break up families. But he tells his followers that if following him leads to a break in family relationships, they will have companions on the journey in his new family.

"Acceptance of Jesus' teaching, and obedience to God's will, is understood as a familial relationship with God," says Anthony Saldini.[46] In Matthew, obedience to the Father's will means carrying out the directives laid out in the Sermon on the Mount (Mt 5, 6). "The group has only one father (Mt 23:9) and its relationship with the Father mirrors Jesus' special relationship with him," adds Saldini.[47] For Matthew's Jewish community, calling God "father" was not unusual. Yet when the "early Christians called upon God as 'father' they were doing something that was quite subversive. In the context of Roman imperial rule, Christians claimed God as the only power in their lives, not the emperor, who claimed to be pater patriae, (the father of the nation) and ruled the empire as the head of a patriarchal family."[48]

What can be said about Mary in this context? While Mary's commitment to God is present in the infancy narrative, she has to learn how this commitment will unfold for her as Jesus sees himself called to, and undertakes his mission among, the people. As in Mark, Mary's visit to her son shows that she, like everyone else, must be exposed to and shaped by Jesus' teaching. God visits her through the teachings of her son. She must learn to hear God's word from him. Like everyone else, Mary, despite her initial commitment to God, must make a choice because of the demands presented in his teaching on the meaning of true discipleship.

Matthew's community and Christians today know Mary as a woman ready to face this challenge. Luke, drawing on Mark and Matthew, has a different perspective on the visit of Mary and the family to Jesus:

> Then his mother and his brothers came to him, but they could not reach him because of the crowd. And he was told, "Your mother and your brothers are standing outside, wanting to see you." (Lk 8:19-20)

Like Matthew, Luke omits any suggestion that Mary and Jesus' family did not understand him. He also alters the text yet again. For Luke,

Jesus' mother and brothers could not reach him because of the crowds. They are on the edge of the circle, unable to get closer. Nor does Jesus ask, "Who are my mother and my brothers?" when he is told of their presence. He simply says, "My mother and my brothers are those who hear the word of God and do it" (Lk 8:19-21).

In Luke, the parable of the sower (Lk 8:4-15), which outlines the different ways people can receive and respond to God's word, has preceded this event. (Mark and Matthew present this teaching afterward.) Jesus' response that his mother and brothers are those who hear the word of God and do it recalls the parable, which explains that the good soil represents those who, hearing the word, hold it fast in an honest and good heart, and bring forth fruit with patience. This refers, then, to anyone in the crowd who has listened to him and accepted his word. According to Raymond Brown, the "Lucan context underlines the fact that the mother and the brothers are examples of the fate of the seed that has fallen in good soil."[49] The person in the crowd who has done this fully is Mary, at the Annunciation: Elizabeth affirms her as blessed at the Visitation because she heard the word of God and acted on it (Lk 1:38, 45). Luke underlines that this is how Jesus sees his mother: he, too, praises her for her ability to hear God's word and do it (Lk 11:27-28).[50] In Luke, from this action Mary derives her status in Jesus' new family.[51]

Luke places the story about Jesus' rejection at Nazareth early in his ministry, and makes no mention of Mary.

The rejection of Jesus in his own village, regardless of where it appears in the gospels, shows the division his mission will cause among his own people. Mary, despite her "Yes" at the Annunciation, would face costly choices that the evolution of his mission was placing on her in her relationship with him and with her own people. In that sense, her visit to Jesus during his public ministry presented in Mark, Matthew, and Luke carries a common thread: the challenges and the choices she would have to make to stand on the side of her son.

John's gospel, on the other hand, tells us that the people question how Jesus can claim that he is the bread come down from heaven. After all, they know that he is Joseph's son. They know his mother, too. Many of Jesus' disciples at this point choose to withdraw from the group (Jn 6:41-51, 66). Mary stays, but faces two major challenges: at the wedding at Cana, and at the crucifixion.

Mary with Jesus at Cana and the Cross

John's gospel, written late in the first century CE, presents Mary at these two significant moments in Jesus' adult life. The wedding feast at Cana (Jn 2:1-13) takes place at the beginning of Jesus' ministry; his death on the cross (Jn 19:25-27) takes place at its conclusion. How were these events, these contacts between a mother and her adult son, times of visitation for Mary?

Turning to the wedding feast of Cana we read:

On the third day there was a wedding in Cana of Galilee, and the mother of Jesus was there. Jesus and his disciples had also been invited to the wedding. When the wine gave out, the mother of Jesus said to him, "They have no wine." And Jesus said to her, "Woman, what concern is that to you and to me? My hour has not yet come." His mother said to the servants, "Do whatever he tells you." Now standing there were six stone water jars for the Jewish rites of purification, each holding twenty or thirty gallons. Jesus said to them, "Fill the jars with water." And they filled them up to the brim. He said to them, "Now draw some out, and take it to the chief steward." So they took it. When the steward tasted the water that had become wine, and did not know where it came from (though the servants who had drawn the water knew), the steward called the bridegroom and said to him, "Everyone serves the good wine first, and then the inferior wine after the guests have become drunk. But you have kept the good wine until now." Jesus did this, the first of his signs, in Cana in Galilee, and revealed his glory; and his disciples believed in him. After this, he went down to Capernaum with his mother, his brothers, and his disciples; and they remained there a few days. (Jn 2:1-12)

Scripture commentaries on this text unfold a variety of theological interpretations. For some authors the Cana story, with its wine and marriage imagery, foreshadows the marriage of Christ, the bridegroom, with his bride, the Church. Others see a sacramental connection between Cana and the Eucharist in Jesus' proclamation "I am the bread of Life. Whoever comes to me will never be hungry, and whoever believes in me will never thirst" (Jn 6:35).[52]

Aristide Serra brought to light the parallel between the Israelites' profession of faith, the covenant at Sinai, "All that Yahweh has said, we will do" (Exodus 19:8; 24:3, 7) and Mary's words to the servants at Cana, "Do whatever he tells you" (Jn 2:5). For Serra, Mary asks of the servants the same unconditional "Yes" in their attitude towards Jesus. In responding immediately to him, the servants represent the new people of God, the disciples of Jesus who faithfully follow their Master and stay close by him. "If anyone wishes to serve me," Jesus says, "let him follow me; wherever I am, my 'servant' will likewise be" (Jn 12:26)[53]

Paul VI concludes his apostolic letter *On Devotion to Mary* with this interpretation. For him Mary's words "Do whatever he tells you" not only echo the covenant at Sinai and the Israelites' renewal of their commitment (Jos 24:24; Ezr 10:12; Neh 5:12), they also harmonize with God's word "Listen to him," spoken to the disciples on Mount Tabor (Mk 8:7; Mt 17:5; Lk 9:35).[54]

When Jesus transforms water that had been set aside for Jewish purification rites into wine, he moves beyond ritual and legalism. He "transforms this water of the ancient law into the wine of the new law, revealing himself in the process."[55] This manifestation of Jesus' glory, the first visible sign of Jesus being God's presence in their midst, leads the disciples to faith (Jn 2:11).

Within these symbolic and theological interpretations, Mary is seen as the catalyst in initiating Jesus' first miracle. She becomes "an associate, a helpmate in Christ's work."[56]

Beyond the symbolic and theological meaning of the text, the presence of Jesus and his mother at a wedding feast provides a human touch, reminding us that they took part in the life and celebrations of the community. Searching the text enables us to uncover nuances not seen when the text is understood in a purely symbolic, theological way. Not having enough food or wine for the wedding guests would not only be embarrassing, it would be shaming. In Jewish society the dishonour would fall on the groom and his family.

Unlike the chief steward and the groom, Mary notices that the wine has run out. For her to be so conscious of a pending embarrassment to her hosts suggests her close relationship with this family. To solve the problem, Mary turns to her son.

It would seem that in Mediterranean society, where relationships were based on reciprocity, honour, and shame, "even in adulthood an 'honourable' son is expected to obey his mother."[57] Jesus' response to his mother – "Woman, what concern is that to you and to me? My hour has not yet come" – challenges the expected relationship between mother and son and his obligation to enhance the family's honour.

Since the gospel gives no indication that Jesus had previously performed miracles, it is unlikely that Mary expected him to perform a miracle. In fact, when Mary says to the servants, "Do whatever he tells you," it seems to indicate that she didn't understand his response and expects him to do something to fix the problem.

This incident at Cana – like the narratives that we considered above in Mark, Matthew, and Luke – challenges normal family relationships and the structures of honour and status upon which this society was built. In particular, the story focuses on the expectation inherent within mother-son relationships in Mediterranean society. For Mary, Cana becomes a visitation with her son in which she is challenged to move beyond her relationship as Jesus' mother into a new relationship shaped by his ministry and within the community of disciples. It is a moment of truth and choice. After the miracle at Cana, Mary joins Jesus, his brothers, and his disciples and goes to Capernaum (Jn 2:12). In John's gospel, the making of a community around Jesus begins here. Mary is not mentioned again until she appears at the foot of the cross.

> Standing near the cross of Jesus were his mother, and his mother's sister, Mary the wife of Clopas, and Mary Magdalene. When Jesus saw his mother and the disciple whom he loved standing beside her, he said to his mother, "Woman, here is your son." Then he said to the disciple, "Here is your mother." And from that hour the disciple took her into his own home. (Jn 19:25-27)

Mary stands at the cross and endures the pain of watching her son suffer and die on a cross – an unjust, humiliating death. In her anguished moments of pain and confusion before the horror of what is happening to her son, the ultimate visitation between them takes place.

The image of Mary standing at the foot of the cross is often linked to the fulfillment of Simeon's prophecy that a sword of sorrow would pierce her heart (Lk 2:35). But Mary's self-emptying, which echoes the moment of the Annunciation, creates in her the inner space to receive his words to her, "Woman, here is your son," and those spoken to the disciple, "Here is your mother" (Jn 19:26-27).[58] The transformation of her relationship to Jesus as his biological mother, begun at Cana, is completed at the cross as she is given the role of mother in the circle of disciples.

For many years, this event was presented to believers as Jesus fulfilling his obligations towards his mother by ensuring that the beloved disciple would take care of her. Yet all the gospels refer to Jesus' brothers and family. Why didn't Jesus entrust her to them?

Some scholars have pointed out that the Greek word translated as "home" should not be interpreted as "house" or "dwelling," but interpreted in a moral sense. The beloved disciple, in his openness in faith to Jesus' last words, accepts to become the son of Jesus' mother. He welcomes her as his own mother and takes her into the intimacy of his own inner life, his life of faith.[59] In recent years, entrusting oneself to Mary as the beloved disciple does has come to be described as the Marian dimension of a Christian's inner life.[60] Simply put, Mary's faith journey becomes the model for any disciple's inner life of faith.

The beloved disciple is different from the other disciples: they would be scattered, while he would stay with Jesus.[61] In having Mary become the disciple's mother, John makes it clear what happens to Mary after Jesus' death. By becoming the mother of the beloved disciple, Raymond Brown says, she "is brought into the relationship of discipleship."[62]

Cana and the cross show that Mary's motherhood and discipleship are not two separate roles: her call to be a disciple grew out of her call to be Jesus' mother. Over time she has learned the meaning of this call for her life. What began at Cana is completed at the cross.

Through Mary's presence at Cana and at the cross, John's gospel shows that relationships in the community of Jesus' disciples transcend the boundaries of family and kinship ties, wealth, ethnicity, and social status. Mark, Matthew, and Luke make the same point by placing her at the beginning of Jesus' public ministry.

For John's community of disciples, the foundation of the Church, the gift of the Spirit, takes place symbolically at the cross as Jesus gives up his spirit in death (Jn 19:30). In the other gospels the Spirit is given to the disciples after Jesus' resurrection.

Mary and the beloved disciple at the cross "represent all of Jesus' brothers and sisters who are there and who will come into the community of believers. Mary is symbolic of this community as its mother," says Bertrand Buby.[63] Together with the women at the cross, they represent the community of disciples called to embrace Jesus' new commandment, "Love one another. Just as I have loved you, so you also should love one another. By this everyone will know that you are my disciples, if you have love for one another" (Jn 13:34-35). For Mary and for all future disciples, this means being willing to lay down their lives for others as Jesus has done for the sake of the kingdom of God.

The time between Calvary and Pentecost, with its darkness and joy, prepared Mary and the women and men disciples for the extraordinary visit of the Spirit that they would experience.[64] With the coming of the Spirit, "Mary's mission as mother shifts from her son to the Church."[65]

Reflection on scriptural references to Mary and the unfolding of her vocation as Jesus' mother further reveals Mary as a woman of visitation, attentive to God, who called her through the events of her life. Let us now consider how her life lived in visitation influenced her growth in discipleship and her faith journey.

Becoming Disciples of Jesus

Part I: Mary's Faith Journey

Demands of Discipleship

All four gospels stress these basic characteristics of discipleship: call; personal attachment to Jesus; and sharing in his life, destiny, and mission. Listening to Jesus, following his way of life, and leaving everything to follow him are inherent in the call (Mk 1:17; Mt 4:22; Lk 5:11; Lk 9:57-62; Jn 13:12-15). Jesus makes the cost of discipleship clear: "If anyone wants to become my followers, let them deny themselves and take up their cross and follow me. For those who want to save their life will lose it, and those who lose their life for my sake will save it" (Mk 8:34-35; cf. Mt 16:24-28). Luke adds "daily" to these requirements (Lk 9:23-27). For this reason, the rich young man goes away sad (Mk 10:17-31; Mt 19:16-30; Lk 18:18-30), and some would-be followers fear the insecurity of this choice or resist the immediacy of the invitation (Lk 9:57-60). All disciples are faced with the mystery of what accepting this call means in their lives.

Jesus shows by example and parable that love of God and neighbour is the mark of discipleship (Mt 22:34-40; Mk 12:28-34; Lk 10:25-28). His teaching about the good Samaritan shows that one's neighbour is not limited by social status, gender, or ethnic background (Lk 10:29-37). In John's gospel, Jesus spells out the exigencies of discipleship at the Last Supper. After washing the disciples' feet, Jesus says, "I have set you an example, that you should also do as I have done to you"

(Jn 13:15). "I give you a new commandment, that you love one another. Just as I have loved you, you also should love one another. No one has greater love than this, to lay down one's life for one's friends" (Jn 15:13).

To become his disciple is to enter into an intimate relationship with him, an attachment to him and to his word. Those who hear him speak God's word and implement his words in their lives become his brother and sister and mother, members of his true family (Mk 3:35; Mt 12:50; Lk 8:21). As Jesus says, "This is the work of God, that you believe in him whom he has sent" (Jn 6:29).

True righteousness is doing the will of God as expressed in his teaching on the Beatitudes (Mt 5–7; Lk 6:46-49). How this plays out in a disciple's life is each individual's sacred story.

The gospels abound with stories where Jesus shows God's unconditional love for people. These include Jesus' gentleness towards the woman taken in adultery (Jn 8:3ff.); his cure of the crippled woman on the Sabbath (Lk 13:10ff.); and his healing of the man born blind (Jn 9:1ff.). Healing the woman suffering from a hemorrhage, which shows his lack of concern for ritual purity laws and admitting women into his circle of disciples (Lk 8:1-3; Acts 1:12-14), are examples of how he challenged the law.

In so doing, Jesus overturned the idea that suffering was punishment for sin (Jn 9:1-3). He portrays a God of love who wants to restore us to wholeness, not a God of wrath and vengeance.

For Jesus, "the sabbath was made for humankind, not humankind for the sabbath" (Mk 2:27). As he gave hope to those on the lower rung of the social ladder, the authorities saw Jesus as denouncing the Law and the Temple. They were unable to see that Jesus was rescuing the commandments from legalism – "there were, at that time, over 600 laws to observe if one wanted to be righteous."[1]

Jesus wanted the authorities and the people to see that God was intimately present among them. God was part of the ebb and flow of life. God, in Jesus, was unconditionally loving, caring, compassionate, and merciful. God, in Jesus, wanted people to be free from fear, ignorance, darkness, and all that imprisoned them.

All the gospels emphasize that Jesus' ascent to Jerusalem entailed hardship, rejection, and opposition from religious and Roman authorities, which result in his betrayal, condemnation, and death on the cross. His behaviour shows all who would follow him that discipleship can make unexpected and difficult demands.

Neither the chief priests nor Pilate wanted the established religious and social order disturbed. They felt threatened by the possibility that those who were poor and dispossessed not only would see that they had rights, but would demand change in the power structure. Jesus, the source of these new ideas, had to be silenced. So they had him crucified.

> Jesus' death on the cross is often presented only as a ransom for our sins. This idea is based on the thinking of Saint Anselm of Canterbury, a twelfth-century theologian, who proposed that God was prepared to forgive human beings, but not without requiring some restitution. Since human beings were incapable of appeasing God, he sent his son, Jesus, to take on the sins of humankind.

> This theology presents God as needing to settle accounts, which is far from the merciful God revealed in Jesus' teachings. The God of Jesus loves freely and always forgives without requiring compensation, leaving human beings free to respond.[2]

Commitment to Jesus means carrying our cross in life – in health, sickness, joy, and sorrow. It means acting for justice and respect for all people, and turning to our neighbour in concern and compassion every day.

Jesus' approach to people and to life shows that following him calls each disciple to conversion – to turn from whatever interferes with a wholehearted commitment to him – and participation in his mission, the building of God's kingdom. Reactions to his teaching by religious and public authorities and many in the crowds show how pride, the need for control, and the inability to make a commitment can and do inhibit a complete gift of self to him.

Jesus gave his disciples no blueprint. He simply asked them to follow him. They were to learn from him how to interact with people, handle injustice, represent God, and call forth the good in people.

The scriptures also show that a disciple's acceptance to follow Jesus and share in his mission does contain joy. The seventy disciples whom Jesus sent ahead of him to do his work returned from their experience with joy (Lk 10:17). In response, Jesus rejoiced in the Holy Spirit for what they had accomplished (Lk 10:21). Turning to them he said: "Blessed are the eyes that see what you see" (Lk 10:23). The implication is that under the guidance of the Spirit they were able to heal as he did. This was a lesson on the mutuality and companionship that he fostered among his followers and wanted them to exercise among themselves. In the light of the resurrection, this narrative also provides hope for the believer who experiences persecution and suffering because of faith in Jesus.

How are these characteristics of discipleship evident in Mary?

Mary's Growth as a Disciple of Jesus

At the Annunciation, Mary meets an essential criterion of discipleship: to hear God's word and to act on it (Lk 1:38). Remembering her Jewishness, her religious formation, and the social climate in which she lived helps us to identify what she left behind at the Annunciation when she said "Yes" to God. Love calls her to let go of the personal plans and wishes she had as a young engaged woman, to risk everything on God's word spoken to her, and to entrust her life to the guidance of God's Spirit. The power of the Spirit enables her to conceive Jesus, which begins her life of intimacy with him. Under the guidance of the Spirit, when she hastens to Elizabeth's house she starts on the road of sharing in Jesus' mission, the call of every disciple. The mutuality of evangelization, which takes place in the Visitation, erupts in the joy-filled cadences of the Magnificat and echoes the promise of God's mercy to all generations. Mary emerges from the Annunciation–Visitation narrative filled with joy and in wonder at the son she has conceived. She is unaware of what life with her child will hold for her, but she is connected to his life and his destiny. The Annunciation–Visitation sets her firmly on the road of discipleship as Jesus' mother.

As perfect as the Annunciation–Visitation motif appears, we must not lose sight of the fact that Mary had no road map to follow. We have read Mary's life in terms of visitation within the context of the infancy narratives, the years known as "the hidden life." Her encounters with Jesus during his public ministry, at Cana and at the cross, enable us to identify her joys and the challenges in her development as a disciple – the self-giving demanded of her when she chose to stand by her son.

Considering her life from the Annunciation on in terms of visitation enables us to see the conversion to which she was called – to change what might interfere with wholeheartedly following Jesus and to participate in his mission. Her encounters with Jesus during his public ministry (Mk 3:31-35; Mt 12:46-50; Lk 8:19-21) and at the wedding at Cana (Jn 2:1-11) reveal the challenges that discipleship made on her. She is called to let go of time-honoured values related to kinship ties, to honour and shame, and to mother–son expectations. Accepting the call to discipleship meant moving beyond the interpretations of the Torah that had previously guided her life. Like everyone else, she was called to discover the pervading presence, love, and compassion of God in herself and in all people.

Identifying with her son meant identifying with all humankind. In listening to and observing him she is gradually led to the awareness that being his disciple would connect her more and more with his mission of establishing God's covenant of justice and righteousness for all. As at the Annunciation, her encounters with Jesus during his public ministry, her interaction with him at Cana, and her stand at the cross present her with moments of decision. Here she must face what is asked of her and continually try to discern the meaning of God's word spoken to her in the events of her life.

Mark's Gospel especially helps us to see the doubts that arose in Mary and in the family because they did not understand Jesus or what he was about. We can appreciate her concern for her son as she became aware of some people's disapproval of him, and her anguish before the imminent danger to her son's life because his teachings and actions threatened the religious authorities of her people and their Roman oppressors. Only a mother who has watched the pain of a child experiencing alienation can truly understand what the marginalization of Jesus must have meant for Mary and the extent to which she also must have felt marginalized. His condemnation as a criminal must have felt like a condemnation of her. Only a mother who has watched a child die can really understand to what extent Jesus' death on the cross, letting go of the intimacy of his physical presence, was also her death.

The evolution of Mary's life as a disciple echoes the self-denial and the taking up of one's cross that Jesus requires of all his disciples. While she doesn't die physically at this point, her experience of his death, her continued love for him, and all that transpired in her life show how she was called to die daily to her personal hopes and dreams.

The Church's emphasis on Mary as a sinless person and the perfect disciple because she heard and acted on God's word at the Annunciation can lead us to overlook the challenges she encountered in her life.

> Describing Mary at the Annunciation as the perfect disciple does not imply that she had reached perfection, shutting out the possibility of further development in her life. On the contrary, the title simply indicates that Mary's response to the word of God that she heard at the Annunciation was as perfect as it could be at that moment. In the following years, as Jesus matured and began to preach his message, the conditions of discipleship for her became increasingly clear.[3]

Mary continually had to decide what living according to the word of God meant in her life. Her presence at the cross and at Pentecost suggests that "she responded to these new demands and increasingly matured in perfection."[4]

Building on Mark's gospel, Luke emphasizes discipleship as a journey (Lk 9:51–19:44). In accepting to be Jesus' mother, says Pope John Paul II, Mary "in a sense becomes the first disciple, the first to whom Jesus seemed to say: 'Follow Me,' even before he addressed this call to the apostles or to anyone else."[5] Every time she is mentioned in the scriptures, we see Mary staying on the journey. This is especially true of John's account of her at the cross (19:25), but we also see it in her presence among the small group of believers gathered in prayer in the Upper Room and at Pentecost (Acts 1:14, 2:1). For Mary to stay on the journey is linked to her initial gift of herself when she said "Yes." This recalls Jesus' words, "No one who puts a hand to the plow and looks back is fit for the kingdom of God" (Lk 9:62), and highlights an essential quality of faith and perseverance in discipleship.[6]

Perseverance in the gospels is born of closeness with Jesus. Closeness with Jesus arises from a prayerful attitude, that continuous reflection on and pondering of the meaning of Jesus and his words and actions in terms of one's own life. Mary had carried Jesus in her womb, given birth to him, raised and educated him, and watched him grow to adulthood. She, who knew him intimately from his conception to his death, pondered her relationship with him and the events that took place in their lives; she is a model of the disciple at prayer.

Mary, the Disciple at Prayer

Mary's prayer life began in childhood. Luke's narrative of the Annunciation provides us with our first image of Mary as a woman of prayer. The way she attentively listened and questioned Gabriel, God's messenger, shows a picture of a woman in relationship with God who opens herself to the action of God's Spirit. Soon after, under the Spirit's guidance, Mary responds to her cousin Elizabeth's affirmation of her and the child in her womb with a prayer of praise. This Magnificat reveals her joy and gratitude for who she is and for her experience of God's tenderness for her.

Most importantly, Luke's narrative of the Annunciation points out that Mary's "Yes" is born of a discerning heart that opens her life to the guidance of the Spirit – an attitude that is described more fully when Luke tells us that she treasured and pondered in her heart the shepherds' words about Jesus during their visit (2:19). After her encounter with Simeon and Anna, and her conversation with her twelve-year-old son when he was found in the Temple, Mary is again said to have "treasured all these things in her heart" (2:51). Luke's use of the word "things" can also mean that she treasured all these events.[7] It is important to connect the verbs treasured and pondered (2:19, 51). This does not imply simply remembering that certain things happened or that certain words were spoken. Rather, these Greek verbs mean to turn over and over again in one's mind and heart in order to understand or interpret their meaning. Using them in relation to Mary shows her "bringing together the individual incidents she has experienced in order to understand their meaning."[8]

Neither text suggests that Mary reached a conclusion. This open-endedness conveys to us that this attitude will permeate Mary's life. Other occasions will call her to listen, to ponder the mystery in her heart, and to wait patiently for understanding as life unfolds.

In many ways this attitude resembles Matthew's advice about closing the door of one's room and praying to God in secret (6:6). This stance before Jesus, as his life and mission evolve, allows Jesus' way of being and acting to fill her, facilitating her growth and maturation as a disciple while she experiences the uncertainty, insecurity, and darkness of the unknown in her life. In Raymond Brown's words,

Mary is the only adult from the Lucan infancy narrative who appears in Jesus' public ministry among those who hear the word of God and do it (Lk 8:21), who is part of the believing community in the Upper Room praying for and awaiting Jesus' promise of the Holy Spirit and at the Pentecost event (Acts 1:14; 2:1).... Luke shows that Mary must have sought to interpret these events surrounding the birth of Jesus and ultimately have succeeded, for she became a model Christian believer.[9]

Mary, Jesus' mother and his first teacher, has become his disciple, "educated into his own ways and according to the requirements of his mission."[10] Her prayerful, pondering, and discerning heart played a significant role in this development.

Discipleship cannot be separated from faith. To follow Jesus as his disciple means to grow in faith. Each depends on the other. To call Mary a disciple of Jesus is to speak of her as a woman of faith.[11] Her life lived in visitation not only unfolds her growth as a disciple of Jesus, but also traces her faith journey.

Mary's Faith Journey

Faith, in Hebrew terms, encompasses two poles: faith-illumination, which is the light received that leads to faith, and faith-adherence, which is one's personal response on a daily basis.[12] In speaking of Mary's faith, it is important to remember that she was formed in the faith of her people. Her faith in God existed before the Annunciation. At the Annunciation, the light of the Spirit led to her faith response of "Yes" to God's word. This is, as Pope John Paul II tells us, "the culminating moment of Mary's faith in her waiting for Christ, but it is also the point of departure from which her whole journey towards God, her whole pilgrimage of faith in relation to Jesus begins."[13] Her "Yes" at the Annunciation marks the beginning of her growth in discipleship and her "personal faith development which takes her further and further away from herself on to a mission which is not hers but which she wholeheartedly accepts in faith."[14]

Mary's life lived in visitation allows us to see that her growth in faith, as in discipleship, unfolds in her social environment. Her faith journey from the Annunciation to Pentecost, as her development as a disciple, is "shaped through continuous interaction with other persons."[15] In committing herself in faith to be Jesus' mother, Mary undertakes the journey for her lifetime.

Looking at her from this perspective allows us to trace her "pilgrimage of faith, a faith shaped by joy, free choice, lack of understanding, obscurity and total commitment," as the encyclical *Lumen Gentium* puts it.[16] We see Mary's personal openness to and receptivity of God's word and her ability to ponder over and to walk in the obscurity of the events in her life that she did not understand. We watch her encounter with Jesus during his public ministry, her experience of Jesus' death as a criminal, her acceptance of the darkness that followed, her journey to and beyond the resurrection to Pentecost, and her life in the Jerusalem community. This shows the two poles of faith – commitment and perseverance – interacting day by day in her life as she grew in faith and in discipleship. Her faith journey also conveys her ability to face and incorporate radical change in her life that lead her beyond the familiar boundaries of her religious and social environment. Through life's experiences, her identity as a believer and as a disciple of Jesus were shaped and developed.

Mary, indeed, walked in faith. The meaning of her role as mother and a disciple of Jesus would become clear only in the light of the cross and Pentecost.

Mary's visitation lifestyle points to the interlocking dynamic that love and suffering play in life, and underlines that choosing Christ is a never-ending process. It also shows Mary as a real woman in the religious and social context of her day. Face-to-face with Jesus – like all the disciples – she had to learn to see, to hear, and to understand from his point of view.

Mary's pilgrimage of faith represents a constant point of reference for every believer and for the Church. In truth, Mary's faith is a model for ours: she leads the way.[17]

Mary's growth as a disciple and her faith journey emphasize that following Jesus is a call into a relationship of ever greater intimacy with God, self, neighbour, and the whole of creation. She becomes the model servant of God for others.[18] Mary brought this maturity to the small group of Jesus' followers with whom she gathered in prayer in the Upper Room as they waited for Jesus' promise that they would be empowered by the Spirit for a new mission (Acts 1:12-14).

A seventeenth-century image of Mary, used by a seventeenth-century theologian, captures this view of her life.

Mary's Journeying Life with Jesus: A Seventeenth-Century Image

Cardinal Bérulle, a seventeenth-century theologian, presented Mary as a model of Christian life.[19] He urged Christians in his day to reflect on Mary's "journeying life" with Jesus, contemplating their relationship each step of the way from his conception to his death on the cross and his ascension. To grasp the heart of his reflections, we must first consider his perception of how Jesus lived. For Bérulle, Jesus, throughout his "journeying life on earth,"[20] in particular during his public life, was always engaged in conversation with his neighbours, looking beyond appearances to their inner heart. In this way, Jesus did not impose himself on them, but responded to them as individuals; he addressed their needs, healed them of their illnesses, and challenged them, when necessary, to change their ways. Jesus' outreach to people was always in view of their liberation, seeking ways to enable them to become free from whatever impeded their understanding of themselves as persons deeply loved by God. Jesus had started a new conversation between God and humankind.

In the seventeenth century, the French word that we translate as "conversation" was still close to its Latin root and meant "to live with." It carried the sense of its verb form, which meant to turn and turn again towards one's neighbour – to be oriented towards and attentive to one's neighbour as a person.[21] This suggests that imitating Jesus in his journeying life or his life in conversation with his neighbour were one and the same, and involved being attentive to others as Jesus was to everyone he met. In Bérulle's opinion, no one had done this better than Mary.

For Bérulle, Mary's prayerful attitude – her treasuring and pondering in her heart her relationship with Jesus as it unfolded through the many events they experienced together, including his death and ascension – had allowed Jesus' way of being and acting to permeate her. He complements this image of Mary with that of her journeying with Jesus throughout his public life, often sitting at his feet listening to his word. This portrait of Mary resembles that of Martha's sister, Mary (Lk 10:38-

42). But, in Bérulle's eyes, Mary the mother of Jesus had already chosen the better part at the Annunciation, when she accepted to be Jesus' mother. For him, her ability to ponder deeply and to listen attentively to Jesus' teachings had enabled her to develop the same mind and heart as Jesus had (Eph 3:14-21; Phil 2:1-11). For this reason, Bérulle proposed that Christians learn from Mary how to love, to follow Jesus, and to imitate his virtues in their lives according to their personal gifts and circumstances.

It is not surprising that, as a result of Bérulle's reflection, Mary "in conversation with her neighbour" became a favourite expression in seventeenth-century spirituality. This expression was used to describe her whole life – the depths of intimacy she entered into with Jesus and her neighbour. Rooted in scripture, it placed Mary strongly within the whole of Jesus' life and mission and conveyed the essence of her entire life on earth. After Jesus' ascension, Mary, empowered anew at Pentecost, drew on the life of the Spirit in her to continue to be intimately connected to her Risen son. Moulded and shaped by Jesus during his life, and now under the guidance of his Spirit, Mary would live her life in the first community in service of others as Jesus had. She was always turned towards the needs of her neighbour, was always in visitation and ready to make Jesus known and loved. Mary, in conversation with her neighbour, was a woman in the world; she was not a cloistered nun steeped in prayer and solitude and set apart.

This seventeenth-century image of Mary in conversation with her neighbour fits well with the Church's emphasis today on Mary's discipleship and her faith journey as a model for Christians, called to be Christ's presence in a world plagued by broken relationships between people and among nations. Life lived in visitation is the best way to capture this reality.

Part II: Faith and Discipleship: Being Christian Today

The Annunciation was a point of departure for Mary's development in faith and as a disciple of Jesus; baptism fulfills the same role for us today. If we were baptized as children, we make a conscious choice to be Christian the moment we confirm our initial yes, promised in baptism, rather than simply attending church because our parents or friends do. We become conscious that our choice for Jesus is a response to our having been chosen first. This moment affirms our faith in Jesus, bringing us into relationship with him on the long road of discipleship.

Baptism becomes a touchstone experience for us – the jewel against which we can reflect on the authenticity of our ongoing efforts to live in communion with God and in intimacy with Jesus. This life is guided by the Spirit, who leads us to internalize the values of the gospel that, in turn, shape us and all we do. As our faith journeys unfold, with our eyes on the encounter between Mary and Elizabeth in the Visitation (Lk 1:39-56), we are mindful that the Jesus we carry in our hearts must be shared with others. We must speak about him in ways that truly show him to be good news for all who receive him.

Disciples of Jesus can find inspiration for their lives in Mary. They know that, like Mary, they are called to live their lives in an attitude of visitation, where intimacy with God and service of neighbour form an intertwining dance.

Mary's life in visitation underlined that her "Yes" was shaped through her relationship with Jesus, the events of their lives, her relationships with others, her service, and her call to share in his mission. Reflection on her journey shows us that hearing the word of God and incorporating it into our lives will bring unforeseen joys and challenges that can alter our lives radically. Her development as a disciple also shows that discipleship is an all-consuming vocation that is always evolving. As life revealed the meaning of discipleship in her very special call as Jesus' mother, so it will do for us. Recognizing her unique vocation should help us to appreciate our own unique call as Jesus' disciples today. Like Mary, we cannot say that we know what it means to be a disciple. But we are called to trust that the Spirit of Jesus – while respecting our person, our gifts, and our limitations – will help us respond as Jesus' disciples in our own place and our own circumstances.

In looking at Mary's lifelong commitment we see that fidelity to her call required her to be able to enter into uncharted territory, to be open to surprises, and to embrace a new community of Jesus' followers. Her fidelity required flexibility, as does ours.

Faith, walking hand in hand with discipleship, progresses and changes through life; it summons us to live in the present and to hope in the future. Faith, like discipleship, is always evolving. Looking at Mary's life helps us to see that maturing in faith and in discipleship is an ongoing process that invites us into an ever-deepening love relationship with God. Reflecting on her life experience with Jesus shows us that God was not, and is not, distant – even in the midst of chaos and catastrophe.

To live in visitation like Mary did summons us to trust in God who, while remaining totally Other, is present in us in our neighbours and in all of creation. To live in visitation calls us to open ourselves to the presence of God in all events: the peak moments, the ordinary events of everyday life, the unforeseen events, and the continuous changes in our lives. To live in visitation helps us to believe that the Holy Spirit can, and does, break through in the good that we and others do.

To live in visitation is to trust that God is with us at all times. We trust as we carry the memories of horrendous evil experienced in the massacres of thousands of people, in human-made famines caused by the abuse of the earth, and in the despair of countless refugees throughout the world.

Mary's life in visitation shows that faith and discipleship call us to mindfulness; we must live in the awareness that every person – and, indeed, the whole of creation – carries a sacred story. Guided by the inner workings of the Spirit, we are called to live life like Mary – open and receptive to the mystery of life as it unfolds in each of our lives. We are called, like her, to see beyond ethnic and cultural differences and to embrace every human being as a child of God.

Reflection on Mary's life from the Annunciation to Pentecost shows a journey in which attentiveness to God's word throughout her life radically changed her life. Mary was shaped by joy, pain, light, and darkness; she let go of time-honoured traditions as she chose to stand with her son. This letting go was not a negation of the past but a movement to new vision as she shared more and more in her son's life and his mission. This was Mary's call to conversion.

The disciple of Jesus can expect no less today. Beyond formulas and creeds, faith and discipleship require that disciples continually pray to know in the depths of their hearts the answer to Jesus' question: "Who do you say that I am?" (Mk 8:29).

Each person is called to let go of whatever impedes living as a disciple of Jesus in today's world. Conversion is never easy, especially when we find ourselves in the middle of conflicting opinions on religious, ethical, moral, and social issues within and beyond our own faith community. Conflicting opinions have alienated members of the

Christian community, caused divisions in families and in the workplace, and set religions and political ideologies against each other. The issue for all disciples is to discern whether, as followers of Jesus, once we have reflected on the gospels and church teaching, we are speaking and acting with authenticity. Mary's life – from the Annunciation to the cross, in the Upper Room, and at Pentecost – proclaims to us that conversion is basic to Christian living.

Reflection on Mary's faith journey and growth as a disciple gives us hope on our own journey. Following Jesus and embracing his mission led her to a new awareness of God. As Jesus revealed God's great compassion and love for all people, Mary was called to a new understanding of family.

Her life enables us to see how interiority – permeated by our belief in God and in the presence of the risen Jesus – transforms every facet of living. Her life shows us what it means to love God with all our heart, soul, mind, and strength, and to love our neighbour as ourselves. Her life lived in visitation shows what it means to live in love. To live in love we must live from the centre of our being, as Mary did.

Living Life from the Centre

The centre of our being is the still point, the place where we touch true joy in the midst of hell, "peace in the midst of storm and turbulence."[22] To live life from the inside out is to live in the awareness that "both levels – the inner and the outer – are the reality of life. It is the inner reality where we know the Advent – the eternal coming of the Spirit of Christ – that allows us to live into and through the outer crucifixions to a New Life."[23] That reality allows us to experience true consolation and peace as we, too, pick up our cross – manifested in the daily stresses of life – and follow Jesus on the Way. Above all, "love at the centre of one's being demands a response – availability, service, action."[24] Mary's journey to the cross reminds us of the interconnectedness of our prayer and worship, our communion with God, and the gift of ourselves for others. Taking the cue from Mary's prayer, alone and with others we can find the way.

Mary's prayer on the journey shows that prayer is the heart of ongoing communion with God and of intimacy with Jesus that enables our lives to be shaped and moulded by his values. From the Annunciation on, she manifests the importance of prayer in a disciple's process of discerning choices, and the need for active listening and patient waiting for light on the journey. Her prayer of pondering things and events over and over again shows us that growth in faith and in discipleship requires inner solitude – that entry into the depths of our being where authenticity is born and shaped over time. Inner silence enabled Mary to hear the Holy Spirit speaking in her heart. Inner silence also opens our hearts to the Spirit's voice.

Mary's prayer on her journey in faith and in discipleship shows us the importance of walking with and waiting out those moments of doubt, questioning, and uncertainty. We experience these times when we seek new clarity and new understanding from God in our lives. Yet, if we can live in the moment, new impulses of the Spirit and a new vision of life can emerge. Such interior availability opens us up to life as an adventure of faith, complete with the awareness that there will be surprises along the way. From this perspective, we see the joys and the sorrows of life, the light and the darkness, for what they are: experiences enabling our development as persons of faith and disciples on a journey, the very fibres that weave the fabric of our lives and help us become the person God wants us to be. They help us make our contribution to help transform our society and our world into a safe and nurturing home for all people and all creation. To live in this manner is to live like Mary, trusting "that all things work together for good for those who love God" (Rom 8:28). It is to pray and not lose heart (Lk 18:1). Living from the centre of our being makes room for Mary's words spoken to the servants at Cana to be heard in our hearts: "Do whatever he tells you" (Jn 2:5). This is the disciple's call to give birth to Christ.

Giving Birth to Christ

Viewing Mary as the archetype of Christian discipleship, rooted in the narratives of the Annunciation–Visitation, reminds us that her virginal heart is a symbol of inner freedom. When Mary opened her heart to the power of the Spirit, she creatively united herself to God's purpose. New life sprang from within her being. Jesus was conceived, born, and shared with others. Like Mary, we are called to become pregnant with the word of God so that Christ can be born in our world today and shared with others along the way.

We need to ask, as did the medieval mystic Meister Eckhart, what good does it do if Mary gave birth to Jesus in her time and place if I do not also give birth to Jesus in my time and place?

The Annunciation–Visitation motif speaks a truth about us and our relationship with God. In the words of John Shea, it means that

> the place from which we do our actions affects their quality and effectiveness. Whether we are acting out of love, duty, guilt, or anger has consequences on our actions and their impact on how others see us, and how they receive what we do for them. Our fruitfulness depends on our union with God who is Love who leads us to act in love.[25]

If we live in visitation like Mary, we will continually be called to move from the inside out, to connect to the inner place of love that is the spiritual source of all our actions. "When action flows from this source, everything we do – our relationships, our work, and our play – will be stripped of anxiety, purged of ego, and free from hidden competitions and subtle dominations that keep us from joy and peace. Christ will be born."[26]

The enthusiasm of a life lived in Love can only help others to reflect on who Jesus is in their own lives and on their own call to give birth to Christ daily. Pope John Paul II reminds us that as long as we believe

> simply on the authority of the Church, without caring what the contents are, we can hardly be enthusiastic about our faith. If we focus on the God of Jesus Christ, as disclosed in the gospel, our faith becomes a loving assent to an extraordinary piece of good news intended by God for all the world. It is a message that we have no right to monopolize, to keep to ourselves.[27]

We will no longer see faith as a private affair but as a gift to be shared with others, a call to participate in the mission to evangelize that Jesus gave to his disciples, and our responsibility as church.

Many in the Church are frightened off by certain approaches to evangelization. How does a disciple of Jesus evangelize in today's world while respecting other religions? Mary's life can shed some light on this Christian responsibility.

The Church's Mission of Evangelization

Through the story of Mary's visit to Elizabeth, Luke tells us that everyone who makes room for God's word within their hearts must carry the gift to others. The phrase "to carry forth God's Word" or "to carry Jesus with us" wherever we go is often used to express the Church's mission of evangelization. Mary's life lived in visitation shows us how to stand before God and be attentive to God's word. Reflection on her encounter with Elizabeth shows that Mary, the visitor, was visited by her cousin; evangelization is a two-way street. Mary's entire life from that moment showed that her faith journey and growth as a disciple evolved as she was evangelized through the events she experienced with her son.

To live our mission of evangelization in visitation is to turn and turn again towards our neighbour, always showing compassion, care, and concern for each person and what they are living at that moment. It is to be available to God's surprise visits to us in our meetings with others, in the daily or unexpected events in our lives, and in creation. To live in visitation is to know that our whole person is an expression of our faith in Christ, and that any person or any event can be a messenger of God.

To participate in the Church's mission of evangelization is to take time to reflect again and again on the scriptures – praying and discerning how we are to live as Jesus did and how we can communicate his message to those we meet. "Evangelization then is not about securing new church members nor becoming a more cohesive body as church as tempting as that may be," says George Wilson. "It is first about being transformed by the good news of Jesus Christ."[28]

For this to happen, we must be open to surprises of the Spirit at work in us and in those with whom we are in dialogue. If we approach others thinking that we possess all truth, then we will be unable to hear the truth that they carry. For our participation in the Church's mission of evangelization to be effective, we must be deeply aware that we stand at all times in the mystery of God's grace and human free will. We must be open, individually and communally, to conversion. Such an attitude will help us greatly as we enter into inter-religious and ecumenical dialogue. To be there in visitation is to listen and to be touched, to challenge and to be challenged, to be open to a change of attitudes, and to stand before the presence of God, the Spirit, at work in other religious expressions. The Vatican II encyclical *Gaudium et Spes* emphasizes that

> God has been, and continues to be active in every culture, even before evangelization; God's presence is experienced in the virtues of people; evangelization discovers these virtues and further enhances them through the people's knowledge of Christ.[29]

We must encounter people first, and listen to their heart's wishes. We must always be in visitation, sensitive to the person and the moment, and attentive to the presence of Jesus waiting to be announced and affirmed in self and in others. To approach evangelization in this manner calls us to enter into the liberating power of true visitation between and among persons and to stand in wonder at all that God is doing in people. Such an approach will facilitate our rediscovering the Incarnation at the heart of the people – a discipleship that acknowledges God's presence and action in others: "God is love, and those who abide in love abide in God, and God abides in them" (1 Jn 4:16). To evangelize is to be attentive to the moments when the Spirit invites us to speak about Jesus. When we do speak, whatever we say about Jesus must address people's lives and relate to their everyday experience.

Mary's encounter with Elizabeth and her experience with Gabriel took place inside a home. While the Temple had a place in their lives, as churches have in ours, Luke emphasizes that God's presence was not confined there. In fact, most of Mary's encounters and her ongoing revelation of God's word take place in the arena of everyday life outside the Temple. The challenge in a post-Christian secular society, where we encounter people of various religious expressions or none at all, is to live in awareness. Wherever we are – any home, street, store, restaurant, community centre, bus, subway, workplace, park, or vacation spot – we may be called upon to share our faith. We may be touched by God's presence in the simple goodness of people and in the beauty of creation that surrounds us.

For evangelization to be effective, it must "always take the human person as its starting point, coming back to the interrelationships between persons and their relationship with God," says the encyclical *Evangelii Nuntiandi*.[30] The Magnificat, Mary's prophetic prayer of thanksgiving and promise, will help us achieve this.

Praying the Magnificat Daily

To pray the Magnificat each day as a disciple of Jesus is to pray in union with Mary in joy, faith, and thanksgiving to God as the source of our being; it is "to sing of God's everlasting love and mercy which extends from age to age [and] to proclaim Mary's hope in the fulfilment of the divine promises in favour of the whole of humanity."[31] It is to claim with Mary that God does not accept a world built on injustice – a reminder of God's tenderness for those who are exploited. To pray the Magnificat is to take the Beatitudes seriously (Lk 6:20-26; Mt 5:3-11) and to see in both the synthesis of the Christian message. It is a daily expression of our availability for discipleship – a confession of faith.

To pray the Magnificat is to make Mary's concern for the poor our concern. It is a commitment to act justly, to promote respect and equality for all, and to nurture our sense of interdependence with people of every nation and with all creation. Our efforts to foster peace in our world begin with how we relate to others in our families, our neighbourhoods, our workplaces, our schools, our churches, and our communities. To pray the Magnificat is to seek ways to address issues in our communities where power in the hands of a few is used against countless anonymous ones: the elderly, the homeless, the working poor, the unemployed, the marginalized, abused women and children, and single-parent families living in poverty.

The heart of anyone who prays the Magnificat seriously grieves the slaughter of innocent people in futile wars around the world, those maimed by exploding land mines, and victims of genocide. The Magnificat, a song of liberation, challenges us to help our brothers and sisters who are in need. Praying the Magnificat echoes our world crying out for compassion and mercy.

Often the global picture is more than we can absorb. The world of multinational corporations can appear impenetrable and too much to tackle, but our own neighbourhoods are not. If each of us finds a way to stand on the side of the poor in our own neighbourhoods, we will be making a statement – small as it is. In this way we recognize that the present situation of poverty in our cities and throughout our world is a sign of a system gone awry. Resisting the temptations of our consumer culture, which urges us to buy more to be happy, and respecting our piece of the earth can be giant first steps at turning things around. Many small efforts at home and around the world can chisel away at the present glaring inequities in which people live.

The Magnificat, at the heart of visitation, summons us to hospitality – to break down the barriers, prejudices, and mistrust that exist in our hearts as well as between and among ethnic, religious, and political groups. Today's disciple of Jesus cannot pray the Magnificat without having petty dislikes challenged and eyes and heart opened again and again to the sacredness of all God's children and all creation. Such is its challenge each time we speak out against the billions of dollars poured into the war machine while people go hungry, say no to the careless disposal of nuclear waste, protest the misuse of funds that makes leaders richer and their people poorer, and enter into honest dialogue with people of other faiths. To pray the Magnificat is an expression of our desire to be honest about the state of our world and shows our conviction that the kingdom of God that Jesus preached is not a vision for an end time but a vision that begins now, in this world.

To pray the Magnificat in union with Mary draws us deeper and deeper into the heart of our baptism – our being sent into the world on mission for the gospel – and assures us that hearing the word of God and keeping it is not a private affair but a commitment to the reality that Christ has no hands or feet but ours.

The Magnificat calls us to enter into the heart of visitation, carrying God's word with us wherever we go; we need to be attentive, listening, and sensitive to the moment when God's love, compassion, and justice can be proclaimed in word and in action. It is our call to be prophetic – to receive the word of God and, under the guidance of the Spirit, be open to speaking God's word in a new way.

As Elizabeth Johnson points out, "It must be made explicit that the word of God that one hears and keeps may well impel the hearer toward conflict with the powers that oppress people not only outside the church but also within it."[32]

Mary, as the archetype of discipleship and her life in visitation, offers Christian disciples a journey – spirituality.

A Journey Spirituality

The journey theme dominates contemporary spirituality. Writers such as Gail Sheehy use it to designate the integration of all dimensions of human life.[33] Gerald O'Collins, among others, speaks about mid-life spirituality as a second journey.[34] According to these authors, journey involves process and movement, light and darkness, joys and risks that move us beyond the comfortable, a willingness to let go of known and secure ways." Psychological interpretations of journey spirituality focus on developmental stages and thresholds."[35]

These notions of journey found in contemporary spirituality fit well with Mary's life as she lived in visitation. They draw our attention to her ongoing openness to the inner guidance of the Spirit that inspired her "Yes" and her ongoing intimacy with Jesus. They indicate her courage to follow him, to grow as his disciple, and to participate actively in his mission to the world. They emphasize her ability to stay the course through ups and downs of her faith journey.

Thresholds, by definition, are places of beginning – like doorways, places of entering into new space. As one writer says,

> Psychologists and anthropologists say that power lies in the thresholds. As random and unpredictable as that power may be we need it. Without it nothing changes – and without that power what does not change does not, cannot endure either. Thresholds are the places of inspiration, of prophecy and the places of beginning.[36]

The Annunciation–Visitation, the cross, and Pentecost are threshold moments in Mary's life: major times of letting go to make way for new life, and places of inspiration, prophecy, and new beginnings. Mary's life in visitation in the ordinary moments of every day as well as during the major threshold times stresses that contemplation and mission – the inner-outer journey of visitation – go hand in hand.

To adopt a journey spirituality that is modelled on visitation will stand us in good stead, permeating the reality of our lives – all we are and all we do – and influence our personal growth as disciples of Jesus and our faith journeys.

We must be careful, though, not to leave Mary's life as the archetype of Christian discipleship for women and men, her life lived in visitation, and her journey spirituality as a model for individual believers. To leave it there is to see only half the picture.

Mary, our sister in faith, was called to take her place in the community of Jesus' disciples – the Church born at Pentecost. So are we. As Clare Thompson says, "Discipleship means participation within a family, a church, a community, an ecclesia: a group of people who have been 'called out.' The building of God's kingdom on earth requires communal, not only individual effort."[37]

Mary, as the archetype of Christian discipleship – who lived in visitation, was attentive to God's ongoing presence in her life, and became part of the circle of disciples gathered in the Upper Room and at Pentecost – points the way.

Part III: In the Footsteps of Mary

5

Mary in the Circle of Disciples

Mary, Woman of Visitation, Woman of Reconciliation

Seeing Mary named among the inner circle of disciples[1] (Acts 1:14) should come as no surprise to us. Luke had already claimed her as the first disciple in the Annunciation–Visitation (Lk 1:26-56); in naming her, along with the brothers of Jesus, as being among those who hear the word of God and do it, he affirms her continuation as a disciple (Lk 8:19-21).[2] Situating Mary among the group in the Upper Room assures us that she has cast her lot with Jesus' intimate followers and roots her in history.[3]

At prayer with the disciples as they wait in faith for the Spirit, she shows her willingness to trust in yet another promise to be empowered by the Spirit for a new mission. This time, the empowerment will involve the group gathered (Acts 1:14). Their gathering together is a strong indication of their commitment to continue the process to which the risen Jesus has invited them.

Mary's presence gives the disciples a strong example of a woman who knew how to wait. From the beginning of her pregnancy she had learned that anything worthwhile takes time to come to life. This woman who pondered events in her life with Jesus over and over again in her heart knew how to wait for understanding to unfold. This same attitude guided her as she searched in her heart to grasp deeply the meaning of Jesus' life, death, and resurrection – for herself and for those with her. Mary is an example of a woman who risked all at the Annunciation, trusting that God's promise to her would be fulfilled (Lk 1:38). Because she had given her "Yes" without knowing the impact it would have, Mary's life shows the disciples the deeper meaning of Jesus' call to follow him – the joys and challenges of her faith journey.

Acts 1:14, the first summary passage in Acts that describes post-resurrection life among Jesus' followers, points to the unity of the group. Luke's description of them gives us an image of people gathered in a circle of silence – content, at one, and at peace. Together, they seem enveloped in mystery as Mary was at the Annunciation.

While they are united, each of these men and women has also had a personal experience of Jesus during his ministry, and has been changed by his death, which ruptured their lives, hopes, and dreams.

Although it may be presumptuous to try to imagine what Mary and the disciples experienced during that time, doing so can help us appreciate the transformation that took place in each of them.

The gaps in the story lead us to wonder what happened when the disciples met up after Jesus' death. In their despair, did they feel uncomfortable with each other? Were they at odds with one another? Did the women reproach the men for abandoning their friend in his hour of need?

And what about Mary? How was she coping with the horror of Jesus death?

Tradition holds that Mary, Jesus' mother, brought the group together after Jesus' death. Setting her own feelings aside, she reached out to comfort them, a source of strength and encouragement. "It is only natural then that Mary who had given birth to Jesus the source of reconciliation would be seen as the 'mother of reconciliation,'"[4] showing the same unconditional love, compassion, and forgiveness to the disciples that Jesus had shown during his ministry and in his death.

Reconciliation gathered them together, broke down division and hostility, and restored them into relationship and into communion with each other.

The power of Jesus' resurrection blossomed amidst their emptiness and desolation. Joy dissipated their fear, bringing light into the pervasive darkness that had enveloped them during and after Jesus' death, and opening their hearts and minds to receive his final teaching. Their confusion and despair gave way to new confidence and hope.

In the Upper Room, the memory of their ecstatic joy over Jesus' resurrection, the comforting assurance of his risen presence, and his final words must have been engraved deeply in each heart. For Mary, her son's resurrection must have unleashed deep peace and joy in her being as she realized that her decision at the Annunciation in putting aside her own plans and risking everything for Jesus had not been in vain.

The resurrection, like the Annunciation, underlined the paradoxical ways of God. In believing that God had raised Jesus from death, Mary and the disciples are brought to a new awareness about themselves. As Robert Ludwig says, "What they believe about Jesus, they come to believe about themselves. They feel themselves chosen, affirmed, claimed by God."[5] Certainly they must have sensed that they stood on the threshold of something new. What it would look like and mean for their lives remained to be seen.

Hidden in the opening verses of the first chapter of Acts are Mary's and the disciples' stories of coming to faith in the risen Jesus, which help us to recall the key events that had marked their lives: walking with Jesus during his ministry and their conversion, letting go of Jesus in death, entering into chaos, regrouping around the risen Jesus, and then letting go of that comforting presence. All these moments prepared their hearts for the creative power of the Spirit.

Mary's presence in the circle of disciples in the Upper Room leads us to believe that even in the darkest moments, she had clung in faith to the promise of the Annunciation that "nothing will be impossible with God" (Lk 1:37). In turning to the disciples after Jesus' death, reaching out to them with a mother's love, she begins to see the new direction discipleship will take for her as Jesus' mother.

Pentecost

> When the day of Pentecost had come, they were all together in one place. And suddenly from heaven there came a sound like the rush of violent wind, and it filled the entire house where they were sitting. Divided tongues, as of fire, appeared among them, and a tongue rested on each of them. All of them were filled with the Holy Spirit and began to speak in other languages, as the Spirit gave them ability. (Acts 2:1-4)[6]

This passage from Luke, which announces the Spirit's presence in Mary and the disciples, followed by their immediate exodus from the

Upper Room to join the crowds in Jerusalem at Pentecost, is charged with excitement, enthusiasm, and courage. Their behaviour suggests that they know in the depths of their being that Jesus' promise has been fulfilled. All fear and uncertainty dissipate. The power of the Spirit impels them to go out and share what they have received.

Anyone who has visited Jerusalem knows that the Upper Room, according to tradition, was located in the Upper City of Jerusalem known as Mount Zion. It was within walking distance of the Temple Mount. Today, in the same area of the old city of Jerusalem, a large room known as the Cenacle stands above the site designated as David's tomb.[7] A stairway leads from the Cenacle to the street below. We can imagine this Spirit-filled group hastening enthusiastically down the steps and proclaiming the mighty works of God to everyone they meet (Acts 2:11). The excitement mounts as the narrative continues.

It is not surprising that the disciples' Spirit-given ability to speak in other languages astonishes those they meet. The result is truly amazing! People who were strangers to each other before, unable to enter into conversation, now understand one another. And yet, although some were amazed, others were skeptical.

To end any misunderstanding of what had taken place in the Upper Room, Luke places a detailed speech on Peter's lips. Although he gives no indication of where the crowds had gathered,[8] this first speech, one of many in Acts, contains the very structures of evangelism. It begins with an explanation of what God has done for them. In this case, Peter explains that what has happened to them is a fulfillment of the last days foretold by the prophet Joel, where all have access to God's spirit (Acts 2:16-21). This announcement is followed by an acknowledgment of what people know about Jesus. Peter then helps them to see the meaning of Jesus' life, death, and resurrection, supporting his claims about Jesus by referring to the Hebrew scriptures.

As the speech continues, he tells his listeners that the kingdom Jesus announced begins with an inner spiritual transformation that leads to freedom from oppressive inner and outer structures. The promise is for everyone whom the Lord God calls (Acts 2:39). The same Spirit that Peter and his companions have received will be given to all believers. He calls them to baptism, "to make a visible and verifiable profession of their acceptance of Jesus," as Raymond Brown puts it.[9] "In terms of the Christian life there will be no second-class citizens."[10] On

Pentecost, many hearts were touched by what was heard and seen. According to Acts, three thousand were converted that very day (Acts 2:41).

Over the years, scripture scholars have interpreted this figure symbolically rather than literally, as Luke's way of indicating the rapid growth of the Jesus movement throughout the first century (Acts 2:41, 47).[11] That the population of Jerusalem would have swelled at the feast of Pentecost (Acts 2:5ff.; 20:16; 21:27) has been proven by recent studies.[12] Though Leviticus states that this feast lasted only one day (Lev 23:15-21), Jews were permitted to bring the appropriate offerings to the Temple for a further seven days thereafter. Apparently there was an unwritten duty to stay in Jerusalem for the week. This information – coupled with demographic and archeological studies showing that first-century Jerusalem was a prosperous, well-populated urban centre – suggests that Luke's figures may not be that inaccurate after all.[13] Regardless of the accuracy of the number, these conversions make it clear that the prophetic Spirit empowering Mary and the disciples to be witnesses of Jesus was spreading. The Spirit and the mission are shared by all who join the group of believers. The formation of the Christian community began at this moment, even though it would be some time before followers of Jesus were known as such.

Luke gives no indication of the number of converts from Jerusalem, the Galilee, or the Diaspora. With the entry of the latter into the group of believers, Acts 2 opens the door for diversity and the development of creative pluralism.[14]

The overshadowing of the Spirit on the group gathered at Pentecost – as at creation, at Sinai, and at the Annunciation – has created something new.[15] The universality of the gift of the Spirit has been set in motion, even though the early chapters in Acts focus on the growth of the community in Jerusalem.

Pentecost: In the Footsteps of Mary

For some time, scripture scholars have remarked on the parallel structures found in Luke and Acts. There is a striking similarity between the story of Pentecost and Jesus' baptism (Acts 2:1-4; Lk 3:21-22). The disciples at Pentecost, like Jesus at his baptism, are filled with courage for the mission ahead. At the same time there is an important connection between the conception of Jesus at the Annunciation and Pentecost, which we identify as the birth of the Church. "The person who links these two moments is Mary: Mary at Nazareth and Mary in the Upper Room at Jerusalem," says Pope John Paul II in *Redemptoris Mater* (Mother of the Redeemer).[16] Mary, empowered by the Spirit at the Annunciation many years before, had conceived and given birth to Jesus. Now, united in prayer with the group gathered in the Upper Room, she conceives and gives birth to the Church with the disciples. The Spirit had not left her; rather, a new infusion of the Spirit was needed for a new mission that involved the gathered community. As Mary had opened herself to the transforming power of the Spirit at the Annunciation, the men and women disciples with Mary at Pentecost do the same. All are filled with the power of the Spirit, no one more than the other (Acts 2:4).

At the Annunciation Mary, through the power of the Spirit, conceived Jesus. From that moment she knew his pervasive inner presence. Now, at Pentecost, Mary and all gathered with her in the Upper Room experienced the pervasive transforming presence and power of the Spirit of the risen Jesus.[17] This was another reminder that "nothing will be impossible with God" (Lk 1:37).

Earlier, the significance of Mary's virginal heart, in relation to every disciple's need for inner freedom to hear and be transformed by the word of God, became clear. At Pentecost, the emphasis shifts to the community. As previously noted, the disciples' inner freedom came at a price. It grew out of their experiences with Jesus crucified and dead, out of buried dreams, out of hope restored in Jesus risen, and through trust in his promise of the Spirit. Pentecost shows that detachment – the ability to wait on God – and inner freedom are prerequisites for receptivity. Jesus was formed in the creative darkness of Mary's womb. The circle of disciples in the Upper Room, gathered in prayer and waiting on God, conveys an image of new life being formed and born out of the group's interior darkness. Together, they form a womb for the Spirit of the risen Jesus to be born and to form community.

The experience of the Upper Room underlines that the disciples – who had travelled with Jesus, had been taught by him during his public ministry, and had received his final instructions – "had all the knowledge they could handle. But the life-change and the power Jesus promised came with Pentecost when the Holy Spirit hit them with the force of undeniable change," says Dimitri Sala.[18] Jesus' promise was fulfilled.

The power of the Spirit that initiated and guided him in his ministry had been passed on. Mary's presence there shows that she was part of this process.[19]

Another striking similarity exists between Mary after the Annunciation and the circle of disciples after their empowerment by the Spirit. After conceiving Jesus, Mary, under the Spirit's guidance, hastens to carry Jesus to her cousin Elizabeth. The Spirit-filled men and women disciples likewise hasten to share the power they received in that transformative moment of liberation. They carry the liberating, saving power of Jesus to their Jewish brothers and sisters celebrating Pentecost in Jerusalem.

The Spirit of the risen Jesus had transformed them into bold, courageous missionaries of the Word – Jesus. A new Visitation erupts – a visitation that will continue in the days, months, and years to follow from one generation to the next and from century to century. Peter's response to the people's mixed reactions (Acts 2:12, 13) contains strong echoes of the Magnificat (Acts 2:14-36; Lk 1:39-56).[20]

Mary opens the Magnificat by expressing her joy over all that God had done for her (Lk 1:47-49). Similarly, the beginning of Peter's speech proclaims what God has done for him and his companions. The new age has come. God's promise through the prophet Joel has been fulfilled. God's spirit has been poured out equally on these men and women servants of the Lord (Acts 2:17-21).[21] Mary, who first described herself as the servant of the Lord at the Annunciation (Lk 1:38), is in the midst of this fledgling community of disciples. These servants of the Lord, like Mary at the Annunciation, have been captured by the paradoxical ways of God's love.

The paradoxical ways of God's love did not stop there. The announcement of Jesus' resurrection affirms several extraordinary reversals. Life has conquered death, and good has triumphed over evil. Robert Ludwig explains,

> This Jesus whom worldly powers have rejected, God has affirmed; this crucified Jesus who was condemned by both religious and civil authority, God has endorsed; this abandoned and God-forsaken Jesus, God has chosen and acclaimed; this broken and beaten Jesus whom oppressive rulers have killed, God has restored and given new life.[22]

In the Magnificat, Mary also sings of a God who saves, who knows no partiality, who is inclusive. In the name of the community, Peter does the same. He announces that Jesus' life, death, and resurrection signify God's compassionate, saving desire for all people. God's Spirit, the Spirit of the Risen Jesus, is available to everyone: old and young, men and women, slave and free. Economic status and rights of birth carry no privilege. What God has done for them this Pentecost day is open to everyone. The universality of salvation – announced in the infancy narrative of Luke's Gospel and foretold in the Magnificat – has been acclaimed.

Pentecost sets in motion a new order of relationships. A patriarchal society hears that the women of Pentecost have received the power of the Spirit directly, as Mary did at the Annunciation, without the mediation of either father or husband.

Pentecost shows men and women praying and giving birth to the Church together (Acts 2:1-4). It lays the foundation for the development of church as a community of equal disciples where every person is respected and has a voice. The group gathered in the Upper Room at Pentecost is indeed an image of what church is to be.

A spirit of shared joy, mutuality, and solidarity in the community arises as the disciples move among the crowds, sharing their conviction about who Jesus was and what he means in their lives. What God had done in each of them they only fully understood as they saw the effects together. This scene echoes what happened during Mary's encounter with Elizabeth at the Visitation (Lk 1:39-55).

At the same time, the first converts who joined them affirmed the truth of the inner transformation that had taken place in the group that emerged from the Upper Room – the Word they carried – as Elizabeth had affirmed Mary. The events at Pentecost, as at the Visitation between Mary and Elizabeth, point out that evangelization is relational, never a one-way street. True visitation comes from the inside out. Mutuality is its fuel.

In its initial response at Pentecost, the circle of disciples, walking in Mary's footsteps, takes on the attitude of the perfect disciple – the responsibility together to hear the word of God and do it. Like Mary's "Yes" at the Annunciation, their "Yes" to God at Pentecost is as perfect as it could be at that moment. The community over time would discover what it means to follow in Jesus' footsteps and how to reflect, like him, the redeeming, liberating power of God's presence and compassion.

The Visitation joins Mary's vocation to intimacy with God and service to others into one call, setting her on the road to discipleship. The interrelatedness of her inner and outer journey is set in motion. Likewise, the visitation that follows Pentecost joins the vocations of the circle of disciples to intimacy with the risen Jesus and his Spirit, and service to others, into one call. The interdependence of the inner–outer life of this fledgling community of disciples makes it clear that intimacy with Jesus is integral to a life of mission for the gospel. Prayer and action were inseparable.

The encounter between Mary and Elizabeth shows that people of the First Testament perceived God's visitation to them in the concrete reality of their lives. What made the encounter between Mary and Elizabeth a visitation was their recognition and acknowledgment of God's presence in recent events of their lives and in the moment they are experiencing together. The same is true for the group at Pentecost. The entire group gathered in the Upper Room recognizes and acknowledges the power of God's presence in their lives. They know that this is a moment unlike any other. God had visited them; Jesus' promise was fulfilled (Acts 1:5, 6; Lk 24:49).

Mary shares this new visitation of God within the circle of disciples. The presence of the Spirit in each one of the group gathered assures them that they will never be left on their own. Jesus, through the power of the Spirit, is with them. From this moment, the fledgling community is called to live in an attitude of visitation.

Mary commits her experience of life lived in visitation to what will unfold in the newborn community of equal disciples. Day by day, month by month, and year by year, the community will be called to be attentive to and discerning of God's presence. Together it will discover how to live in faith as disciples of the risen Jesus.

The unfolding of events on Pentecost day points out that the group has indeed followed in Mary's footsteps. Mary, in the Annunciation–Visitation, conceives God's Word and hastens to share it with Elizabeth. In response to Elizabeth, she interprets the Word she had conceived in the Magnificat. At Pentecost, the community of disciples conceives God's Word, Jesus. The Spirit of the risen Jesus is unleashed in them. Impelled by the Spirit, they hasten from the Upper Room to share the

Word about Jesus that they had received. The disciples' ability to speak in a variety of languages enables those who listen to hear what they are saying (Acts 2:4-8). Finally, Peter's speech expresses an ability to interpret their own behaviour and their message about Jesus so others can understand why faith in him would be good news for them (Acts 2:14-36). The Annunciation–Visitation and Pentecost events are truly one and the same motif: to be sent in Jesus' name.

The parallels between these two events invite us to take a second look at Mary in the circle of disciples.

Mary in the Circle of Disciples: A Second Look

When Mary takes her place in the circle of disciples, she is the only one who has known Jesus and his needs from the moment of his conception, to his birth, and through each stage of his life. She enters the circle of disciples as the mother who had followed her son during his years of ministry, listened to his teachings, witnessed his suffering, and watched him die. Along the way, she gradually discovered the heart and the meaning of discipleship for her.

In the Upper Room, Mary is the same woman whom tradition and art through the centuries have portrayed holding the body of her dead son in her arms as tenderly as she had held him as an infant. It is not difficult to imagine her cradling the infant Church in her heart in the same way.

Among the disciples, Mary is present as the remembering mother, the one who pondered and sought understanding of the events of her life with Jesus (Lk 2:19, 51): the meaning of his teachings and of his loving care and concern for all he met. Despite the conflicts he encountered, he maintained his freedom to love, forgive, and be faithful to his mission. Surely, with Pentecost, Mary became aware of the extent to which Jesus enabled a God of love and compassion to be personally present to her and to her people.

Mary enters the circle of disciples as a woman with her own history. Her faith journey and evolution as Jesus' disciple clearly shows that she, like every other human being, experienced joys and struggles. She knows how to walk in faith in times of light and darkness.

She is there as the woman of prayer par excellence – the only one present whose prayer life, modelled on the Psalms and on personal reflective prayer, is recorded in the gospels.[23] She enters the community as a prophetic reminder that the attitudes of justice, inclusivity, and equality announced in the Magnificat (Lk 1:46-55) – and actualized in her son's ministry – are to be emulated.

She is present as a woman of faith. Nurtured in the faith of her people, Israel, Mary, from the Annunciation on, sets out on her journey of faith with Jesus. At Pentecost, she shares not only in the founding grace of the Church, but also in that moment marking, in the words of *Lumen Gentium*, the "point of departure of the Church's journey of faith."[24] Casting her lot with the disciples, Mary chooses to continue her journey of faith within the community. At the Annunciation, Mary, in her "Yes" to God, committed herself to live her life under the guidance of the Spirit. At Pentecost, she chooses to continue her life in the Spirit with the emerging church.

She enters this community as a mature woman, the disciples' sister in faith, mother, teacher,[25] and colleague. She is among them as a Spirit-filled woman of prayer, a woman of visitation, the first disciple of the Word, the remembering mother, and a unique and "exceptional witness to the mystery of Christ."[26]

Mary's faith journey is longer than that of the others who had gathered with her in the Upper Room and those who became believers after Pentecost. Mary goes before them, leading the way.[27] From Pentecost onwards, the faith journey of this woman who responded to God with an undivided heart and her growth as a disciple become a beacon for the community of disciples – the fledgling church.

Pious tradition, which is not based on historical data, holds that Mary lived fifteen years in the Jerusalem community. According to this tradition, the early Christian community, in seeing and hearing Mary, saw the Church unfold before their very eyes. How did this community, following the Spirit of the risen Jesus, walk in her footsteps?

6

Mary and the Jerusalem Community: Life in Visitation

Like Mary, Called to Conceive, to Share Jesus, the Word of God

In shaping the stories of Jesus, the disciples turn to their scriptures in an effort to interpret his crucifixion, death, and resurrection. All the speeches interspersed at strategic moments in Acts show how the disciples begin to see Jesus in a new way (Acts 2:16-21; 3:12-26; 4:8-12; 5:29-32; 10:34-43). Prophetic interpretation enables them to tell their Jewish brothers and sisters how Jesus is the fulfillment of the Scriptures. They explain who Jesus is in the context of their own religion and culture.

Over time, these first disciples identify Jesus as the anointed one, the Messiah, the prophet, the Lord and Saviour, the Son of God, the servant of God. They are clear that, in Elizabeth Johnson's words, "Jesus' crucifixion, death, and resurrection gave these symbols new meaning.... No longer was the Messiah simply the triumphant king of the Davidic line, but the crucified and risen one."[1] They announce that faith in the risen Jesus brings an assurance of new life in the Spirit. Jesus' crucifixion, death, and resurrection – like the Israelite exodus from Egypt – offer freedom from inner and outer oppression.

In their totality, the speeches in Acts reflect the first-century believers' faith in Jesus.[2] As at Pentecost, all reflect themes of the Magnificat: recognition and praise of what God is doing in and through them, and an interpretation of the message to help listeners receive the good news.

The speeches provide a background for the countless numbers of Jewish men and women, and later Gentiles, who come to faith in Jesus and join the community (4:4; 5:14; 6:1, 7; 9:42; 10:44).[3] As on Pentecost day, the continuous addition of men and women into the community affirms the inner transformation that takes place in people who accepted Jesus. This transformation is so readily observable that the community soon earns the respect of other Jews and Gentiles – their neighbours in Jerusalem – who choose not to believe (Acts 2:43, 47).

The dominant story, told at the beginning, centres on Jesus' crucifixion, death, and resurrection, and on the meaning these had for the life and mission of his followers. Only a general reference is made to the many signs and wonders Jesus did. The gospels, which arose out of different communities, attest to the fact that the disciples, including Jesus' mother and new members of the community who knew him during his ministry, would have shared their memories of Jesus: his teachings; the ways his tender touch healed so many people afflicted with physical, mental and moral ills; and how he reached out to and spoke on behalf of so many men and women who were marginalized by oppressive political, social, and religious structures. At the heart of their stories was their memory of a man whose passionate love of God and of his neighbour had sparked the ire of the authorities and led him to crucifixion. His life, his death, and his resurrection assured them that his very presence was truly a sign of God's endless love and compassion for every man, woman, and child.[4]

Unfortunately, Luke's literary style makes it easy to forget that the Spirit had empowered and commissioned all the men and women gathered in the Upper Room, creatively opening up their ability to communicate what God had done for them in Jesus (Acts 2:4). You have to read between the lines in Acts to uncover the influence and involvement of women and men believers in the emergence and growth of the post-Pentecost community.

As the community grew, new followers of Jesus likely resulted from the disciples' interaction with individuals and groups as they visited their neighbours and shopped in the markets in the Upper and Lower sections of Jerusalem.[5] We can imagine the conversations that would have taken place; the more wealthy believers likely spoke about their new-found faith in Jesus to their day labourers who did domestic work and cared for their children and the sick.

At the Portico of Solomon, the walkway leading to the entrance to the Temple, Jews and Gentiles, men, women, and children could congregate. Here members of the first community probably mingled and shared their stories about Jesus with the crowds, the money-changers, and the carpenters and stone masons still engaged in rebuilding Herod's temple.

As these men and women disciples walked the streets and went to the Temple they would not have ignored the beggars – some lame, some blind, and some terribly ill – who wandered through the city streets and markets. Stories of these people include Peter's cure of the lame man at the temple gate (Acts 3:1-8) and the great signs and wonders Stephen performed among the people (Acts 6:8). Raising Tabitha, a disciple devoted to good works and acts of charity (Acts 9:40), is an example of one of the signs and wonders done in Jesus' name (Acts 2:43; 5:12).

Acts provides us with a model for storytelling.[6] The ultimate story is the "breaking of bread" that took place in the disciples' homes (Acts 2:42). When the community gathered for the breaking of bread, Eugene La Verdiere tells us, "they were continuing a Jewish ritual gesture associated with family meals. At the beginning of the meal, the head of the family or a special guest took bread, spoke a blessing, broke it and gave it to them at table."[7] But for the community, the memory of their meals with Jesus during his ministry, his last supper with them, and the times he ate with them after his resurrection bring new meaning to the breaking of bread. This is not just any meal together, not just any ritual. According to La Verdiere, it is "Jesus' breaking of bread and Jesus' sharing of it as an expression of his very person. For the Christians, the bread was broken in memory of Jesus."[8] It is the ultimate expression of living out their sacred call to intimacy with Jesus and with one another. To be in communion with Jesus and with one another is to be united in mind and heart.

It isn't long before the community begins to feel the cost of discipleship. Peter and John have conflict with the Temple priests, the scribes, and the Sadducees, who did not believe in the resurrection of the dead (Acts 4:1f.). They arrest the two men, then release them the next day, warning them not to speak or teach about Jesus and his resurrection again. The community is undeterred. Reunited with Peter and John, they pray, pleading with God: "Grant to your servants to speak your word with all boldness" (Acts 4:29). To their surprise, the place where they are gathered together is shaken, and a new energy of the Spirit fills their hearts. They continued to speak the word with boldness (Acts 4:31), even when Peter and John are imprisoned again (Acts 5:17-18).

Their perseverance confirms the community's inner conviction about the truth of Jesus and his message.

From the very beginning, the community is faithful to the teaching of the apostles (Acts 2:42). This expression does not refer to a body of apostolic teachings, but to the activity of apostolic teaching by the community. Devoting themselves to the teaching of the apostles meant that all the disciples, men and women, were faithful to their mission of apostolic teaching. "The community did have special teachers, such as Peter and John (Acts 4:2, 18), indeed all the apostles (Acts 5:21, 25, 28, 42), but the whole church identified with their teaching mission and made it their own," says La Verdiere.[9] In the new community, being an apostle, a missionary, was to represent Jesus. This meant that as people joined the community, older members would tell them stories about Jesus and how faith in him had brought them new life. As stories were passed on, the power of the Spirit opened up the ability of disciple after disciple to share their faith in Jesus.

As the days and months passed, Acts reports that "Great grace was upon them all" (Acts 4:33). They could not keep from speaking about what they had seen and heard (Acts 4:20). "Every day in the temple and at home they did not cease to teach and proclaim Jesus as the Messiah" (Acts 5:42). These terse statements tell us that the stories they tell and all their actions have one goal: to witness to the risen Jesus and, in the process, help others to come to faith in him as their Messiah. These others would, in turn, share the freedom and joy of the first believers. It would take internal conflict and a new persecution for the word about Jesus to spread to the ends of the known world.

Within the first five years, the Jerusalem community experienced difficulties between two groups divided along lines of language and culture: Aramaic-speaking Hebrews and Greek-speaking Jews, the Hellenists, who had returned from the Diaspora to live in Jerusalem. There was a conflict over the way daily food was distributed to widows in the Greek-speaking community (Acts 6:1); then, when this was resolved, a disagreement on the place of the Temple in their lives. On one side, the Hebrews felt called to live as exemplary Jews, worshipping in the Temple daily until Jesus returned. An attack on the Temple was an attack on their identity. On the other side, the Greek-speaking Jews – represented by Stephen – began to take seriously Jesus' words about destroying the Temple and rebuilding it in three days. Stephen challenged the customs from Moses (Acts 6:13-14). For Stephen, God did not want a permanent dwelling place (Acts 7:44-50).[10] His assertions enraged the high priest and the council, and he was stoned to death. The result was persecution.

A man called Saul went from house to house, dragging to prison every man and woman follower of Jesus he could (Acts 8:3). Those who escaped were scattered throughout the countryside of Judea and Samaria without property or possessions. Fearless in the face of persecution and alive with the Spirit of the risen Jesus, they went from place to place, proclaiming how faith in Jesus had changed their lives (Acts 8:4).[11] Out of this period of darkness, new life was born. Many accepted their message. More and more men and women throughout Judea, Galilee, Samaria, Phoenicia, Cyprus, and Antioch became followers of Jesus, and were in turn empowered by the Spirit to become his witnesses and apostles.

The Jerusalem community shaped, shared, and nurtured the memory of the risen Jesus. Mary is clearly within the community as a disciple among disciples. She is also present as Jesus' mother, the one who knew him best.

From its founding moment at Pentecost, the Jerusalem community, like Mary at the Annunciation, shows that it has become good soil in which God's word can take root and flourish (Lk 8:11-15; Mk 4:9; Mt 13:9). Like Mary, the remembering mother, the community becomes an exceptional witness to the mystery of Christ. It testifies to the human reality of Jesus: his birth, his mission, his suffering and death, and his resurrection. Together, the disciples witness to Jesus' continued presence through his Spirit and in breaking bread together.[12]

The community of disciples, of which Mary is a member, has assumed its maternal role: to give birth to Christ and to be the memory of Jesus in the world, day by day. The significance of this is profound.

Pentecost established the equality of men and women. When the community assumes its maternal role to give birth to Christ, the generativity of men and women disciples is affirmed.

The community of disciples, like Mary, lives in visitation; they are intimate with the Risen Jesus, share their faith in him, and interpret how their message about him is to be communicated.

In conceiving, shaping, and sharing their memories of Jesus, the community interprets their meaning for their lives and acts accordingly.[13] The Magnificat rises from their hearts.

The Magnificat of the Jerusalem Community

With the opening verses of the Magnificat, Mary announces to Elizabeth that she has discovered her true identity in God. She would no longer define herself by the social and religious conventions of her day. The gift of God's Spirit has brought her joy, power, and strength; she has gained the courage to accept a pregnancy and conceive Jesus, despite any misunderstanding or danger it might cause her. She has named herself God's servant, willing to trust totally in God's promise to her.

As Mary praises God, she represents the primitive community that has discovered, through faith in the risen Jesus, that their true identity and status derives from their relationship with God. Because of Pentecost, the community has become God's servant, called to place their trust totally in God.

It is dangerous to underestimate the challenges these first post-Pentecost believers faced. Faith in Jesus called them to repent (Acts 2:37; 3:19). Within their historical and religious context, conversion was a choice to be ruled by God's wisdom and not, in Robert Ludwig's words, "the oppressive political, social and religious structures which up to this moment had governed their lives, and defined who they were (Acts 2:38; 3:19).[14] Jesus' life, and Mary's, showed them that being under God's wisdom meant being directed by the inner law of love – the double commandment to love God with their whole heart, mind, and soul, and to love their neighbour as themselves.

Like Mary, the community is called to live in visitation – attentive to God's presence in their midst.

Her heart filled with joy, Mary praises God, who upset distinctions between rich and poor, and the powerful and the lowly (Lk 1:52-53). The Magnificat does not suggest that God hated the powerful and the rich. Neither does it suggest that the poor will become the oppressors of the rich. Rather, it proclaims that "God upset the perceived maps which indicated who enjoyed God's favour and who was in the circle of God's elect."[15]

Mary, who had prophetically interpreted the meaning of the child whom she carried in her womb, observes the fulfillment of this prophecy in her son's actions and words. As a representative of the community, she speaks for a people who had become aware that the resurrection of Jesus is God's assurance that Jesus – who had blessed the poor, the hungry, the afflicted, the downtrodden, and the persecuted (Lk 6:20-22) – is the in-breaking of God's healing presence.

Faith in the risen Jesus, then, is not an intellectual exercise: it means, as Albert Nolan puts it, "receiving Jesus' word as God's word, his Spirit as God's Spirit, recognizing that what Jesus stood for was exactly the same as what God stood for." God's unconditional love for all people, God's compassion, and God's justice are not for some future time but for life now. The community worked hard to live that way.[16]

It became a people of one mind and heart (Acts 4:32) – one with God and one with their neighbour. Members held all their goods in common. No one claimed private ownership of any possessions. No one was in need (Acts 2:33; 4:32-35).

There seemed to be an equality between rich and poor. While people did not have to sell everything they owned, those who owned lands or houses sold them and brought the proceeds to the community (Acts 4:34).

By Acts 4:32, it is evident that the community had grown to the point where they lived in separate houses. Some believers, like Mary the mother of John Mark, shared their homes with the community (Acts 12:12). People would have had their own clothes, their own housing, and their own household articles. But in laying no claim to private ownership, the more affluent among them gave up the power and the prestige that accompany ownership. In sharing their goods in common and seeing that no one was in need, the Jerusalem community broke down the system of patronage that prevailed in that society.

Communal sharing of goods contradicted a commercialized society in which relationships were structured by patron and client, honour and shame. It was, in John Dominic Crossan's words, "a far more radical criticism of commercialized community than patronal sharing, because the more individual almsgiving is increased, the more systemic justice is ignored."[17]

Two narratives in Acts contrast two types of givers, showing the importance of equality among members and of holding all goods in common to maintain harmony within the community.

Barnabas sold a field and brought the money to the apostles (Acts 4:37). Ananias and Sapphira also sold a piece of property, but kept some of the money from the sale (Acts 5:1-10). Their punishment was severe. Each died in their own lie.

The severity of Ananias and Sapphira's punishment sent shockwaves through the community. It even startles the reader today. The point of the narrative is that by lying about the value of the sale, Ananias and Sapphira have betrayed their calling as disciples of Jesus. Crossan says, "Claiming an absolute gift was also claiming an absolute right to receive what one needed, an absolute right to share in the eucharistic share-meal of the community."[18] In lying to the community, Ananias and Sapphira break communion with the men and women – their brothers and sisters – with whom they share a common faith. They are no longer of one mind and heart with the rest of the community. The community's integrity is threatened from within. This is the greatest tragedy.

The story of Ananias and Sapphira brings home the cost of discipleship. Jesus, in life and in death, had shown that following him required being ready to give up everything one owned, even one's life, so no one would be in need.

Discipleship also called the community to welcome all who were sick, needy, destitute, and socially, spiritually, economically, and politically marginalized. All are welcome in God's kingdom. Together, the disciples overturn the popular theology that God favoured the rich and that sickness was a punishment from God. They show, as Jesus had, that God is impartial.

Sharing of goods in common[19] and distribution of food to those in need depend on the daily gathering of the community (Acts 2:44-45; 4:32). The Hellenists, as noted earlier, complain to the Hebrews that their widows are being neglected in the daily distribution of food (Acts

6:1), which likely took place during the daily meals taken together (Acts 2:46). The community resolves the conflict by appointing seven deacons among the Hellenists to assume responsibility for the task (Acts 6:3).

Those appointed deacons serve the poor and continue to witness to the power of the risen Jesus. Stephen is singled out as one who preached the word of God and did great wonders and signs among the people (Acts 6:8).

Although people came to have separate functions, they continued to share their faith with everyone they met, even after the stoning of Stephen (Acts 8:4) and their exile from Jerusalem. They took seriously their responsibility to make Jesus known.

The Jerusalem community shared its resources and food. Their fellowship was heightened by sharing meals and breaking bread together (Acts 2:42, 46). Being at table together was the ultimate sign of inclusivity. People of one mind and heart (Acts 4:32) who are called to be one with God and with their neighbour cannot have an elite centre that leaves the rest on the margins of the community.

In the Middle East, people would never eat or drink with persons of lower class or status or with anyone of whom they disapproved, not even out of politeness. "Eating together was a sign of intimacy, of welcoming, and, if appropriate, of forgiveness and reconciliation," say Marianne Race and Laurie Brink.[20] "Not done lightly," adds Elizabeth Johnson, "this action makes people into friends, colleagues, family."[21]

During his ministry, Jesus made it clear that hospitality went far beyond one's relatives or immediate friends. For Jesus, "God's mercy included hospitality and inclusivity," according to John H. Ashworth.[22] Consequently, he shares his table with a variety of people, including Pharisees (Lk 7:36-50; 11:37-54) and tax collectors (Lk 5:27-39; 19:1-10).

Jesus also welcomes to his table those whom one would not ordinarily invite: the poor, the crippled, the lame, and the blind – people who could not reciprocate the invitation. Even the Pharisees observe that he shows neither deference nor partiality to anyone (Lk 20:21; Mk 12:13-14; Mt 22:16). "When you give a banquet," Jesus says, "invite the poor, the crippled, the lame, and the blind. And you will be blessed, because they cannot repay you" (Lk 14:13-14). In multiplying the loaves and fishes, Jesus shows that no matter how little food you have, there is always plenty when it is shared (Lk 9:10-17; Mk 6:30-44; Mt 14:13-21; Jn 6:1-14).[23]

Jesus also eats with his friends Martha, Mary, and Lazarus when he visits or stays at their home in Bethany, on the outskirts of Jerusalem (Lk 10:38-42). With a heavy heart, he eats his last supper with his disciples during the Passover celebration in Jerusalem on the eve of his death. After his resurrection, he continues to show the importance of a meal in reconciliation and building relationships. He breaks bread with two of his disciples, who were confused and distraught over his death as they headed home to Emmaus. In his encounter with them along the road, Jesus shows how dialogue helps people to understand the scriptures. But it is only when he breaks bread with them that they realize who he is. Their spirits lifted and their hope restored, they hurry back to Jerusalem to share their news with the other disciples (Lk 24:13-35). Even as they speak, Jesus appears to them, but only during the meal do they truly understand his presence among them. In those moments together Jesus promises them that his Spirit will provide them with everything they will need to carry on his mission (Lk 24:36-53).

Through his openness to and acceptance of every person – even those marginalized by their society – Jesus shows the importance of unconditional hospitality. The early community must have learned, in the stories about Jesus shared by the disciples, that breaking bread together and unconditional hospitality were inseparable. Thus, it is not surprising that Acts reports that the community, following in Jesus' footsteps, "broke bread at home and ate their food with glad and generous hearts" (Acts 2:46). They share meals with people with whom they ordinarily would not have associated.

The Jerusalem community was born within the climate of first-century Jerusalem, with its pluralistic social, political, and religious structures.[24] As a result, people who had been strangers to one another were called into a new family. Sharing faith and life together, they became brothers and sisters. They were companions on the journey, equally empowered by the Spirit of the risen Jesus.

Their behaviour must have been counter-cultural in this highly stratified and diverse society where wealth, status, positions of power, and a system built on reciprocity determined social relations. As one scholar explains, reciprocity required that "any recipient of another's largesse was expected to repay in some way. Where reciprocity does not govern social relationships, the power aspect which allows some to lord it over others is removed."[25] An inclusive community – where all were welcome and equal, had equal access to God, and experienced the power of God's Spirit – could not consider some members as patrons and others as clients.

The very concept of holding goods in common was not limited to sharing material possessions. It encompassed openness, hospitality, interdependence, mutuality, equality, and concern for one another.

Faith in the risen Jesus and the power of his Spirit brought rich and poor together in a community of life-giving relationships. The Magnificat expressed the joy of all who found their way into this community, especially the poorest of the poor, who had been deemed worthless and exiled to the fringes of society. Together they understood their gatherings as the ongoing presence of Jesus. "The wisdom and compassion of God continued to be embodied in these 'healed healers,' who gathered for the breaking of the bread, continuing Jesus' table-fellowship and celebrating their ecstatic experience of his risen presence among them," says Robert Ludwig.[26] In the early community, the Beatitudes announced by Jesus are fulfilled (Lk 6:20ff.).

It was likely this witness of community and life in the Spirit that attracted countless people from every stratum of Jewish society. The community would soon discover that they were called to extend hospitality to their non-Jewish neighbours, the Gentiles, as well.

To his surprise, a hungry Peter is told through a vision that he must not call anything profane or unclean (Acts 10:15). Mindful of Jewish law that stipulates what foods Jews can eat, he objects, only to be given the same message again. Peter soon discovers that this command from God extends beyond food to acceptance of the Gentiles into the community, as represented in the person of Cornelius, the centurion. Peter comes to understand that "God shows no partiality, but in every nation anyone who fears him and does what is right is acceptable to him" (Acts 10:34-35). To his amazement, he sees Cornelius and his household receive the power of the Spirit just as he and the small group had in the Upper Room at Pentecost (Acts 10:44-45).

The admission of the Gentiles gives rise to new concerns. Some members of the Jewish-Christian community who belonged to the sect of the Pharisees demand that the men be circumcised and that the

Gentile community observe the law of Moses (Acts 15). They cannot comprehend how the Gentiles could belong to the Christian community without embracing Jewish practice. Peter feels otherwise. He argues eloquently against making such demands on these new members, and the assembly decides not to require that Gentiles be circumcised.[27] They ask only that the Gentiles abstain from things polluted by idols, fornication, whatever had been strangled, and blood (Acts 15:20).

While these stipulations may seem like a strange mixture to us today, they were not so in the eyes of the Jewish believers who were vitally concerned with the origin of the food they ate. In their minds, for the Gentiles to follow these rules – especially those concerning food – would ensure that all believers, regardless of ethnicity, could eat together. Table fellowship, an essential characteristic of communal life, would therefore not be threatened.

As James H. Neyrey puts it, "The outpouring of the Spirit on the unclean Gentiles as in the case of Cornelius (Acts 10:44-47; 11:17); earlier on the Samaritan Jews (Acts 8:14-17); later on the Ephesians (Acts 19:2-7) is a clear indication of God's surprising action evident in the reversal of their unclean states."[28] Everyone is equal in God's sight. Everyone must be made to feel welcome in the community.

In the early Christian community, says John Ashworth, inclusiveness and impartiality "involved welcoming those who were excluded from the Jewish community from within (the sinners, the poor and the oppressed) or from without (those such as the 'Samaritans', the Gentiles who did not belong to the community in the first place)."[29]

Hospitality had broken down all the artificial barriers that people had set up. For the community, it was a symbol of the inclusivity and impartiality to which the community was called, and a sign of the community's life lived in visitation.

Over time, the community comes to realize that faith in the risen Jesus and baptism determine membership – not circumcision and observance of the Law of Moses (Acts 15:1-5). The community expresses this new life in their baptismal formula. With the admission of the Gentiles, they can proudly proclaim that in this new community there is no longer any distinction between Jew and Gentile, free and slave, or male and female, but that all are united in Christ Jesus (Gal 3:28ff.). The community rejoices that women, slaves, and Gentiles could be full and equal members in their community, and that all are called to the same missionary task.

Jesus sending out the seventy is a clear example of the disciple's mission in a community of equals. As John Dominic Crossan explains, he sent them out

> to speak as he did, to act as he did, to live as he did.... They are told to invite others to do likewise. The mention of pairs is very significant, because it means that women could also participate travelling either in two's or simply with a man; both customs and safety concerns kept women from travelling on their own.[30]

It is impossible to consider the Magnificat in relation to the Jerusalem community without touching on leadership in the community and the role of women.

Shortly before Jesus' death, the disciples argue about who would be the greatest among them. Jesus uses this moment to tell them that power in God's kingdom is service, not the force and violence used by the leaders of nations in their day to dominate people. This comparison would not have been lost on them, for this was how the Roman oppressors governed their nation. "The greatest among you," Jesus says, "must become like the youngest, and the leader like one who serves" (Lk 22:26; Mk 10:42-45; Mt 20:25-28). Pointing out that the greatest one is the person being served, he says that he is among them as one who serves (Lk 22:27).

The most passionate expression of Jesus' teaching is in John's gospel, where he describes Jesus washing the feet of his disciples at the last supper with them. "If I, your Lord and Teacher, have washed your feet," he tells them, "you also ought to wash one another's feet" (Jn 13:14).[31]

In Mediterranean society, children, women, slaves, and servants had neither status nor power. Servants washed the feet of their masters every time they returned home so the dust from the roads would not be brought into their houses. In calling his disciples to be servants of one another, Jesus affirms that mutuality and interdependence must be at the heart of their relationships. Although the community may have leaders and people of honour according to societal norms, they will have "no different status from the young and those who serve at tables, that is, they will have no power and special honour."[32]

Jesus' teaching must have brought home a startling reality to the men in the community. The way they are to exercise their role as leaders in the community is compared to serving food at tables – a function reserved for the "confines of the home, performed by women and servants, at the periphery of a society dominated by free men."[33]

In gathering around him a small group of men and women during his ministry, Jesus has indeed turned the tables upside down. The patriarchal, hierarchical system of governance that institutionalized power over others will have no place in his new community – whether the leaders were men or women.[34] After all, "the basic concepts which would define the Christian community were forged and initiated" at Pentecost. From that moment, "reconciliation, unity, loving service among a community of equal disciples, and the power of the Spirit – who sends disciples forth in Jesus' name – would be signs by which the Christian community would be known.[35]

While the evolution of the church in Acts does indicate the rise of specific roles, the importance of the power of the Spirit residing in the community is preserved.

From the very beginning, the community gathered in Jerusalem prays for perseverance as they try to understand what the first persecution means for them (Acts 5). When a conflict arises, Peter gathers the whole community to resolve the situation (Acts 6). When Peter escapes from prison he goes immediately to the home of Mary the mother of John Mark, where the community is gathered in prayer (Acts 12). Those who listen to Paul and Barnabas relate what God had done through them among the Gentiles are the "many" – the community in general (Acts 15). The decision not to require that male Gentile believers be circumcized is made by the whole church (Acts 15:22). Luke's interspersed observations of communal involvement in decision-making show that authority was not vested in a few individuals but in the community.

There is a danger in romanticizing the first group of believers. Faith in the risen Jesus, and membership in the community, did not exempt them from the daily demands of life. Certain moments in the life of the community show this all too well: recall the story of Ananias and Sapphira, and the persecutions and resentment between the Hebrew- and Greek-speaking Christians over the distribution of food to widows. Other problems included the struggle over how to incorporate the

Gentiles into the community, their apprehension of Paul at the beginning, and the conflicts that arose with him. In light of these unexpected demands, what stands out is that the community, like Mary before them, was faced "with the sword of deciding what doing the word of God means." The community discovered, as every disciple does, that it could never say, "Now we know the way." New wine always needs new wineskins.

Eventually, these first believers became known as "followers of the Way" (Acts 9:2; 19:9, 23; 22:4; 24:14, 22). A "way" is "a totally encompassing mode of life."[36] Life in the Jerusalem community made that clear. To follow the Way meant that faith in the "risen Jesus and making every effort to live as he had would bring them close to God and lead them to salvation."[37]

Being followers of the Way distinguished them from other groups that lived in various forms of community life in and around Jerusalem and throughout Israel: the Essenes, the Zealots, the Pharisees, and the Sadducees, to name a few. It distinguished Gentile believers from their neighbours who worshipped their own gods.

The Jerusalem community conceived, shaped, and nurtured the memory of the risen Jesus. At the heart of the community, Jesus' life, teachings, and ministry were for imitation. The community in word and in action interpreted the meaning of their new-found faith in the risen Jesus. The countless numbers of men and women who joined the community had heard the disciples, observed them, and discovered for themselves that the message of Jesus was indeed good news. Every effort to live as Jesus had done meant that the community was the presence of God's love and compassion in the world.

From the very beginning, the community of disciples fulfills two fundamental criteria of discipleship for which Jesus had praised his mother: to hear the word of God and to do it (Lk 8:19-21).

The Magnificat expresses the reality of the first Jerusalem community. Mary must have recalled it as she watched the community in Jerusalem grow. She must have experienced great joy as she saw the poor, the destitute, and the so-called weak of her society find their dignity and their place in the community. In its evolution, Mary saw her son's deepest desire fulfilled: that every person would know they are loved and treasured by God.

In the Jerusalem community, Mary is also present as a woman of the Spirit. Beginning with the Annunciation, the presence of the Spirit in Mary guides her growth as a disciple of Jesus and her faith journey – her life in visitation. Her encounter with Elizabeth at the Visitation showed Mary the power for good that can be released when two people meet in the Spirit. As we follow her growth as a disciple of Jesus and her faith journey, it becomes obvious that the Spirit's life in Mary was progressive. It was the power of love – "a love which the Greek tradition calls her 'parresia,' her audacity of spirit."[38]

She observes this same love in her son. Jesus is in such close relation to the power of God's Spirit in him that he heals the blind, the infirm, and the lame. Appealing to the good in each person he meets, he is able to guide people to inner freedom and away from behaviours and outer social, religious, and political structures that imprison their spirits. With the release of the Spirit of the risen Jesus at Pentecost, Mary commits herself to live in a community that has been initiated by the Spirit of her risen son. Under the guidance of the Spirit, the community would be formed and shaped over time into Jesus' likeness – empowered to carry on her son's mission in his name.

Communal Life in the Spirit

Beginning at Pentecost, the faith journey of the community is under the guidance of the Spirit, who sends forth the disciples, transformed into courageous witnesses of the risen Jesus, to accomplish a missionary task.

The Spirit guides them to preserve creatively the memory of Jesus and to act as he had done during his ministry. A people of the Magnificat, they experience the power of the Spirit profoundly. Through their interaction with each other, they see how faith in Jesus and life in the Spirit change their lives. Observing the Spirit's impact on one another, the community knows that God works in everyone – male or female, rich or poor, sick or healthy.

The Spirit guides people of diverse social, political, and ethnic backgrounds to the community. Baptism releases the power of the Spirit in each new member, marking their entry into the group of believers (Acts 2:38; 8:15-17; 15:8; 19:5-6). The outpouring of the Spirit on all members of the community – men and women alike – continues to embody the fulfillment of Joel's prophecy announced by Peter at Pentecost (Acts 2:17-21). This is a community united in the Spirit.[39] They are all sisters and brothers of the same Christ, sons and daughters of God.

The power of the Spirit in each member and in the community gives them the courage to stand steadfast in the face of persecution. When Peter and John are arrested, the community prays that they will continue to speak God's word boldly. Even as they seek to discover why their own people would oppose them, "the place in which they were gathered together was shaken; and they were all filled with the Holy Spirit" (Acts 4:31), giving them the strength to continue their mission fearlessly.

Acts underlines that from Pentecost on, each new mission initiates a new empowerment of the Spirit. We see this empowerment in Stephen as he faces death by stoning, and in the courage of the people who, despite being scattered because of persecution, never hide their faith in Jesus. Later, Acts reports that the Holy Spirit falls on the Samaritans in the same way as on the initial group in the Upper Room (Acts 8:14-17), and on Cornelius and his household (Acts 10:47). This doesn't mean that the Spirit isn't present and active on a daily basis. But it does point out that at certain moments, a new and more powerful impetus of the Spirit is needed.

Peter makes it clear to the circumcised believers in Jerusalem, who criticized him for going among uncircumcised men and eating with them, that his actions are the result of listening to the Spirit. "The Spirit told me," he said, "to go with them and not to make a distinction between them and us" (Acts 11:12). In essence, Peter tells them that life in the Spirit means being open to a God of surprises. Admitting male Gentiles into the community without requiring that they be circumcised results from communal discernment under the Spirit's guidance. In outlining the community's rules to the Gentiles, the spokespersons say, "It has seemed good to the Holy Spirit and to us to impose on you no further burden than these essentials" (Acts 15:28).

The faith journey of the community, under the guidance of the Spirit, shows that the risen Jesus is continuing his work in the world through all who come to believe in him. The principles that Jesus taught and lived were alive in the Jerusalem community. The Spirit now calls the community to apply these principles – inclusivity, impartiality, and equality for all God's people – to new situations. The community discovers that they cannot control the Spirit's activity: they are at its service.

When the Spirit empowers men and women equally in the Upper Room, this emphasizes that every person is needed to carry on Jesus' ministry. Every member is needed to build up the community. Following Jesus and his Spirit means service for all and by all.

Acts provides little evidence that men and women were co-workers in ministry,[40] but we can presume that Priscilla and Aquila, who explained the Way of God to Apollos, represented many couples who were teachers and leaders of house churches (Acts 18:26). Acts also mentions Mary the mother of John Mark, in whose home the community gathers for prayer (Acts 12), and Lydia, who comes to faith in Jesus along with her household (Acts 16:14). She likely became a leader of a house church. We need to turn to Paul's letters to hear about other women who were actively engaged in ministry as teachers and leaders.

It is important, though, to read Acts for what it does say: the power of the Spirit transformed all believers. Alive with the power of the Spirit, these first believers – men and women – enter a new way of life that calls them to carry on Jesus' ministry. Reflection on the Magnificat shows that "their way of life included service extending the kingdom of God into the needy, turbulent world even as it brought about the new religious law of love."[41] After his conversion, Paul writes passionately,

> Now there are varieties of gifts, but the same Spirit; and there are varieties of services, but the same Lord; and there are varieties of activities, but it is the same God who activates all of them in everyone. To each is given the manifestation of the Spirit for the common good. (1 Cor 12:4-7)

The Pentecost event laid the foundation for this community of equal disciples. Every follower of Jesus was called to live in an atmosphere of mutuality and interdependence: to be attentive to the Spirit speaking through others, to appreciate the gifts the Spirit gave each person, and to recognize their need for each other.

Life in the Spirit brings faith into the marketplace. In imitation of Jesus, his followers are called to act with justice and compassion, to treat every one they meet with dignity and respect, and to do their work conscious that their life is to be Eucharist, or bread broken for others. They are to speak passionately about Jesus, the source of the new life and joy.

There is no question that some members of the community are called to specific ministries. Acts identifies the predominant ministries of Peter and Paul, along with a few others, such as Stephen, Philip, Barnabas, and Silas. For a more complete picture of what took place from the very beginning, we must turn to Paul's letters. On different occasions Paul identifies ministries of men and women, such as apostles, prophets, teachers, and evangelists, as well as the power to heal and the ability to speak wisely (1 Cor 12:8-11, 28-31; Eph 4:11-12). These ministries have arisen out of the growing community, a response to its needs, and all are important.

According to Thomas O'Meara, "ministry is not simply organization and work but the activity of the Spirit in co-workers."[42] For Paul, no matter how one served, the greatest gift of the Spirit to each member was love (1 Cor 13:13) – love of God and of neighbour.

Communal life in the Spirit is strengthened in the homes where they gather to praise God and to break bread together. The focus is no longer just on the Temple, as Sean Freyne explains:

> For all of Judaism the Temple was the focal point where God's presence might be experienced. Various groups defined themselves in relation to it: Sadducees, controlling it; Pharisees extending its sphere of influence to everyday life. Essenes substituting the desert community for it. Zealots extending it geographically and politically to control of the land. While Jesus frequented the Temple and observed Jewish holy days, he made it clear that God's presence was available outside the Temple and its ritual. He proclaimed that the kingdom was already present in his own person, in his life and ministry. For him it was characterized not by judgment but by God's mercy for all – and especially for those who might be thought of as unworthy according to the ideals of the Hasidim and their heirs within the religious parties.[43]

The pervasive presence of God's Spirit is found in the Annuciation in Nazareth (Lk 1:26-38); the Visitation in Ain Karim (Lk 1:39-56);

the Nativity in Bethlehem (Lk 2:1-20); at Jesus' baptism in the Jordan river (Lk 3:21; see also Lk 4:18-19); and at Pentecost in Jerusalem.

The early Jewish-Christians continue to go to the Temple for certain prayer times and for ritual sacrifice, but they see the homes where they pray and break bread together as sacred spaces, because there the community gathers. The gathering of the community is sacred, not the place.[44] This is why, before Paul's conversion when he was persecuting Christians, he looks for them in their homes and not in the Temple (Acts 8:2).[45]

The communal household redefined the nature of religious and social relationships, setting aside the system of reciprocity and creating a community of equal disciples. It was "the dwelling place of the Spirit; the sphere of God's activity; the main social symbol of the kingdom of God and Christian holiness."[46] Prayer nurtured the activity of the Spirit in the members of the first community.

Prayer at the Heart of the Community

From the moment the small nucleus of Jesus' followers gathers in the Upper Room to await the Spirit (Acts 1:13), prayer is the source of their unity. Beyond Pentecost, Acts clearly tells us that prayer is central to the early Christians. At home, they are faithful to the prayers and the breaking of bread (Acts 2:42); they also take part in the Jewish practices of prayer and go to the Temple daily for public worship (Acts 2:46; 3:1; 5:12). "Their presence at the Temple for prayer at the time of sacrifice probably enabled the Christian community to maintain a distinctive presence"[47] among their Jewish neighbours, says Daniel K. Falk.

The prayer of the Magnificat, already seen as representative of the community, spills over into the community's day-to-day attitude of praising God with joy-filled hearts in response to God's saving action among them (Acts 2:47) and among those who receive God's mighty works through them (Acts 3:9-10). Prayer permeates their table fellowship: "They ate their food with glad and generous hearts, praising God" (Acts 2:46-47).

As time goes on, the community gives praise to God because the Gentiles had been empowered by the Spirit (Acts 11:15). The Jewish believers praise God for all Paul has done among the Gentiles, even during controversy over how the Gentiles will be admitted into the community (Acts 21:20). When Paul and Silas' jailer becomes a believer, his whole household rejoices (Acts 16:34).

Nowhere in Acts is the power of prayer more obvious than when the entire community faces persecution. The community, hearing of the arrest of Peter and John, gathers to pray. When Peter and John are released, the community "prays for boldness to continue to proclaim Jesus' name" (4:31). To their surprise, they receive a new empowerment of the Spirit. As at Pentecost, the power of the Spirit is born in prayerful, discerning hearts.

Rooted in prayer, the community continues to witness to the reality that Jesus, who had suffered the shameful death of crucifixion, had been raised by God and was the Messiah. Eventually, Gamaliel convinces the Sanhedrin that if this movement was of God they could not stop it, for they would be fighting God (Acts 5:34-40).

Some time later, Stephen is filled with the Spirit as he prays that God will forgive the people who are intent on killing him (Acts 7:60). When the community faces persecution again because of Peter's arrest, they gather for prayer at the home of Mary the mother of John Mark (Acts 12:12). Years afterward, Paul and Silas – persecuted and in prison – pray and sing hymns to God (Acts 16:25).

All these moments emphasize that prayer sustains intimacy with the risen Jesus and his Spirit, who helps them to discern and understand events in the light of faith. This, in turn, provides them with the courage to face persecution and even death. Through prayer, the community comes to understand what it means to take up the cross and follow Jesus.

The prayer of the community moves back and forth between the privacy of their homes and the public sphere represented by the Temple. This back-and-forth movement between Temple and home is symbolic of the interlocking outer-inner dynamics of prayer and mission present in the community's life.

Since the Jewish believers continued to go to the Temple for prayer and worship (Acts 2:46; 3:1),[48] one can presume that they also continued to recite the Shema, Israel's prayer of praise to God, when they rose and retired. But prayer at home also gave the community its distinctive identity. In the community's fidelity to prayer (Acts 2:42), one senses the emergence of distinctly Christian prayers.[49] Over time, the community composed prayers to express the meaning of their new-found faith in the risen Jesus.

Breaking bread together becomes the community's response to Jesus' command to his disciples at the Last Supper: "Do this in remembrance of me" (Lk 22:19). The breaking of bread (Acts 2:42), surrounded by prayers of thanksgiving and praise (Acts 2:47), is "closely associated with the early Christian experience and ideal of the Eucharist."[50]

Here is the ultimate expression of the community's fidelity to their call to share faith, to carry out their mission to witness to the risen Jesus, to be companions to one another on the journey and people of one heart and soul (Acts 4:32). Such unity "depended first and foremost on the way the members of the community were prayerfully attuned to the Spirit of the risen Jesus and thereby actually empowered to continue the mission of Jesus as members of his Body, the Church."[51] In a spirit of unity,

> each person's maturing life of prayer also called for a sharing of faith insights with other members of the community. Through such prayerful sharing and dialogue, the community grew in their ability to discern where and when and how the Spirit of the risen Jesus was prompting them to carry out the mission of Jesus.[52]

As prayer became an essential element of the community's life, the first disciples would have recalled that Jesus regularly set aside time for prayer. But in Bertrand Buby's words, "Mary is the only disciple present 'among the disicples' who has actually given witness to a prayer-life modelled on the psalms and to personal reflective prayer."[53] She enters the Upper Room and joins the fledgling community as a woman of prayer.

Mary knew that prayer was essential to her growth as Jesus' disciple and to her faith journey – her life lived in visitation under the guidance of the Spirit (Lk 1:26-39; 2:19, 51). She had seen how important prayer was to her son as he discerned the direction his mission was to take.

As a member of the community, Mary would likely have shared her experience with the other disciples, helping them to see how important prayerful listening, reflection, and dialogue with God were to enable the community to really hear and carry out God's word (Lk 8:19-21).

Mary, at the centre of the community's life in the spirit, is also at the centre of their life of prayer, "the model for the disciples in the prayer of the emerging church."[54]

Communal Life in Visitation: A Journey Spirituality

We have seen how Mary's life, lived in visitation, fits well with the journey theme dominant in contemporary spirituality. Her growth as Jesus' disciple and her faith journey to Pentecost highlight characteristics that are integral to life's journey: process and movement, light and darkness, joys and risks that move us beyond comfortable and known secure ways.

Her life journey included "threshold moments" that psychologists say are key to any person's growth. The same dynamics can be detected in the life of the early Christian community described in Acts.

For the circle of disciples, Pentecost is a threshold moment: a place of inspiration, prophecy, and new beginnings. As Mary passes through the doorway with the disciples, impelled by the power of the Spirit, the faith journey of this fledgling community – the nascent church – begins. As Mary had done years before at the Annunciation, they set out on an unknown future, trusting that the Spirit will always be with them. They cross the threshold aware that the gift of the Spirit establishes the inclusivity and equality of men and women in the community that is forming. Indeed, Pentecost is a place of inspiration and prophecy, and of opening a door to a new future.

In the visitation that erupts after Pentecost, the community's call to contemplation and mission is set in motion. Intimacy with Jesus, the power of his Spirit, and service to others are united into one call.

As more and more people join the community, these characteristics become the pulsing heart of the community. Like Mary before them, they are called to live in visitation.

To live in visitation is to be a people on a journey. Descriptions of life in the emerging community point to a people on the move. They are eager to share their news about Jesus, to enter into dialogue with their listeners, and to interpret the message so others can understand. As a people of visitation they are always attentive to God's presence – at home, in the Temple, travelling the roads in Jerusalem, shopping in the market, and going from house to house.

On the journey, the community experiences light and darkness, joys and risks. The success of the community never leads them to ease up on their profession of their faith. In times of darkness and persecution, they do not withdraw but go forward, meet the danger, and continue to be a prophetic community. The power of the Spirit draws them on, providing energy and courage for the journey.

Hospitality calls the community to move beyond a static notion of how to live the Way. Each arrival of people with whom they do not ordinarily associate brings about major changes in their lives. The need to change and adapt to new ways is ongoing in the community's life as they carry out Jesus' mission. They are called to change whatever might result in the rupture of the unity of mind and heart of the community.

In relinquishing circumcision as a requirement for Gentile men who had come to faith in Jesus, and revising the rules about food, the community is called beyond the legalism of the law of Moses.[55]

This enables Jewish and Gentile Christians to mix with one another and to eat together. The courage of this move cannot be underestimated: through it, unity in diversity was established.

All these events are threshold moments in the life of the community. For the community to live its life in visitation under the guidance of the Spirit was to accept that life is open ended and that God's visitation often happens in unexpected ways.

These early Christians learned that living under the guidance of the Spirit and being attentive to God's visitation called them communally, again and again, into uncharted waters and into new ways of being and acting in Jesus' name. In 70 CE, the Romans destroyed the Temple in Jerusalem and sacked the city. Jerusalem's inhabitants, including the Christians, fled for their lives. Eventually, Jewish Christians from Jerusalem and neighbouring areas, deprived of their temple, would need to cross another major threshold – the separation of synagogue and church.

The Spirit of the risen Jesus shaped their lives as a community of equal disciples, leading them beyond the security and comfort of knowing the way.

The men and women disciples gathered with Mary in the Upper Room received the Spirit and went out to evangelize. As others joined them, they were formed to do the same. Our call today is to continue this mission, for each generation of Christians must discern how to be a visible and influential presence of Christ in the world. In taking up our responsibility, we remember Mary's presence in the Upper Room, at Pentecost, and in the fledgling church.

Mary was at the centre of the group at Pentecost that formed the nucleus of the community of equal disciples, the church in Jerusalem. Luke compares the Annunciation–Visitation, including its challenging Magnificat, to Mary being with the disciples at Pentecost. These parallels, along with evidence of how the early Christian community lived its faith, support the claim of tradition that Mary reflected in her own life all that the Church is to be. What is possible for the Church community today that chooses to follow Jesus in Mary's footsteps?

Part IV: New Wine, New Wineskins

7

Mary and the Transformation
of the Church

Towards a Community of Equal Disciples

For Mary to influence the transformation of the Church into a
community of equal disciples[1] in our time, she must be as present
to us now as she was to the disciples united with her in prayer in
the Upper Room and at Pentecost.[2]

As we have seen throughout this book, the scriptural memory of
Mary helps us to remember this historical woman for who she was: the
first disciple of Jesus, who took her place among the disciples in the
Upper Room. She was a woman who walked in faith, trusting in God
in the midst of the oppressive Roman powers that surrounded her and
her people. She learned step by step what being a disciple of Jesus
meant for her as his mother; and her faith journey involved times of
joy, pain, and uncertainty as she chose to stand on the side of her son.
She was a woman who watched her child suffer and die unjustly as a
common criminal. As a woman, she made the supreme offering in giving
her child back to God, while Jesus made the supreme sacrifice of his
life for us. She was a woman whose presence in the Upper Room roots
her among the small group of Jesus' followers and in the community of
equal disciples, the Church born of the Spirit.[3] Mary, after her death, is
alive within the communion of saints, providing hope and
encouragement for Christian disciples struggling to be faithful to Jesus
today.[4]

Holding this memory of Mary, the first disciple of Jesus, clearly in our minds and hearts enables us always to see her as a real person and to enter into relationship with her, "our sister in faith who has gone before us."[5] It allows us to keep before us the image of this woman who emerged from her experience of the Annunciation–Visitation as the archetype of Christian discipleship for women and men.[6] Her presence among the disciples at Pentecost (Acts 1:14; 2:1-4) invites us to treasure the memory of her being "within the church, a disciple among disciples."[7]

Earlier we saw the parallel between Mary's experience of the Annunciation–Visitation, including her prophetic song, the Magnificat, and Mary and the disciples' participation in the birth of the Church as a community of equal disciples (Lk 1:26-58; Acts 2:1-4). Luke's memory of Mary's presence and involvement in the founding moment of the Church makes it clear that what is said of Mary in scripture is said of the Church. Her continued life-giving presence among us today is a constant reminder that, then and now, Mary represents all that the Church is to be,[8] a community of equal disciples[9] that hears the word of God and puts it into practice.[10] Like the Church born at Pentecost, Mary summons the Church born in our times to be a community of equal disciples, and to be, like her, "the listener, receptive to God, to Christ and to the Spirit."[11]

Looking at Mary with the disciples at Pentecost, the Church – the community of equal disciples – knows that discipleship, following Jesus in her footsteps, is not limited to the realm of interior, private spirituality. Mary was one of the disciples at Pentecost who, empowered by the Spirit, made an immediate exit from the Upper Room to share their experience of the risen Jesus. Her presence shows the community that intimacy with God, being a faithful witness of Jesus Christ, and service can never be separated. Jesus – the word of God conceived and born of the virginal heart – and the inner freedom of the community must be shared and interpreted so that this can become good news for others.

Mindful of Mary's example, the Church as the community of equal disciples, like the early Church, recognizes that it, like Mary, is called to be the perfect disciple – the good soil into which the word of God can take root and flourish.

As we recall Mary's life from the Annunciation to Pentecost, and the life of the fledgling Church, the community of disciples today is aware that the call to be the perfect disciple is not a static concept. Rather, as life unfolds and the community strives to follow Jesus, to hear the word of God and put it into practice, the Church knows that it will learn again and again what being the perfect disciple means.

Disciples of Jesus know that they are called to be learners together who journey with one another in faith. The memory of Mary's ongoing openness to the Spirit, her growth as a disciple of Jesus, and the fact that she joined her faith journey to that of the Church born at Pentecost will remain a point of reference for the community and a beacon on its journey of faith. The community will choose to live as a people of visitation, like Mary. It will be attentive on the journey to God's presence among them in daily life, in all people, and in creation.

For Mary and the disciples at Pentecost, and for the early Church in Jerusalem, the Spirit grasps the very core, the very essence of their being, "their spirit with the very Spirit of Christ."[12] The unleashing of the power of the Spirit in Mary and in that small group of Jesus' followers "hit them with the force of undeniable change."[13] Together, they become a new people in Christ, members of Jesus' new family – his sisters, his brothers, and his mother (Mk 3:31-35; Mt 12:46-49; Lk 8:19-21). What God had done in them was only fully understood in community as they saw the effects together.[14]

From that initial experience of the Spirit's empowerment of Mary and the disciples at Pentecost, it was evident that life in the Spirit did not lead them into a selfish, insular, and comfortable life among themselves. Rather, the Holy Spirit empowered them as church "to make them actors in the kingdom...with power."[15] According to Thomas O'Meara, "New life in the Spirit brought ministry. As the Church spread beyond Jerusalem to the ends of the earth (Acts 1:8), ministry flowed out of the community, and nourished and expanded the community"[16] which had grown to include Gentiles.

Acts, as we have seen, affirms that those first disciples understood that all were needed to carry on the ministry of Jesus. Their communal life witnessed to their belief in Jesus' promise that the presence of the Spirit in them would lead them into all truth, helping them to discover how to be faithful to Jesus (Jn 14:15-17; 16:13-14) in all circumstances, even persecution. That same promise of Jesus, the assurance of the abiding presence of the Spirit, holds true for the community of equal disciples that is the Church born today.

The empowerment of the Spirit in Mary and in the disciples gathered in the Upper Room at Pentecost is recognized as the birth of the Church. It was "the way God wanted to act in that and every generation"[17] – this transforming power of the Spirit was not for them alone but for all "whom the Lord our God called to him" (Acts 2:39). In imitation of Mary, discipleship rooted in Jesus becomes the common identity of the Church.[18] The sacrament of baptism regains its central place in the life of each community of equal disciples.[19]

With every baptism, the community will celebrate every man's and every woman's "Yes" to God's love, which embraces them from all time (Eph 1:1), and their acceptance to begin, like Mary, the journey of being and becoming a disciple of Jesus.[20] Baptism also indicates their commitment to be guided by the Spirit at work in them and in the Church, the community of equal disciples into which they have been received.[21]

The Spirit in Every Disciple

Today, as in the beginning, the gift of the Spirit belongs to every disciple. Within this context, the sacrament of baptism will be an ongoing celebration that God's Spirit continues to be poured out equally on all of God's servants today – men and women, young and old, strong and weak (Acts 2:17-18).[22] The community of equal disciples, as the early Christians did, will celebrate that in Christ Jesus they are all children of God through faith. All are clothed with Christ, all are equal, for "there is no longer slave or free, there is no longer male and female; for all of you are one in Christ Jesus" (Gal 3:28).[23] All are called to holiness, sharing equally in God's life.[24]

The community rejoices in the equal relationships among men and women disciples of Jesus that baptism continually brings about in the life of the community. Conscious of their equality as men and women disciples, the community cherishes its life in Christ and rejoices that the Spirit – present in each of them – ensures that the gifts needed to build up the Church are there.[25]

As in the beginning, "there are varieties of services, but the same Lord; and there are varieties of activities, but it is the same God who activates all of them in everyone" (1 Cor 12:4-11; see Eph 4:11-12).

The community knows that no one person has a claim to any gift, for the Spirit distributes gifts among all the faithful as the Spirit sees fit (1 Cor 12:11). In Paul's words, each person has a gift according to the grace given to each one (Rom 12:6).[26]

With each gift of the Spirit comes the responsibility for every disciple and for the community to grow more and more into the image of Jesus – to put on the mind and heart of Christ (Phil 2:5). Indeed, the community does not take this lightly, for the gifts of the Spirit are never for oneself alone. Gifts received are for ministry to others. Spiritual maturity is not evidenced by possessing spiritual gifts, but rather by being possessed by the Spirit in such a way that all are moved toward ministry to others.[27] What matters is that every disciple in the community walks in a manner worthy of the vocation they received in baptism and the ministry into which they have been called (Eph 4:1).[28] The same is true for the community as a whole.

In bringing their gifts into the community, disciples bring their whole person – their joys, their pain, their virtues, and their sin. A community of equal disciples, says Avery Dulles, "recognizes disciples' humanity, their limitations as they try to live out gospel values in a world being saturated more and more by greed and competition."[29]

The action of the Spirit in the community allows disciples to identify those "tendencies in themselves and around them which run counter to God's endeavour to bring the world to a good end."[30] This awareness opens their minds and hearts to the need for God's healing in their lives as much as in those of the people they serve.

Paul provides the community with a wonderful tool to gauge the authenticity of disciples' ministry. In Paul's view, the very being and actions of disciples of Jesus that flow from the Spirit bring love, joy, patience, kindness, generosity, faithfulness, and self-control (Gal 5:22-23). What is not of the Spirit brings jealousy, anger, quarrels, and dissension, to name a few counterforces (Gal 5:19-21).

The significance of each disciple and the vital contribution that each one can make to the community is fully grasped in Paul's analogy of the Church as the body of Christ. Speaking to the community at Corinth, where dissension had arisen, Paul stresses the importance of unity in the body. For Paul, this means that different members must care for one another, not work against each other. "If one member suffers," he says, "all suffer together with it; if one member is honoured, all rejoice together with it" (1 Cor 12:26); he reminds them that all are baptized in Christ, "and we were all made to drink one Spirit" (1 Cor 12:13; cf. Eph 4:5, 6).

In Godlind Bilke's words, "In the Church, the whole community of equal disciples is entrusted with ministry and service; different functions and gifts are meant for serving one another in reciprocity."[31]

For disciples of Jesus, reciprocity means a capacity to love and be loved, to give and receive, to empower and be empowered.[32] This requires that all members live in a spirit of mutuality, rejoicing in each other's gifts and trusting that the Spirit, acting in the heart of each disciple, will bring about unity in diversity (Rom 12:4-8).[33] In relation to the mission of the Church, this means that disciples do not act as "individual ministers who collaborate on projects. Rather they are called to be collaborative ministers whose quality of interaction with one another, in all they do, is to be characterized by mutuality and reciprocity."[34] Mary, in her experience with Elizabeth at the Visitation (Lk 1:39-58) and with the disciples at Pentecost (Acts 1:4), goes before the community; she is a witness to the power for good that reciprocity can have on the life of the Church.

At the heart of the community's call to reciprocity is a call to union with Jesus and with God, whom he called "Father."

Mary and that small group of Jesus' disciples gathered in the Upper Room (Acts 1:14; 2:1-4), along with the early Christian community, remind the Church that unity of mind and heart is born from reconciliation, mutuality, interdependence, and loving service among a community of equals.[35] They show by their lives that unity requires flexibility, a spirit of sacrifice that seeks the common good, knowing that no way is *the* way. This is not an easy task, but the community of disciples can find courage to follow Jesus, who did not regard equality with God as something to be exploited, but gave of himself to the point of dying on the cross (Phil 2:6).

Such generosity was born of love. It is not by chance, then, that Paul names love as the greatest gift (1 Cor 13:13). In his letter to the Ephesians, he "placed the gifts to the church in the context of a ministry of 'speaking the truth in love'" (Eph 4:15).[36] He urges the community in Ephesus to put away all bitterness, wrath, anger, wrangling, and slander, together with all malice, and be kind to each other, tenderhearted, forgiving each other as God in Christ had forgiven them (Eph 4:31-32; cf. Gal 5:1, 13-15).

Love for God and neighbour should be the glue that holds together the Church as a community of equal disciples. In Jesus' words, everyone will know that we are his disciples if we love one another (Jn 13:35). All the rest hinges on this attitude.

But unity in the community is not enough: the very heart of the disciples' vocation, alone and together, is to bring Christ's love to the world "to show with our lives that God loves the whole of humanity."[37] This is not romantic love, but loving each other as Jesus has loved us, even unto death (Phil 2:6-8).

When the going gets tough, the community of disciples trusts that intimacy with Jesus, and the ongoing presence of the Spirit, will enable them to stand firm – alone and together – in taking up their cross and following Jesus.

The Church, as a community of equal disciples alive in the Spirit, moves from being "a traditional 'church for the people' to a living 'church of the people,'"[38] "a church of participation."[39]

Participation in the Community of Equal Disciples

Beginning with Pentecost, participation was a reality in the early Christian communities. As Mary in the circle of disciples at Pentecost and life in the primitive community showed, all are needed to build up the community.[40] As one scholar says,

> Participation then is not a new fad, a desire on the part of some members to turn the church into a democracy. It is disciples taking ownership for the faith community and their responsibility to participate in the mission of Jesus, carrying his message of God's compassion, mercy and justice for everyone wherever they are involved in the world. In essence, participation is nothing more than the members coming alive and fulfilling their functions according to their gifts.[41]

Individuals participate in this equal community by sharing their unique gifts. Paul urges the community to use these gifts "that differ according to the grace given to them." "Prophecy, in proportion to faith; ministry, in ministering; the teacher, in teaching; the exhorter, in exhortation; the giver, in generosity; the leader, in diligence; the compassionate in cheerfulness" (Rom 12:6-8; cf. Eph 4:11-12; 1 Cor 12:4).

In contemporary terms, Paul could speak of disciples "having the ability to listen compassionately, to speak with eloquence, to oversee, to heal divisions, to create the worship environment, to make the liturgy come alive with music and song, to make justice and peace, and so forth,"[42] Robert Ludwig says. One thing is certain: in a community of equal disciples, authentic gifts ensure fidelity to Jesus and to the mission he gave the Church.

"Participation means that the whole body is alive and active; that members have the same care for one another as Paul wished the Corinthians to have (1 Cor 12). It is about communion in the community, a process of being of one mind and heart, a people coming together concerned about the common good."[43]

For the Church, participation reaches its fullness in the celebration of the Eucharist – the source and summit of the Christian life.[44] This is much more than attendance at a ritual, or the fulfillment of a weekly obligation. Rather, participation in the Eucharist expresses the ongoing desire of the community of disciples to be transformed into Christ – to be the presence of his body, and the memory and meaning of his passion, death, and resurrection for the world today.

The Church, as a community of equal disciples, affirms the presence of the Spirit in all disciples and trusts that the gifts of the Spirit needed to build up the community are to be found in all disciples. The Church community respects the vocation all disciples receive in baptism; to visibly represent Jesus, the Church accepts its vocation to be a priestly people who are called to participate in the priestly, prophetic mission of Jesus.[45]

Sharing in the Priestly, Prophetic, Royal Mission of Jesus

Vatican II, returning to the scriptures, described the Church as a chosen people, a royal priesthood, called by Christ to be the new People of God (1 Pt 2:9).[46]

In emphasizing the common priesthood of the faithful, the Council identified the priestly character of all God's people, calling the Church to live as a people consecrated to God. For "through the anointing of the Holy Spirit in baptism, all disciples of Jesus are consecrated as a spiritual house and a holy priesthood in order that they might proclaim the mighty works of God who called them out of darkness into his marvellous light."[47]

"Priesthood expresses the fundamental human vocation 'of all disciples'...the gift of self to God," says Daniel Cere.[48] This gift of self does not happen in a vacuum, but arises out of disciples' awareness that they have been called, chosen, and loved by God. Mary shows us the way.

From the first moment of her "Yes" to God at the Annunciation, Mary freely consented to co-operate in the mission of Jesus, her son. She shared fully in Christ's priesthood through her faith in God and her willingness to be transformed into a disciple of Jesus. She also shared in his suffering and death on the cross, and in the continued offering of herself in union with the disciples at Pentecost, and in the early Christian community.[49]

For Mary, sharing in the priesthood of Jesus was at the heart of her sense of self as a servant of God. This great act of love was service patterned on the mission of Jesus, the Servant of God himself.[50] Looking at Mary can help the community of disciples grasp how participation in Christ's priestly office is connected to the way we share in Christ's priestly ministry. It comes by offering ourselves to God, in union with Jesus moment by moment, as we carry out our duties relative to our personal vocations.

Recognizing that deep joy often accompanies such fidelity, the community of disciples, looking at Mary, becomes aware that participation in Christ's priestly office also "involves a willingness to encounter and enter into difficulties, sufferings, failures and poverty of life."[51] In this way, the community of disciples as a priestly people "perseveres in prayer and praise of God, and presents itself as a living sacrifice, holy and pleasing to God."[52] In the communal celebration of the Eucharist, the priestly mission of the Church, the new People of God, in union with Jesus, reaches its climax.[53]

In celebrating the Eucharist, the community remembers and gives thanks to God for what Jesus did at the Last Supper and through his death on the cross. In eating the bread and drinking the cup, the body and blood of Christ, the community proclaims his death until Jesus comes in glory (1 Cor 11:26). It also expresses its desire to be the body of Christ in the world and to be like Jesus – bread broken for others.

Mindful of this understanding, the community realizes that being a priestly people can never be separated from its call to participate in the prophetic, royal mission of Jesus. Wanting to be like Mary, the community will pray to be continually transformed as she was through her relationship with Jesus. It will seek to be imbued with the same burning charity that she exemplified in her desire to share Christ and receive the liberation that belief in him – his life, death, and resurrection – offers everyone.[54]

Like Mary, who hastened to visit her cousin Elizabeth (Lk 1:39-45) and who shared the empowerment of the Spirit with the disciples at Pentecost (Acts 2:1-4), the community of disciples becomes a servant of the gospel according to the gift of God's grace (Eph 3:7). Aided by the Spirit, the community rejoices that all disciples have the power to help others along the way.[55] Mary co-operated with Christ in our salvation through faith and obedience, attentive listening, and response to God's word as it unfolded in her life;[56] the community of equal disciples recognizes its responsibility to follow her example.

The community therefore sends disciples to their families, friends, co-workers, and neighbourhoods to be courageous witnesses to the meaning Jesus brings to their lives. In the words of Vatican II, "everywhere on earth disciples of Jesus are called to bear witness to Christ and give an answer to those who seek an account of that hope of eternal life which is in them."[57]

Holding the prophetic prayer of the Magnificat in its heart (Lk 1:46-55), the community learns from Mary the relationship between praise and gratitude to God in whose image and likeness they are created. Their actions work for the liberation of all people, which includes a preferential option for the poor.[58] Mary – of the Annunciation–Visitation, in the circle of disciples at Pentecost, and in the life of the early Christian community – constantly reminds the community that these two elements cannot be separated.

The Magnificat, prayed and practised in the community of equal disciples, will announce to the world that "they don't have a religion in which all they can offer is intellectual truths or promises for a better future – offers which don't necessarily change lives now."[59] Rather, the Magnificat calls the community to believe and to trust that through faith in Jesus and through the power of the Spirit, they can do the works Jesus did. It must be the compassionate, healing, and merciful presence of God in the world that contributes to freedom from oppression (Jn 14:12).[60]

To share in the priestly, prophetic, and royal mission of Jesus means trusting that the light of Christ can pierce the pervasive darkness that surrounds so many situations in this world, and knowing that the resurrection holds the promise that good does conquer evil.

In the community of equal disciples called to share in Jesus' priestly, prophetic mission, labels like "clergy" and "laity" are not important. What brings status to the community is the call of all disciples to participate in this ministry of Jesus[61] – not titles or offices.[62]

The Spirit's empowerment of the community is always given to carry on the mission of Jesus.[63] This means that the Church can, like Mary, give birth to Christ in their midst. In this way, the community is like a sacrament of Christ's presence in the world: bearers of Christ who bring his values into every area of life.[64] The Annunciation–Visitation and the challenging song of the Magnificat echo through the life of the community today, making concrete its vocation to share in the priestly, prophetic, and royal mission of Jesus.

8

The Annunciation–Visitation Motif
in the Life of the Church

Sharing the Story of Jesus Today

Like Mary, the Church that is called to be a community of equal disciples[1] and to be faithful to its priestly vocation in Jesus' name recognizes the central place that reflection on God's word must have in the life of the community.[2] Inspired by Mary's prayerful, pondering heart, the community of disciples will return again and again to the scriptures. We will listen, reflect on God's word, and pray that God's Word – Jesus – can be conceived and born in the heart of the community, so that we can be transformed into his likeness. Following Mary's examples in the Visitation and with the disciples at Pentecost, we pray that the power of the Spirit will enable us as a community to witness without hesitation to Jesus in a culture that tries to relegate faith to the private sphere of life: we know that the truth about Jesus, interpreted in the light of his life and mission, must be presented to people today in language they can understand.[3]

On Pentecost day itself – as in the early days, months, and years of the Church – the first disciples turn to the scriptures to understand and interpret Jesus' life and mission. They realize that Jesus was the Messiah – the anointed one, the suffering servant who took on his shoulders the sins of the people and was raised up by God (Is 42:1-4; 49:1-7; 50:4-11; 52:13–53:12). For Jewish men and women, to say that Jesus is the Messiah and the anointed one captures the very essence of Jesus –

his life and his mission. Eventually, this leads the Church to a break from Judaism.

As Gentiles began to believe in Jesus, the Church needed to find titles that conveyed the same truth about Jesus in language to which Gentiles could relate. In the process, the Gentiles came to speak of Jesus as Lord and Son of God.

In saying that Jesus was Lord,[4] Gentile Christians intended to say something close to what their Jewish brothers and sisters meant in claiming that Jesus was the Messiah: that is, that Jesus had been sent by God to save the world. In claiming him as Son of God, they transformed a title by which the Emperor Augustus was known,[5] leading to a rupture with the Emperor and all that he represented.[6]

Behind all the titles was one person – Jesus. His life and ministry, death and resurrection showed him to be the incarnation of God's love, compassion, mercy, and justice. Faith in Jesus brought life and freedom to people regardless of age, gender, and culture.[7]

When the first disciples shared their faith in the risen Jesus, they were conscious that their listeners "wanted not only to know who Jesus was, but also what following him and membership in the group had to offer in relation to the uncertainty of their times."[8] The same is true in our time, and is even more urgent today.

Being faithful to the scriptures and to tradition, the community of disciples today is called to find ways to express the same truth about Jesus. What language can be used to convey the meanings of Messiah, Lord, Son of God, and Saviour so that people today can understand and relate to the meaning of what is preached?[9] As in the beginning, people today must be able to say that they hear the message about God's deeds and power and about Jesus in their own languages and culture. This search for contemporary language to convey the truth about Jesus can be inspired by the memory of the Magnificat, through which Mary interpreted the meaning of the Word of God – Jesus – whom she had conceived. Other inspiration in this search comes from the experience of Pentecost and the early Church.[10]

The Roman Catholic Church, along with all Christian traditions, faces this challenge today, says one writer: "how to allow the gospel-event to shed new light on our religious tradition, understood in radical newness, so it can be as fresh and challenging today as it was for those who first heard the gospel."[11]

Many Christians today speak of themselves as being in a process of conversion. In conversations over coffee or in small groups, they venture to reveal their changing images of God and of Jesus, their new understanding of their faith in God and in Jesus, and of their own religious tradition. These changes have been influenced by recent developments in theology, psychology, spirituality, and science; new information about the origins of our universe; and the events and circumstances of their lives.

Recognizing their need for salvation, their reflection has led them to perceive that the gospel and our tradition call for a radical new expression in a world rapidly becoming a global economic community with seemingly no ethical guidelines. While they do not deny the truth contained in credal statements, many find that this language does not adequately express their changing perception of God, Jesus, sin, and the Christian heritage they cherish. These Christians seek new language to express their faith. They want a liturgy that connects to their life experience, reminds them of God's presence on the journey, and makes them aware of the Spirit that calls them to become fully human and unleashes the divinity within them – women and men made in the image and likeness of God (Gen 1:27).

Their changing perception of God makes "the idea of a God ruled by wilfulness and caprice unacceptable."[12] They desire that other biblical metaphors, such as God's motherhood, be introduced into our tradition. At the same time, as Pope John Paul II says, these Christians agree that

> the idea of a divine father, prepared to make the generous gift of life and providing for its necessities, but who at the same time is severe and punishing, and not always for an obvious reason, is linked in ancient societies to the institution of patriarchy and transfers the way 'this image of God' is most commonly conceived to the religious level.[13]

How to be a catalyst and bring about change in the patriarchal mindset that prevails in the Church is an ongoing challenge, but an essential one.

It is clear that disciples today cannot speak about Jesus in the abstract concepts and language suited to another culture and time. Mindful of this reality, and conscious that the word of God is always living and active, the community of equal disciples will search for new ways to express their faith in God and the truth about Jesus. It will look for new language and new images so that the message can truly be good news for all people.[14] The way we speak about faith in God and in Jesus must arise out of the community's reflection while safeguarding the scriptures and tradition.[15]

Faith is much more than believing what we are told. As the lives of Mary and the fledgling Church show, faith, like discipleship, is never static. It demands that we be wide open to God and to Jesus revealed in and through the community.

Disciples of Jesus must always be open to changing perceptions and understandings of God.[16] There is always more to discover and more to say about who God is and what Jesus means in our lives. But where do we begin?

Just as the first disciples announced and interpreted the meaning of the passion, death, and resurrection of Jesus for their lives and those of their listeners, disciples of Jesus today might begin by doing the same. For Jesus' passion, death, and resurrection to be good news for many today, his life must relate to people's search for meaning and understanding. This can be difficult in our rapidly changing society and world.

Praying with Mary standing at the cross, seeing her son in pain (Jn 19:25), will speak to the experiences of many parents today whose children are dying from suicide, cancer, HIV/AIDS, drug overdoses, growing gang violence, and needless wars – to name but a few modern-day crucifixions.

Today's world is experiencing incessant and futile wars between nations, resulting in constant streams of refugees, as well as famines that are often caused by human greed. Women and children are exploited as sex objects or slaves used for pornography and productivity. Many people suffer the ravages of disease. In all the suffering experienced around the world today, we are called to hear Jesus' cry from the cross. Like Jesus, we are to be constant witnesses to the tenderness and mercy of a compassionate and loving God.[17]

Disciples of Jesus – in sharing how the passion, death, and resurrection of Jesus brings meaning to their lives today – can be a source of encouragement to others struggling under the weight of life's demands.

Faith grows in community, through disciples sharing stories of faith and articulating how Jesus challenges their lives. In the sharing, the community continually faces – both personally and communally – Jesus' question, "Who do you say that I am?" (Mt 16:15). Together they can listen and respond to Mary's directive to those servants when the wine ran out at the wedding in Cana: "Do whatever he tells you" (Jn 2:5).

As the community reflects together on the word of God, it will be mindful that Jesus didn't give his disciples a blueprint for responding to each situation they would meet along the way. Guided by the Spirit, they were to interpret how to be faithful to him and to his mission as new situations and problems arose. They did not just repeat the oral tradition about Jesus, but interpreted it in relation to what different communities were experiencing.[18]

Disciples of Jesus today are called to read the scriptures knowing that they do not provide easy, ready-made answers for the global moral dilemmas of our times: issues around sexuality, reproductive techonologies, abortion, euthanasia, threats to the environment, and nuclear weapons. Trusting in Jesus' promise of the abiding presence of the Spirit, the community will look at Jesus' life and pray for discerning hearts to find out how to stand on the side of life for the universe and especially for all of God's people, from conception to death.

Immersed in gospel values, the community, like Mary, becomes the good soil – the virginal heart in which the word of God can take root and flourish again and again (Lk 8:15; Mk 4:20; Mt 13:23). In this way the story of Jesus, the story of God with us (Mt 1:23), remains ever new.

Mary and those first disciples in the early Christian community identified with their teaching mission and made it their own. For them, fidelity to the teaching of the apostles did not refer to a body of apostolic teachings, but to the apostolic teaching by the community. There were special teachers, such as the apostles, but the whole Church identified with their teaching mission.[19]

The community of disciples was on fire with their love for Jesus and empowered by the Spirit. Convinced that following Jesus enabled them to find meaning in their lives, the community hastens to send its disciples forth to share him with others.[20] At home, at work, at play, and before all creation, they know that they are called to be faithful witnesses of Jesus. In so doing, they embrace their call to live the fullness of their priesthood.

Disciples, ultimately, tell the story of Jesus' life, death, and resurrection in the Eucharist. In breaking the bread and sharing the cup they commit themselves to be like Jesus – bread broken for others – over and over again.

"In the long run is there any other way of handing on the Gospel then by transmitting to another person one's personal experience of faith?" asks Pope Paul VI.[21] At times the disciples were discouraged and felt like giving up. Yet, intimacy with Jesus and his promise of the abiding presence of the Spirit assures the disciples that they will have the grace they need. Mary's life witnesses this truth to the community.

In sharing their faith, the community realizes that Pentecost happens daily. This is when the community becomes like Mary, "the remembering mother."[22] She gave birth to Christ and witnessed to the whole of his life – his suffering, his death and resurrection, and the power of the Spirit at work in their midst. As the Church, a community of equal disciples – like the fledgling Church born at Pentecost – shares its faith, it affirms men and women together giving birth to Christ, the Church, in these times.[23]

The Church – in conceiving, sharing, and interpreting the story of Jesus today – is called to follow Jesus and imitate the pattern of his life as it walks his Way.[24] The Magnificat arises from their hearts in prayer and makes gospel values concrete.

The Magnificat in the Church

Mary's song, the Magnificat, has ceaselessly echoed in the heart of the Church through the centuries, and continues to do so today in the community of equal disciples.[25] As in the beginning, the words of her song, rising from the community, announce that they have discovered, through faith in the risen Jesus, that their true identity and status derive from their relationship with God. In praying the Magnificat, the community rejoices in God and proclaims that God has done great things in them and in the whole universe.[26] They are a new creation (2 Cor 5:17), "a liberated people, a people whose life will be centred on the Spirit of Life."[27]

In many ways, this song is a prayer

that God will continue to grant that they, men and women, be strengthened in their inner being with power though the Spirit,

that Christ may dwell in their hearts through faith, as they are
being rooted and grounded in love…[and that they may] have
the power to comprehend with all the saints, what is the breadth
and length and height and depth, and to know the love of Christ
that surpasses all knowledge so that they may be filled with the
fullness of God. (Eph 3:14-19)

The Magnificat looks at Mary's faith journey, her growth as a disciple
of Jesus, and her presence among the early community, and remembers
the witness of the Church – those countless faith-filled women and
men disciples of Jesus through the centuries. The Magnificat presents
a daily call to conversion for every disciple and for the community.

The nature of conversion will differ for each community. Yet,
Christian disciples throughout the world are increasingly aware of the
challenges they face in withstanding the demands of the prevailing
secular consumer global culture that offers a variety of other gods to
worship in every part of the world.

Resisting the desire of the consumer culture to own the latest
technological innovation and refusing to be defined by increasingly
oppressive political and social structures, even in democratically ruled
nations, may be radical decisions today. They are, however, no less
radical than decisions to follow Christ that Mary, those first disciples,
and generations of men and women have made ever since. The
Magnificat, at the centre of the community, challenges each generation
to accept the cost of discipleship, as Mary did.[28]

With Mary and the disciples at Pentecost, the Church as a
community of equal disciples recognizes the resurrection as God's
assurance that what Jesus stood for – compassion for the poor, the
hungry, the downtrodden, and the marginalized in his society – was
exactly what God stood for, and makes every effort to live that way
today.[29]

While they recognize the movement of the Spirit to renew the
face of the earth through individual disciples,[30] the community of
disciples knows that, as in the beginning, communal witness is far more
radical than what can be accomplished by individuals.[31] For this reason,
the community chooses to live by God's wisdom – the inner law of
love, that double commandment to love God with their whole heart
and soul and their neighbour as themselves.[32] United in God at the
centre, and turning again and again towards their neighbour, the

community lives in visitation – intimate with God and in service to their neighbour.

In a touching statement, the Second Vatican Council noted that

the joy and hope, the grief and anguish of the people of our time, especially of the poor and afflicted in any way, are the joy and the hope, the grief and anguish of the followers of Christ as well. Nothing that is genuinely human fails to find an echo in their hearts.[33]

For the Council, the Church must offer hope to people; it must not only proclaim the truth about Jesus but also work diligently to ensure that freedom, peace, and justice will prevail for all humankind. The Magnificat, in prayer and practice, enables the community of equal disciples to fulfill this desire. In carrying out its priestly, prophetic, and royal mission, the community will have the courage to denounce unjust structures in society, its own community, and the institution of the Church. In so doing, it becomes a "church of solidarity" and a "church of poverty."[34]

The Magnificat summons the community to walk in solidarity with God and with the victims of the global market economy, which values technology over people; uses war, "ethnic cleansing," and genocide to maintain power over others; and risks planet Earth for the sake of profits for a tiny minority. Desiring that God's "kindom"[35] of right relationships, justice, and peace be established, the community addresses current issues such as corporate wealth, increased returns to shareholders, company mergers, and downsizing.

In a church of solidarity, the Magnificat challenges the developed world to uncover the reasons for the diminished work opportunities rather than blame refugees, immigrants, and women for job scarcity.

A community of disciples, as a church of solidarity, "not only prays for the poor, but also with them, is not only pious for the burdened and oppressed, but also with them."[36] In this way, the community listens to the experiences and pain of the increasing number of people who are poor, oppressed, and marginalized. It hears the cry of Jesus from the cross rising from every corner of the world as the gap widens between those few who are rich and the majority who are poor.[37] This gives poverty a human face. It brings together those who have and those who have not in discerning how to speak out against injustices and make demands through non-violent actions of dissent that can bring about change.[38]

In a community of disciples, a church of solidarity that is a church of the poor, the social teaching of the church takes root. In the celebration of the Eucharist, the breaking of the bread, the drinking of the cup, the church of solidarity becomes a church of hospitality.[39]

For the early Christians, sharing goods in common meant more than sharing their material possessions. It opened the community to show concern for a diversity of people and to give and receive hospitality from those with whom they ordinarily wouldn't have related. In so doing, the community transformed the idea of reciprocity which, within their society, required them to pay back in some way any favour received.

Inspired by the early Church, the community of equal disciples will continually welcome the stranger, see ethnic differences as gifts people bring to the community, and invite everyone to cross the threshold into the community as full participants and partners. In the process, the community will become a countercultural witness to the present trend in many nations across the world to keep strangers out through limiting immigration. This trend makes it difficult for the increasing number of refugees to find safe havens from wars and dictatorships.

The Magnificat asks that the community of disciples move together, in solidarity with their sisters and brothers of other faith traditions and all people of good will, to address the global injustices of our times.[40] Working with others, they can pressure governments and multinational corporations to develop the political will to work towards a new world order that sustains life and offers freedom from all that oppresses humankind and the earth.

Mary, in her Magnificat, is totally dependent upon and oriented towards God, at the side of Jesus. This is "the most perfect image of freedom and of the liberation of humanity and of the universe,"[41] says Pope John Paul II in *Redemptoris Mater*.

The Magnificat frames Mary's experience of God at the Annunciation, her encounter with Elizabeth at the Visitation, and her experience at Pentecost with the disciples. It announces that the solidarity to which the community of disciples is called arises from intimacy, communion, and interdependence on God and one another.

It is the community's continuous call to discipleship – the ongoing, inward-outward spiral of intimacy with God and service to others in action.

In the Magnificat, Mary also proclaims "the radical dependence of God on humanity; the other side of disciples' dependence on God," says Rosemary Radford Ruether. "Only through a free human response to God is God enabled to become the transformer of history. Without such faith, no miracles happen."[42]

Many today note that the various crises of our times are found within the world's poverty. We see nuclear weapons, racism, sexism, human rights' violations, corporate greed, increasing violence among teenagers, child labour, and the sex trade. Other conflicts exist over who and what define family, the impact of globalization, a breakdown in governments, lack of corporate accountability, mistreatment of the earth, and the unrelenting war machine that creates more problems than it was supposed to solve.[43] It is becoming increasingly clearer that these crises are interconnected.[44] They merge into the "cry of the earth; cry of the poor."[45]

Pope John Paul II offers a way to resolve these crises: "Promoting a culture of peace," he writes, "ensures respect for all other rights, since it encourages the building of a society in which structures of power give way to structures of cooperation, with a view to the common good."[46] In a culture of peace, says Elise Boulding, "love is the prime mover of all behaviour. It is a gift from the Creator, or Creative Principle. Women and men share with one another, as brothers and sisters, each person equal to every other. The weak are cared for and trouble-makers reconciled."[47]

The culture of peace is not a new fad. It already exists in families; intentional church communities; international peace-building centres; interfaith peace groups; and the daily interaction of people getting on with their lives and work, negotiating differences, and seeking reconciliation and forgiveness in a non-violent manner.[48] But here again, the witness of community has a greater chance of bringing about change in society than individual efforts can.

The community of disciples therefore joins continuous efforts for peace with their sisters and brothers of other faith traditions so a community of nations will be born.[49]

Mary is a constant source of inspiration and encouragement for the community in its efforts on behalf of peace in the world. The Magnificat, echoing in the prayer and life of the community, reminds disciples of the woman of the Annunciation who conceived Jesus, the Prince of Peace, and shared him with Elizabeth at the Visitation. Disciples remember the woman who found a quiet solution for the lack of wine at Cana and the mother who stood beside her son through his life, ministry, death, and resurrection. They also remember Mary of Pentecost, whose forgiving, reconciling heart led her into the circle of disciples to pray for the Spirit of unity, peace, love, and joy.[50] The community prays with Mary for peace and takes actions so that peace can become a reality in the world.

Any accusation by critics that the community is moving into an arena where it does not belong is an affront to the gospel of Jesus Christ. The pivotal moments of Mary's discipleship remind us that disciples of Jesus are called to enter the world and change it.

The Magnificat is about being in right relationship with God, with ourselves, and with our neighbour. In a community of equal disciples – a church of solidarity and of hospitality that is characterized by unity, equality, reconciliation, and forgiveness – a culture of peace has a chance.

The elimination of sexism, which ignores the full humanity of both women and men, also has a chance. In recent years, psychology has shown that women and men share the same capacities to be rational and emotional, compassionate, nurturing, and receptive; "receptive" was noted earlier as a prerequisite for hearing the word of God and being transformed by it. Their expression differs by personality, not by biological difference.[51] This awareness breaks down the stereotypes of men and women ingrained in a patriarchal society that identifies men with the outer world and women with the inner. Unfortunately, these distinctions are still fully alive in the Church.[52] As the archetype of Christian discipleship for women and men, Mary can help the community to reverse this patriarchal heritage.

Mary's presence with the men and women at Pentecost frees the community from the old dualism of male domination and female subordination and shows that men and women together can be pregnant with prophetic life, acting in mutuality and reciprocity. She represents this community – men and women created equally in the image and likeness of God, equal partners through baptism who share in the universal priesthood of all believers. What should distinguish women and men in a community of equal disciples is discipleship, lives in sync with the gospel message, not gender.[53] The entire community of disciples growing continuously into Christ's likeness becomes the mirror in which the world sees the face of Christ.[54]

It has been said that the struggle against sexism is basically a struggle to humanize ourselves, to salvage the planet, and to be in right relation with God.[55] In a community of equal disciples modelled on Mary in the Visitation and at Pentecost, with the Magnificat rising from its heart, sexism has no place.

The Magnificat, rooted in the Church, the community of equal disciples, is about the transformation of relationships. Jesus makes it clear that whoever among them wants to be great must be their servant (Mt 20:25-28; 23:8-12). The Magnificat still calls forth servant leaders to serve the community.

Servant Leaders in the Community of Equal Disciples

Servant leaders recognize that the Spirit resides in the community, forming and shaping it into the likeness of Jesus. In a community of equal disciples, the responsibility to lead the community will be received as one gift among many needed to build up the body of Christ. The role of the leaders is to help disciples recognize the presence of God and the action of the Holy Spirit at work in and around them, and to draw forth the gifts present in all members. In the words of Vatican II, they are to help the community understand the events of the times in the light of gospel values "so that their love will overflow with knowledge and full insight and they can choose the action that seems best" (Phil 1:9).

"Effective servant leadership means directing and co-ordinating the energies and resources of the people of God whether they develop ministries to serve the community of disciples to build up the body of Christ, or to answer a need crying out in the neighbourhood, in the world for attention," Roy Anderson explains.[56] In this way, communities of equal disciples become centres where people can find fulfillment and appreciation of their gifts and reach their potential.[57]

Servant leaders and the community, working together, identify and call forth gifts of leadership present in other disciples that are needed to assist the community to fulfill its mission. The goal of sharing power, responsibility, and decision-making is to create a genuine partnership among the disciples so the mission of Jesus – the establishment of God's kingdom of peace, justice, and mercy – can be furthered.[58]

In a community of equal disciples, the sacrament of ordination places the ordained minister as servant leader at the service of the community to nurture men and women disciples who are on fire with their priestly, prophetic, and royal vocation. The ordained minister encourages them to live that vocation to the full – not only in the faith community but in the world where they live and work.[59]

The Magnificat, in prayer and in practice at the centre of the Church, not only calls forth servant leaders, but invites the community of equal disciples to rethink its call to be servants of God and of Jesus, a servant church in the world.

Rethinking Our Call to be Servants of God, a Servant Church

In response to God's great love for her, Mary, at the Annunciation–Visitation, identifies herself as the servant of God – a prophetic servant of the Word, Jesus. With God's male and female servants at Pentecost, she becomes a member of a prophetic community of equal disciples: "It is a sign that the community is composed of persons who through baptism, in response to God's love, have freely chosen to fully surrender themselves to God and to the ministry of the gospel."[60] At both moments, Mary shows us that being God's servant is an act of discipleship.[61]

In the scriptures, being a servant of God is a metaphor for our relationship with God; this role leads to freedom, not oppression.[62] For Mary and the first believers, this freedom was not licence to do whatever they wanted. Rather, it was an inner freedom, born of the Spirit, that enabled them to overcome the obstacles that prevented them from entering wholeheartedly into the service of Christ.

Yet many people in the Church today are uncomfortable with servant language. Despite the transformation of the term "servant," slavery was condoned, both inside and outside of the Church, for many centuries. In many parts of the world today, this word continues to indicate subservience and, in some cases, slavery (even though world governments have officially condemned it); this is especially true for women and children.

Within the Church from very early on, the understanding of equality among women and men in the community of disciples – inherent in their self-identity as servants of God – was co-opted into hierarchical power structures. Even now, within the Church "service is preached in ways that has different implications for both women and men, lay and ordained."[63] This practice continues, even though Vatican II emphasized the common vocation of all baptized male and female disciples of Jesus to participate in the priestly, prophetic, and royal mission of Jesus.[64]

The Greek word for service – ministry – comes from the root word for servanthood.[65] Vatican II, returning to the Church's scriptural roots, emphasized that the Church must be like Jesus – in the world not to be served but to serve.[66]

Jesus' priestly, prophetic, and royal mission flowed from his identity as God's servant, as did Mary's participation in his mission. If the Church – a community of equal disciples – is to feel comfortable in reclaiming its identity as servants of God and a servant church, such terminology cannot be used independently of the community's vocation, received in baptism, to share in Jesus' ministry.

Jesus' outreach to the poor and the marginalized in his society showed him to be God's chosen servant; he was the one to whom God had given "the tongue of a teacher" so as to know how to sustain the person who is weary (Is 50:4; Mt 12:15-21). The Church realizes that by making the Magnificat concrete in its life, it will be doing for the people of our time what Jesus did for people of his time. In this way, modern disciples can recognize themselves as servants of God. They, like Jesus, are anointed to "bring good news to the poor, to proclaim the release to the captives, recovery of sight to the blind, and freedom to the oppressed" (Lk 4:16-19; cf. Is 61:1).

Reclaiming Our Call to be Servants of God, a Servant Church

In reclaiming our call to be servants of God, a servant Church, the community of equal disciples must use the word "servant" carefully. This word must never slip back into "ways that are oppressive for people of colour, for women, for poor people, ways that contribute to passivity, powerlessness, and resentment."[67] The Church must find the key to sustaining the real meaning of "servant" in the practice of foot-washing performed by Jesus at the Last Supper (Jn 13:1-20).[68]

In John's gospel, Jesus' command to wash one another's feet is not just for the leaders but for the entire community. Barbara Bowe explains:

> Here the Christian paradox confronts disciples. The paradox, of course, is that the one who performs the action is thereby cleansed, even more than the one who has been "washed." And, for the author of John, this mystery is the key to eternal life. Thus, Jesus tells his disciples, "If you understand this, blessed are you if you do it" (13:17).[69]

As Jesus washed the feet of his disciples, he initiated a new pattern of relationships that originates in the common meal at the heart of the community – the Lord's supper[70] – and showed that being servants of God and one another are inseparable behaviours.

For the community of equal disciples, foot-washing is a call to serve one another with whatever gift they have received (1 Pt 4:11). Rather than being service over others, this service with and to others breaks down isolation inside the community, within families, and within neighbourhoods; it opens the community to interaction in the world. As reflection on the Magnificat showed, this means embracing all men, women, and children of every nation as brothers and sisters with the same love that Jesus showed to all people.[71]

A community of equal disciples recognizes that following Jesus can be costly. A servant church is a church about life with the same passion that Jesus had, knowing that this resulted in his being marginalized by the religious and civic leaders and led, ultimately, to his death.

Throughout the centuries, and up to today, many disciples have lost their lives working against systems of domination that provide privilege, excess riches, and unlimited access to and use of the world's resources for a few.[72]

In the West, we live in a culture that goes largely against our faith as Christians. The media and the corporate and political structures go to great lengths to neutralize the influence of the mainstream churches and limit religion to the private arena of life.

Today's community of disciples can take heart from Mary and those first disciples of Jesus. Facing conflict and persecution, they turned to prayer for the courage to be faithful servants of God and to continue to speak in Jesus' name. To their surprise, they received a new impulse of the Spirit, providing them with the courage and perseverance they needed to remain faithful to Jesus. The Church today can expect no less.

In the Book of Revelation, Mary, the woman who gave birth to Jesus, has been seen in recent years as a symbol of the people of God of the new covenant initiated by Jesus that overcomes the darkness in any age (Rev 12:1-2).[73] As the community of equal disciples – servants of God and a servant church – enters into the darkness that surrounds it as church in these times, it enters into the mystery of the cross.

There is no question that our time calls for courage to enter into the darkness, the ambiguity, and uncertainty of today just as Mary and the disciples faced the darkness that surrounded them after Jesus' death that Good Friday more than two thousand years ago. What those hours of grieving and the time waiting in the Upper Room tell us, says Andrew Britz, is that

> the experience of the resurrection for Mary and for that small group of women and men disciples with her, despite whatever limitations they had, gave them the courage to wait on the Spirit, to live with ambiguity not knowing what they would become, confident that Jesus would hold true to his promise, to believe that what he called them to was greater than they could imagine. The greatest challenge facing the church today is to believe that this promise holds true for God's male and female servants today.[74]

The memory of the resurrection calls them to trust that out of the darkness of the womb, new life is being shaped and will come to birth.

This is not a call to passivity; it is an invitation to attentive listening and inner seeing. It means touching the moments of resurrection – the power of the Spirit at work in their lives and in the world each day.

No matter how the community is called to serve, the promise of Jesus rings true: in serving others, we serve him (Mt 25:40).

Servants of God in the World

For the Second Vatican Council, "faith is not lived in the sacristy but in the world: in family, culture, economics, politics, peace making"[75] – in all areas of life. At the heart of the pastoral constitution of *Gaudium et Spes* (The Church in the Modern World) is "the realization that God's kindom is in our midst now. At times it may appear to be only a mustard seed, but its growth is fostered when disciples of Jesus work together to transform society by the values of the gospel."[76]

In the words of Pope John Paul II, every member of the community is called "to participate actively in the whole life of the church; not only are they to animate the world with the spirit of Christianity, but they are to be witnesses to Christ in all circumstances and at the very heart of the community of humankind."[77] In this spirit, the community of disciples, attentive to the Spirit, takes up its mission to be the salt of the earth and the light of the world (Mt 5:13-16).

Ministry, then, is not something a disciple does within the confines of a church structure, but a way of life. The community of equal disciples, supporting each other in the challenging task of being God's servants in the world, will help one another make the connections between the sacrament of the Eucharist and family life, work, and leisure.[78] They will together discover the holy in everyday life as well as the sacredness of all creation.

Sacraments, seen in this way, are lived out in the very fabric of life. Everyday life is sacramental. Work is sacred and holy. Disciples enter into their daily activities conscious that they are co-creators with God. Through taking up their responsibilities in their families and at work, they co-operate with God in the emergence of God's kingdom, the transformation of the world. Their workplaces become an altar on which they celebrate the liturgy of their work.[79]

As in Mary's experiences – with Elizabeth at the Visitation, with the disciples at Pentecost, and in the life of the primitive community – dualism has no place in disciples' lives outside the church community. They are called to stay focused within, centred in God, and turned towards their neighbour as they work.

Called to live their priestly, prophetic, and royal vocation in the footsteps of Jesus in the marketplace of everyday life, disciples will strive to emulate Mary – attentive to God's Spirit in all they meet and receptive to the gifts of each co-worker. In this way they will empower others even as they allow the other to contribute to their own growth.

The encounter and dialogue between Mary and Elizabeth at the Visitation and between Mary and the disciples at Pentecost spoke to the early disciples. They knew that mutuality, equality, interdependence, unity of mind and heart, reconciliation, and loving service among equals were important not only for their life in the community of the Church, but in their lives as a whole. In the same way, the Magnificat, in prayer and practice, urges us to allow these characteristics to guide our lives in the office, the factory, the trenches, the store, the restaurant, the courts, and the chambers of government. It guides the way we interact with others at home and on the road.

There is no question that fostering these qualities takes time, a precious commodity in this fast-paced world. They are, nonetheless, essential. In the world, disciples are intent on ensuring that mutuality and co-operation – a circular model of work relationships – thrive among workers. Disciples wish to change the patriarchal structures that foster a top-down, hierarchical mode of operation in which control, competition, and exploitation – regardless of the cost to others – can flourish.

These relational qualities are essential if workplaces – where a person's gender, colour, or ethnic origin often result in discrimination – are to become places of hospitality where male and female workers are treated equally, differences are respected and various gifts appreciated.

Servants of God in the world, encouraged by their experience in the community of equal disciples, can assist co-workers who are also trying to bring those key qualities into their work environment. Together they can nurture healthy and ethical corporate behaviour that respects all those involved. Where a true team exists, women and men co-operate, share responsibility, and mutually respect each other. In such an environment, the shadow side of people and of the institution can be allowed to surface and be addressed; forgiveness and reconciliation, when needed, can take place. To this end, disciples know that fostering the capacity and the climate to listen intently and reflectively are skills that they, their co-workers, and leaders need[80] for the mission of their work to be accomplished in a just manner and for a genuine life-giving community to be built among workers.

We have seen that Mary, in the circle of disciples at Pentecost, opens a window on the transformation of the Church into a community of equal disciples. She helps rekindle the disciples' desire to be servants of God and a servant church in which all take seriously their vocation, received in baptism, to participate in the priestly, prophetic, and royal mission of Jesus. With the Annunciation–Visitation and Mary's prophetic song, the Magnificat, echoing through its life, the Church today, like the early Christian community, fulfills two fundamental criteria of discipleship for which Jesus praised his mother: hearing the word of God and putting it into practice (Lk 8:19-21).

But Mary's influence on the transformation of the Church doesn't stop here. Through her presence in the circle of disciples at Pentecost and her life lived in visitation, the Church, a community of equal disciples, will find the inspiration and courage to make the necessary structural changes to support its life and its mission.

9

The Ongoing Transformation
of Adult Disciples

Creating Upper Rooms

Mary's entire life showed that her initial call and response at the Annunciation was shaped and deepened by the joy of being Jesus' mother, the challenges she experienced in her growth as his disciple and his mother, and the sufferings that included his death on the cross. These challenges, along with her experience with the disciples in the Upper Room at Pentecost, called her beyond what was familiar in her culture and her religion.[1]

Like Mary, the Church would be shaped and deepened through circumstances and through the evolution of the disciples' vocations and the integration of new disciples into the community.

Remembering Mary at the Annunciation and with the disciples in the Upper Room at Pentecost, the community knows that it must journey within to God before journeying out to neighbours. Like the Church born at Pentecost, the Church today will carry the Upper Room always in its heart. To this end, the community will create spaces[2] where disciples can reflect together on their experience of God in light of the scriptures and be attentive to the voice of the Spirit guiding them through discernment towards decisions for the common good of the community. In these sacred spaces, the community, reflecting on the scriptures and the social teachings of the Church, can discern how God's word is calling them, in Jesus' name, to participate in the transformation of the world. Here, also, the community can discover how to communicate the truth about Jesus to others.

Seeing Mary with the disciples in the Upper Room at Pentecost, the Church knows that disciples need to take time together to enter into the deep centre within. There they can yield to the transforming power of the Spirit and shape the community into the likeness of Jesus.

The Church, the community of equal disciples, sees small faith-sharing circles as sacred spaces where the virginal heart of the community can be fashioned over and over again, creating the inner freedom that allows disciples in the community to let go of personal agendas and move away from all that prevents them from following Jesus freely.

Remembering the whole of Mary's life – especially her experience with the disciples at Pentecost – the community can find the inspiration and staying power to engage in prayerful discernment.

Prayer and Discernment in the Community of Disciples

The image of Mary as the woman of prayer whose pondering heart throughout her life enabled her to turn over events again and again in her heart (Lk 2:19, 51; Acts 1:14) shows the meaning of faith seeking understanding. She exemplifies the ability to listen and to respond to God's word and to be attentive to the Spirit within and around her. She demonstrates the capacity to wait for clarity. As a result, she becomes for those first men and women disciples, the fledgling Church, an image of the model disciple – a woman of prayerful discernment.

Mary is a woman of faith who knows how to take God's side in the midst of the counterforces swirling around her. This quality reminds us that we need to sift through the forces and voices that arise in the Church, society and the world. These voices are many and varied. Some of them are considered to be on the right or the left of the mainstream religion or politics, and are often labelled as conservative or liberal.

But in the church community of equal disciples centred on unity, mutuality, interdependence, and loving service, one hopes that such labelling will be set aside. Instead, each disciple's piece of the truth needs to be heard, and time taken for honest discernment.

Mary's life, and life in the early community, show that this process is never easy.

In our society, entering into it is a major challenge. Waiting is becoming more and more difficult in a world built on speed, where technology has made worldwide communication possible at every moment of the day. In this world, immediate answers are expected and demanded. In the West, standing in line – whether at the bank or the grocery store – or being delayed on the expressway is becoming more and more intolerable. But the whole of Mary's life, especially the hours after Jesus' death and the time spent with the disciples in the Upper Room, shows the community of equal disciples that they cannot bypass this process. Her prayerful, discerning heart encourages the community to enter into continuous prayerful dialogue with God and each other and to pray for discerning hearts so that their "love may overflow more and more with knowledge and full insight" so can they can "determine what is best" (Phil 1:9).[3]

Prayerful discernment in community opens disciples to "the adventure of following Jesus in new and ever changing situations."[4] Such a community will be intent on reaching a point where the community can act through consensus and, in the spirit of the early Christian community at the Council of Jerusalem, say with enthusiasm, "It has seemed good to the Holy Spirit and to us..." (Acts 15:28).

Disciples within these small faith communities often see the community as a reference point in making personal decisions: the community does not substitute for personal responsibility, but becomes the vital medium in which this arises and develops.[5]

As we saw in Chapter 2, Mary could experience the presence of the divine outside the Temple and its ritual rites of purification. In the creation of small faith-sharing communities, centres of prayer and discernment, the local church also recognizes that God's communication, the action of the Spirit, and the presence of Jesus are not confined to the church building. The gathering of disciples in community is sacred, not the place (cf. 1 Tim 3:15). As Jesus said, "Where two or three are gathered in my name, I am there among them" (Mt 18:20).

In the gathering of disciples we understand Peter's description of the Church as made up of real people, whom he calls living stones, with Christ as the cornerstone (1 Pt 2:4-9). The community of equal disciples gathered becomes as God's temple, where God's Spirit dwells (1 Cor 3:16).

In small faith-sharing communities – centres of prayer and discernment – using the Annunciation–Visitation motif, including the Magnificat, in prayer and practice will enrich the community of disciples and strengthen its call to live their vocation to discipleship as Mary did: uniting intimacy with God, Jesus, and the Spirit with service as they participate in the priestly, prophetic, and royal mission of Jesus. The creation of such faith communities will provide opportunities for members to reflect together on God's presence at work in their lives and in all creation.

In the process, the local church (or parish) becomes a community of communities, a microcosm of the universal church in which unity in diversity is respected.[6] The Church, the community of equal disciples, thus accepts the challenge to be a Church of communion with God, with each other, and with their neighbours beyond the community. Here, too, Mary shows us the way.

A Church of Communion

Mary, at the Visitation, shows us that her vocation to intimacy with God and service of her neighbour are united into one call. With the disciples at Pentecost, she reminds the community of equal disciples that they are called to be a Church of communion with God and with their neighbour.[7] Her communion with God, with Jesus, and with the Spirit points the Church to the Trinity, wherein the community will discover how to be intimate with God and with their neighbour.

Life in the Trinity has always been seen as relational, where interaction is guided by respect for differences that lead to unity of purpose. Like Mary, the community finds in Jesus the summit of all communion between God and humankind.[8]

In many ways, the Trinity – the source of life – reveals the principles that govern the universe: individuality, differentiation, and communion.

This is not an attempt to push trendy language onto the Church, but to indicate that the life of the Trinity, which we hold sacred, points to the sacredness and uniqueness of each person. Differences are to be celebrated and received as gifts that enrich the community and advance the mission of Jesus.

Communion within the Trinity shows us that where mutuality and interdependence among sisters and brothers exist, communion is born among them and unity of mission is established.[9]

Communion in the Church reaches its climax in the celebration of the Eucharist. In Paul's words, "Because there is one bread, we who are many are one body, for we all partake of the one bread" (1 Cor 10:17).[10]

This communion in the church among disciples extends also to all those who have gone before us.[11] As Elizabeth Johnson puts it,

> As early Christian writers describe it, other holy persons who are now with God are comrades, fellow disciples, fellow pilgrims with us who follow after the one love. The saints are not situated between Jesus Christ and believers, as noted earlier, but are one with their sisters and brothers in the one Spirit.[12]

Their continued presence among us, highlighted in the liturgy, enables us to pray with Mary and with all the saints that God's reign of love, peace, and justice for all humankind and the whole universe will take root and flourish.

Communion is not limited to life within the Church. It extends to all the brothers and sisters in the human family, moving us beyond racial and cultural differences into dialogue as we seek together a humane and just life for every person. Here the Magnificat merges with the Church of communion, for the unity born of communion with Christ cannot be separated from the community's call to be a Church of solidarity – bread broken for others.

Communion reaches out to the way we work together in and beyond the community of disciples – trusting one another and recognizing that the gifts of the Spirit are given to all the Church. All Christian churches, in the spirit of the Second Vatican Council, have the quest for unity; together these churches – rooted in the same creed and faith in Jesus – can be his united presence in the world. Communion also calls the community into a relationship with people of other faiths that is characterized by love and respect.[13]

This approach may seem idealistic, for no community of disciples will be able to completely avoid conflict within or beyond it.[14] Disciples bring their limitations and their egos to the community as well as their gifts. In Mary, woman of Visitation, the community has a model of the power of reconciliation and forgiveness.

Forgiveness and Reconciliation
in the Community of Disciples

Throughout his ministry, Mary sees Jesus continually manifest the forgiving, reconciling, and compassionate power of God. Walking in his ways, Mary the disciple turns her sorrowful, wounded heart towards the confused and fearful disciples after Jesus' death, joining them in the Upper Room (Acts 1:14). As the woman of Visitation turning again and again towards her neighbours – becoming one with them in mind and heart – Mary shows the power of reconciliation[15] and forgiveness to heal divided hearts and to restore unity. Empowered by the Spirit with the disciples at Pentecost, she hastens with them from the Upper Room; she is a member of the community of equal disciples, the Church that was entrusted with the ministry of reconciliation (Acts 2:1ff; Jn 20:19-23; Mt 18:15-20).[16]

She remains the model of reconciliation and forgiveness for the Church.

Although we may not admit it, we often see one another according to the wrongs committed and the hurts experienced; we see only the failures, prejudices, envy, stereotyping, betrayal, abuse, or sin.[17]

Without question, anger, upset, and confusion exist at times in the Church. Disciples of Jesus are called to walk the extra mile and to take the necessary steps to restore unity between neighbours and in the community.[18] This is no easy task, but Jesus reminds us that God, who alone is the judge and searcher of hearts, forbids us to pass judgment on the inner guilt of others.[19] For the the community of equal disciples, living like Mary in visitation, turning again and again towards their neighbour within and beyond the community, means being a force of forgiveness and reconciliation within and outside the community.

Knowing that mistakes can happen, the community will acknowledge that there are times when unity and solidarity in and beyond the community call for forgiveness. Such a community will be a "sign that points to the God they worship as a forgiving God and actually makes God's forgiveness present and active in people's lives."[20]

A reconciling community is one without walls that is intent on building right relationships with God, oneself, and others. The prayer to Our Father, which the community of disciples prays daily, is a reminder that God's forgiveness of us is linked to our forgiveness of others.

There is no limit to situations requiring healing, forgiveness, and reconciliation in the community today. Creating safe spaces for people to share their stories is one way to approach this process. This is not a substitute for therapy, but a place where the community can show the compassion and love of God for people suffering as a result of separation, divorce, and sexual and physical abuse. In these spaces, hidden family conflicts that may surface around the celebration of sacraments, especially baptism and marriage, can find healing. Here, refugees, who carry the loss of their homeland and support system and often the memory of the murder of a family member, can rise from the darkness of their experience with the help of a compassionate, welcoming community. These sacred spaces can also ensure that patriarchy and the sterile forces of economic downsizing that devalue the full worth of women and men do not have the last word. In these sacred spaces, the richness of social and cultural differences can be honoured and respected.

Mary's prayerful, discerning, and reconciling heart – evident by her presence in the Upper Room and at Pentecost – are a reminder that when anger, confusion, fear, and hurt are brought into prayer, the light of the risen Jesus can pierce the most seemingly irreconcilable differences.[21] Peace can return to troubled hearts, and unity and the passion for mission are restored in the community.

Rather than diminishing the importance of the sacrament of reconciliation, this approach points to the communal face of sin and the need for the community to own its mistakes and its failure to represent Christ to the world.

The Church – as a community of equal disciples, a church of discipleship, a church of participation, a church of solidarity, and a church of communion – will also find in Mary's life lived in visitation a journey spirituality for communal life as a pilgrim people.

Communal Life in Visitation: A Journey Spirituality for a Pilgrim People

Mary, in joining her faith journey to that of the Church, the community of equal disciples born at Pentecost, becomes the archetype for the Church's pilgrimage of faith.[22] We have seen that her faith journey contained characteristics that psychologists and anthropologists say are integral to life's journey: process and movement, light and darkness, and joys and risks that move beyond comfortable, known, and secure ways. Her life lived in visitation offers a "journey spirituality" not only for individual disciples, but for the Church beginning in Jerusalem.[23]

As in the beginning, her continued presence among us – a disciple among disciples and the archetype of all that the Church is to be – offers a journey spirituality for the Church today.[24] In fact, all that has been written here about the Church becoming a community of equal disciples like Mary – a church of discipleship that is called to pattern its life on Mary's life – could be described as a call to be a church of visitation. For our faith journey as church is not lived in a vacuum, but within the evolution of the history of our world.

The community, in choosing to live a faith journey modelled on Mary's life in visitation, takes ownership of it. Inspired by her faith journey, the community sees itself as disciples on the move and active participants in the drama of everyday life. Like Mary and the Church born at Pentecost, the community knows that their faith in Jesus and their call to discipleship are constantly evolving as communion and intimacy with God and their neighbour deepen.

Led by the Spirit and nurtured by prayer, reflection on the scriptures, the Eucharist, and the sacraments, life lived in visitation calls the church community of equal disciples to be contemplative, mindful that God, through Jesus becoming one with us, remains God with us (Mt 1:23) at every moment of every day.[25]

Life lived in visitation summons the community to be attentive to the action of God's Spirit and God's presence in their midst in all people, in every situation, everywhere in creation, throughout the world, and in the whole universe. It is a constant reminder that God's presence – God's visitation – is not limited by gender, colour, nation, or religion. In God's eyes everyone and everything is sacred, even though the evil in the world often tries to hide God from our view.[26]

For the Church to journey in faith, in visitation, is to open itself to "divine love present in the ongoing drama of existence, to the pain and the violence, to exhilaration and the sublime, to death and new life."[27] In the journey, the community can expect to experience process and movement, light and darkness, and joys and risks that move beyond comfortable, known, and secure ways.

Exploring Mary's faith journey from the Annunciation to Pentecost showed that her life contained threshold moments – places of power, inspiration, prophesy, and new beginnings that opened the door to an unexpected future full of promise and hope.[28] Without these moments, psychologists say, life stagnates in people and in communities.

These moments in Mary's life called her beyond the religious and cultural world view of her times to embrace the vision and the mission of her son in a discipleship of equals. At Pentecost, Mary crossed a major threshold with the disciples as they gave birth to the Church. Life in the Spirit challenged this committed community of disciples beyond the comfortable and secure ways of being together (Acts 6:2ff; Acts 12; Acts 15): as the Church opened to the Greco-Roman world, the community was led to creatively interpret their Jewish past.

The Second Vatican Council was a threshold moment in the life of the Church in our time – a new Pentecost in which the Spirit ignited a passion for new life, power, inspiration, and prophecy, and opened a door to a future of promise and hope.

The Council encouraged the reawakening of the vocation received in baptism by all disciples to share in the priestly, prophetic, and royal mission of Jesus, and spoke to the presence of the Spirit in all disciples and their right of participation in the life of the Church. It also recognized that God's Spirit was not confined within the Church and made major changes to the way the liturgy is celebrated to foster lay participation on many levels.

With these new attitudes, the Council promoted a return to the understanding of the Church as a church of communion, a notion that prevailed in the first ten centuries. In doing so, Walter Kasper says,

> the Council set aside its one-sided view of unity, where the church throughout the world had to be cast into the same mould, a perception that had prevailed since the second century. Unity as union in community opened the door for a legitimate variety of local churches within the greater unity in the one faith, the same sacraments and the same ministries.[29]

It paved the way for the Church to be a community of communities united in the one faith and mission of Jesus. Unity in diversity was possible and acceptable.

No one who has lived within the Church since Vatican II would deny that the action of the Spirit in the life of the Council moved the Church beyond comfortable, known and secure ways. How the Council's vision of the Church is to be truly implemented in a constantly and rapidly changing world is a question that nudges us to this day.[30]

As for Mary and the first Christian community, communal life in visitation urges the Church to be attentive to the action of the Spirit, which calls us to let go of the way we thought everything should be to embrace the life that is trying to work its way into our being. Holding onto Jesus' promise that he will be always with us and that the power of the Holy Spirit will guide us on our way,[31] the community of equal disciples finds the courage to live their faith amidst ambiguity and uncertainty.

Choosing to follow Jesus in Mary's footsteps, the community of equal disciples inwardly and outwardly will be a Marian Church.

Conclusion

A New Springtime for the Church

Our journey through the scriptural memory of Mary has ended – or has it just begun?

In suggesting Mary as an image of discipleship for Christian women and men that would relate to their call to live out the mission of Jesus in this continually evolving and complex world, I have reconnected Luke's account of the Annunciation–Visitation with its challenging song of the Magnificat (Lk 1:26-55).

A close examination of these narratives unveiled a portrait of Mary as a strong woman of faith, a disciple of Jesus, a woman on a journey with a mission for the gospel.

In fact, Mary emerges from the Annunciation–Visitation narratives as the archetype, the original model, of Christian discipleship. She shows us by example that after hearing the word of God and allowing it to take shape in our hearts, we must share it with others – not simply by repeating it, but by interpreting it so that Jesus can be good news for others.

Drawing on the parallel structure of Luke and Acts, we examined the connection between Mary as the archetype of Christian discipleship and the story of Pentecost (Acts 2:1-4ff), which share the motif of being sent in Jesus' name. We considered how this renewed image of Christian discipleship, rooted in Mary, is a guide for the transformation of the Church into a community of equal disciples. This community redresses the present imbalance in the Church, which was created from patriarchal structures.

What are some challenges and implications, and what questions arise, if we take seriously this Marian archetype of Christian discipleship? What will happen if we dare to cross the threshold and move from reflection to action?

While we are not to read the scriptures literally, they provide us with truth about how to live. If we allow Luke's accounts of the Annunciation–Visitation and the Magnificat to shape our lives as disciples and as Church, we will own our baptismal call to become pregnant with God's Word, Jesus. Individually and communally, every day, we will face the challenge of finding time for the Jesus of the scriptures, his approach to ministry, and his values to be conceived and take root in our hearts. Then the passion to share Jesus from the depths of our hearts will inspire us to interpret and communicate our experience of Jesus in language that enables him to be good news for others. Our challenge will be to speak about Jesus who reveals a God of compassion, love, and justice for all people, and who is the very centre and heart of our being Christian, in ways that do not put others down or trivialize other systems of being.

Making such a move may mean letting go of some traditional language about God and Jesus that rises from a number of our credal statements. In doing so, we might well discover that new language about who God is, and what God means in our lives, lies deep within us waiting to be born. This new language would truly speak to the spiritual longing for meaning so evident in women and men in these times.

Of course this approach would contain some risks. As new language to express our understanding and our experience of God and Jesus transforms us, how will that be reflected in our creed? The Church moves slowly and carefully in embracing changes in language: do we have the courage to be bridge-builders, linking the old with the new in a creative and effective way? We can take inspiration for this challenge from the first Christian community, which shows the whole Church identifying with their teaching mission and making it their own (Acts 4:2; 5:21). When the time came to proclaim Jesus to their non-Jewish neighbours, they sought language to help these neighbours understand who Jesus was and what his life, death, and resurrection could mean for them. Our responsibility as disciples of Jesus is to do no less today.

The more this Marian archetype of Christian discipleship shapes our lives, the more we will promote Mary as a model of discipleship based on much more than her "Yes" to God at the Annunciation, and foster an understanding of her influence as a disciple of Jesus far beyond the realm of a personal relationship with God. We will speak out against interpretations of Mary that relegate women's Christian vocation to virgin or mother and limit their full participation in the life and mission of the Church.

Allowing the dynamic motif of the Annunciation–Visitation and Magnificat to shape our lives as disciples of Jesus, we will integrate our private spiritual life with our public lives each day. Like Mary's, our vocation to intimacy with God and service of neighbour will be united into one call. As this unity shapes our lives, we will be contemplative disciples in action, engaged in an interlocking dance of intimacy with the love of God, and of God's son, Jesus, and we will call ourselves as Church to do the same.

Mary in the Annunciation and Mary and Elizabeth in the Visitation display radical openness to the Spirit; their example urges us to trust the presence of the Spirit in ourselves. We will then turn towards others, attentive to the Spirit speaking to us through all those we meet and drawing us into fuller life in ways that may surprise us.

The interaction between Mary and Elizabeth also highlights the importance of hospitality, mutuality, and equality between persons – our interdependence with one another and with all creation. With the Spirit's help, our commitment to the mission of Jesus will lead us to join people of every faith and every nation who treasure mutuality and own their interdependence with each other and with the earth. In our own neighbourhoods, we can become a grassroots movement creating a world community of communities.

To choose Mary in the Annunciation–Visitation as the archetype of Christian discipleship also calls us to read our life experience through the lens of visitation – seeing God present in and visiting us through life events. This approach has many implications. The most obvious is viewing life as a journey wherein process and movement, light and darkness, joys and challenges, and the risks we take move us beyond comfortable, known, and secure ways of being. But mindfulness of and attentiveness to God's presence and God's word in the midst of the chaos of our world is not always easy. What word is God speaking to us as wars continue to be waged and the threat of violence lurks on all sides? What signs do we see of the presence of a loving, compassionate, and just God as countless men, women, and children die each day as a result of war, famine, and AIDS? What indications do we have that God is calling forth what is new in our families, our friends, our world, and even ourselves as threats to our existence arise from various quarters of the globe?

Reflections on the Magnificat, at the heart of this Marian model of discipleship, point to our call to be a people of the Beatitudes, a prophetic presence of Jesus in our world. Like Jesus we are to denounce the unjust systems – our workplaces, our governments, our places of worship – that diminish people's worth. If we look closely, we will see how hierarchy, rooted in patriarchy, operates in our homes, our marketplace, and our schools.

Crying out for our attention are corporate greed, which causes increasing poverty, famine, and the growing rate of trafficking of women and children, and which contributes to the increase of warring factions within and between nations and the hijacking of God for personal and political ends. Luke's account of Mary in dialogue with Elizabeth and of the first Christian community urges us to seek out the wisdom in the group gathered to discover non-violent solutions to conflict and inequality, and to work for communal action for peace and to save our planet for future generations.

What a challenge! Disciples of Jesus who have dared to put their lives on the line by questioning unjust structures in the Church and unjust systems in corporations and government have often been ostracized. Some, like Jesus, have lost their lives. Clearly, discipleship is a heavy responsibility.

Turning to Mary, we see that her "Yes" at the Annunciation, in response to God's great love, was connected to her self-identification as God's servant (Lk 1:38). The question before us is this: Are we willing to identify ourselves as God's servant, knowing that to do so means patterning our lives on Jesus' life and embracing his mission? Are we willing to move out of our individualism to stand up together for the values of Jesus and risk the consequences? Here, too, we can find inspiration in Mary.

Deep within the image of Mary is her growth as a disciple of Jesus – her faith journey. In choosing to stand on the side of her son and his mission, the scriptural memory of Mary shows ways in which she was called to conversion – to let go of certain time-honoured traditions of her religion and her people. In following Jesus, she had to broaden her understanding of family to embrace those who had no status and no voice. Our call to conversion as disciples of Jesus is the same today. Each one of us knows in the depths of our hearts what prevents us from such radical discipleship. If we were to embrace radical discipleship individually and together as Church, what traditions might we be called to set aside?

In learning to live with this difficult question, we find comfort in Mary, whom Luke describes as treasuring and pondering events – turning them over again and again in her heart in order to seek understanding (Lk 2:19, 51). He does not say that she ever found an answer. Her presence among the disciples in the Upper Room after the death of Jesus (Acts 1:14) suggests that she was a woman of strong faith who was willing to commit herself with the disciples for the journey of life, trusting that Jesus' promise of the Spirit would be fulfilled in them. That same promise of the Spirit is available for us today. In accepting Mary as the archetype of Christian discipleship, to what extent are we willing, like her, to walk in faith, to live with ambiguity and uncertainty, to embrace a certain powerlessness, and to move forward with no map for the journey?

By unlocking the biblical memory of Mary, we see her at Pentecost, a disciple among disciples and the archetype of all that the Church could be. The whole community of equal disciples is called, like Mary, to hear the word of God and put it into practice.

This vision of church rooted in Mary's discipleship cannot be separated from her motherhood. While her motherhood is unique to her, it is transferred to the Church at Pentecost.[1] Consequently, the whole Church is called to be like Mary – the remembering mother giving birth to Christ and witnessing to the whole of his life, his death, and his resurrection.

When Pope Paul VI named Mary as Mother of the Church at the Vatican II – mother of the entire people, both pastors and faithful – he also claimed her to be the archetype of the Church.[2]

Mary's motherhood provides us with an image of the body of Christ, which is the Marian metaphor for the Church. It is not focused on juridical form, binding and loosing, but co-operating with a maternal love in the birth and education of the faithful.[3]

The Church, a community of equal disciples acting with maternal love, will affirm the good in all God's people and recognize their weakness rather than their sinfulness. It will provide opportunities for disciples to grow, to integrate the strength and weakness of the shadow side of their personality and to deepen their faith and commitment to Jesus throughout every stage of their lives.[4]

In this way, the Church will present a face of maternal, compassionate love towards all God's people, mindful that while everyone is called to the "kindom" of God, not everyone may be called to the Church as we define it.

Emphasizing the maternal dimension of Christian discipleship will not create a new imbalance in our Church. Rather, it will call men and women forth into their full humanity; it will integrate the masculine and feminine in both women and men who are created in the image and likeness of God.

By embracing the maternal dimension of Christian discipleship, men and women disciples, gathered together as Mary and the disciples gathered in the Upper Room (Acts 1:14), will symbolically form a womb. Into this symbolic womb the word of God, Jesus, can take root and transform us into being the presence of Jesus and his values in our world. When and where this takes root, the feminine will become visibly present in the Church. The motherhood and fatherhood of God will be honoured equally. The generativity of men and women ministering together will call the community to new life.

The Annunciation–Visitation motif provides a lens through which we can understand our baptismal call to carry on the priestly, prophetic, and royal mission of Jesus. The deeper our priestly identity as disciples of Jesus becomes, the more we will honour that all are consecrated in baptism and ordained to carry on the ministry of Jesus in their families, their communities, their workplace, and their leisure. Our personal challenge will be to broaden our present, limited understanding of ministry to embrace the whole of our lives, patterned on the mission of Jesus. In this climate, personal call discerned within the community, not gender, will determine a vocation to servant leadership of the community. The whole community of equal disciples will be called to live in a climate of vocation and will take responsibility to help their sisters and brothers in faith to discern their personal vocation.

Since theology is a reflection on lived experience, what theology of church must be written to embrace this priestly vocation – the universal call to ministry of all disciples of Jesus? In the interim, how will those who own their priestly identity received in baptism and believe that ministry encompasses the whole of their lives find shelter in their Church? What new structures must emerge to support the community of equal disciples as it carries out its mission in Jesus' name?

Where do we begin? Mary, by her example of discipleship, reveals a church "structured in communion at all levels wherein disciples are partners, united in the one mission of Jesus."[5] A Church in communion suggests a circular structure – a round table where everyone is equal and everyone equally represents Christ.

To entertain this image is to invert the present hierarchical pyramid that is the structure of the Church.[6] This is not a negation of authority. Rather, it captures the vision of the Church as the new people of God – a church of discipleship in which authority gains its competency from radical discipleship. Authority, in this sense, is exercised at all levels in communion with the disciples of Jesus and in a spirit of shared responsibility and decision-making, rather than in the present top-down modality.[7] In Raymond Brown's words, "New ideas and constructive insights from disciples in relation to their faith expressed in the Creed, the one faith, the same sacraments that unites disciples are welcomed."[8] All disciples of Jesus are thus seen as partners with the pope, bishops, and ordained ministers, sharing responsibility for the life of the Church and discerning together how to be church in their times. Honouring the presence of the Spirit in all disciples will require that we become a discerning people so that in our search for truth together, powerful voices do not overwhelm or dominate.

Structured in this way, the Church could provide a strong, countercultural challenge to present hierarchical structures in government and in multinational corporate enterprises in every nation where leadership exercises domination over the people. It could be a major influence in developing a spirit of communion among nations that could lead to the world becoming a community of nations.

Reflection on Mary as the archetype of Christian discipleship has unfolded a rich image of discipleship for Christian women and men and offered a guide for the transformation of today's Church into a community of equal disciples. Rooted in the Annunciation–Visitation and Pentecost, this Church, in imitation of Mary, would be a church of discipleship, a church of participation, a church of solidarity, a church of the poor, a church of communion, and a servant church on fire with its priestly, prophetic, and royal mission in Jesus' name.

Conscious that the Spirit blows where the Spirit wills, a Church modelled on Mary will not be a new movement. This Church will not be born of a revolution but will rise from the hearts of individual disciples. Like water springing up inside us, it will flow out, bringing about change in ourselves and in the way we live church. At its heart, it is a call to radical Christian discipleship in shaping a new Church for a new world – a quantum leap into the future.

Notes

Chapter 1
Setting the Stage: Luke and Acts

1   Passover and Booths are the two other pilgrimage festivals. Passover commemorated the Exodus from Egypt. The Feast of Booths was the final harvest festival of grapes and olives, falling within the month of October. It was called 'booths' because the harvesters lived in the field in makeshift tents or booths. "Glossary." The Catholic Bible, Personal Study Edition, *New American Bible*, New York: Oxford University Press, pp. 427, 434.

2   Colin Brown, ed., "Pentecost." *Dictionary of New Testament Theology*, Exeter, UK: The Paternoster Press, 1976, Vol. 2, p. 784.

3   Anna Marie Erst, SHCJ, Director, "Shavuot"(Pentecost). One of a series of leaflets describing Jewish Feasts prepared for The National Institute for Catholic-Jewish Education, Chicago, IL.

4   Joachim Jeremias, *Jerusalem in the Times of Jesus*, London, UK: SCM Press, 1969, p. 32.

5   Richard J. Dillon, "Acts of the Apostles." *The New Jerome Biblical Commentary*, Raymond E. Brown, S.S., Joseph A. Fitzmyer, S.J., Roland E. Murphy, O. Carm., eds., Englewood Cliffs, NJ: Prentice Hall, 1990, p. 731.

6   Raymond E. Brown, S.S., *The Churches the Apostles Left Behind*, Mahwah, NJ: Paulist Press, 1984, p. 68. Brown is among the scholars who maintain that in Jesus' time the feast of Weeks (Pentecost) served to commemorate the giving of the covenant to Moses on Sinai. Brown also notes that the Essenes who gave us the Dead Sea Scrolls chose this feast for admitting new members into their community of the new covenant.

7   Later Paul will urge Christians "to pursue love and strive for the spiritual gifts, especially that you may prophesy. Those who prophesy [he says], speak to other

people for their upbuilding and encouragement and consolation" and build up the church (1 Cor 14:1, 3, 5).

8   This response on Peter's lips likely echoed the early baptismal ceremony, as it echoes ours today.

9   Anna Marie Erst, SHCJ, p. 68.

10   Peter Van der Horst, "Hellenistic Parallels to the Acts of the Apostles 2:1-47." *Journal for the Study of the New Testament*, No. 25 (1985). For his reference to wind and fire see p. 49. For his discussion on similarities between Acts 2:6 and the Homeric Hymn to Apollo see vv. 156–164, p. 50.

11   The Essenes originated in Babylon as a reaction against the religious laxity, which, in their view, had provoked the exile of the Jewish people from Jerusalem during the sixth century BCE. Some of the sect returned to Judea about 164 BCE. Finding themselves at odds with the religious establishment in Jerusalem, they settled in rural areas, especially around Qumran, where they remained until they were dispersed by the Romans in 68 CE. Jesus was probably very aware of this community and their ideals. The discovery of the Dead Sea Scrolls, in early 1947, and the subsequent excavation of Qumran threw new light on the Essenes. Jerome Murphy-O'Connor, O.P., *The Holy Land: An Oxford Archeological Guide from Earliest Times to 1700*, New York: Oxford University Press, 1998, pp. 250–252.

12   Peter Van der Horst, "Hellenistic Parallels to the Acts of the Apostles." References to parallels with the community of the Essenes, and to common property in Greek and Latin literature, are found on pp. 58–60.

13   Raymond E. Brown, S.S., *An Introduction to the New Testament*, New York: Doubleday, 1997, p. 282.

14   Carolyn Osiek, "Women in the Church." *The Bible Today*, Vol. 32, No. 4, July (1994), p. 228.

15   See Jane Schaberg, "Luke." and Gail O'Day, "Acts." *The Women's Bible Commentary*, pp. 275–292; 305–312; Elizabeth Tetlow, *Women and Ministry in the New Testament: The Status of Women in Greek, Roman, and Jewish Society*. New York: Paulist Press, 1980, chapters 1–4; Elizabeth Schüssler Fiorenza, *In Memory of Her*, New York: Crossroad, 1984, pp. 161–168. Recent studies support the possibility of Acts having been edited to downplay women's leadership role and missionary activity in the founding days of the Church. See Ben Witherington, "The Anti-Feminist Tendencies of the 'Western' Text in Acts." *Journal of Biblical Literature*, 103 (March 1984): 82–84; Curt Niccum, "A Note on Acts 1:14." *Novum Testamentum XXXVI*, 2 (1994): 196–199.

16   Raymond E. Brown, S.S., *Peter in the New Testament*, Minneapolis, MN: Augsburg, 1973, p. 10.

17   For further discussion of the disappearance of the majority of the apostles from Luke's narrative and on the fact that the early Christian community makes no attempt to maintain a distinct group of Twelve, see Raymond E. Brown, S.S. *The Churches the Apostles Left Behind*, New York/Mahwah: Paulist Press, 1984, p. 14. Also

Schulyer Brown, "Apostleship in the New Testament as an Historical Theological Problem." *New Testament Studies*, Vol. 30 (1984), p. 479.

18 Judith R. Baskin, ed., *Jewish Women in Historical Perspective*, Detroit, MI: Wayne State University Press, 1991. Carolyn Osiek, "Women in the Church," pp. 233. Elisabeth M. Tetlow, "Women and Ministry in the New Testament: The Status of Women in Greek, Roman, and Jewish Society." pp. 5–29, and, Amy L. Wordleman, "Everyday Life: Women in the Period of the New Testament." *The Women's Bible Commentary*, Carol A. Newsome and Sharon H. Ringe, eds. Louisville, KY: Westminster/John Knox Press, 1992, pp. 390–396.

19 St. John Chrysostom, "Homily IV: Homilies on The Acts of the Apostles." *Nicene and Post-Nicene Fathers*, Peabody, MA: Hendrickson, 1994, Vol. II, pp. 25–26.

20 Ibid., p. 26.

21 Ibid., Homily III, p. 18.

22 Ibid., p.18.

23 Ibid., "Homily on Matthew 23:14, LXXIII." Homilies on the Gospel of Matthew, *Nicene and Post-Nicene Fathers*, 1994, Vol.10, p. 443.

24 Ibid., p. 443.

25 Jane Schaberg, "Luke." *The Women's Bible Commentary*, p. 281.

26 The Greek text of Acts says "in prayer with women" and "Mary, the mother of Jesus and his brothers." What led translators to insert "certain" before women (Acts 1:14)? Not naming them can convey that they just happened to be there rather than that their presence was normative.

27 Carla Ricci, *Mary Magdalene and Many Others*, Minneapolis, MN: Fortress Press, 1994, pp. 176–177. A complete development of her position on the possibility of twelve women around Jesus is found on pp. 163–177. See also Catherine Barry, *Des femmes parmi les apôtres, 2000 ans d'histoire occultée*, Montréal: Éditions Fides, 1997. Barry discusses the information on women disciples in the manuscripts discovered at Nag Hamadi in Upper Egypt in 1942. Among the manuscripts were the Gospel of Thomas, the Gospel of Philip, and the Gospel of Mary. For a discussion on women's place as leaders and prophets in the early Christian communities see Elaine Pagels, *The Gnostic Gospels*, New York: Vintage Books, 1981.

28 Matthew and Mark in their gospels identify women at the cross and as witnesses to the resurrection by name (Mt 27:56, 61; Mk 15:40, 47). What is common in the synoptic gospels is they were "women from Galilee who had followed Jesus." John places Mary, Jesus' mother, along with three other women, including Mary Magdalene, at the cross. In Matthew, Mark and Luke the women are the first witnesses of Jesus' resurrection. In Matthew, the Risen Jesus appears first to the women (Mt 28:9). In the longer ending of Mark, Jesus appears first to Mary Magdalene. This is true also in John's gospel (Jn:20:11-18). Luke does not include Jesus' appearance to the women alone or to Mary Magdalene.

29 Mary's presence in the group of Acts 1:14 and at Pentecost also raises the question as to why Luke never mentioned her among the women at her Son's painful death on the cross (Lk 23:55). While a later gospel portrays her standing at the cross of her son (Jn 19:25), the reader of Acts must make the leap from Luke's mention of her as being among Jesus' new family who hear the word of God and do it (Lk 8:19-21) to Acts where she is united in prayer with the women and men disciples in the Upper Room (Acts 1:14).

30 Paul mentions this couple as having a house church in 1 Cor 16:19; he names them as co-workers with him in Christ Jesus, and notes that they had risked their lives for him (Rom 16:3).

31 For further discussion of this point, see Raymond E. Brown, S.S. "Roles of Women in the Fourth Gospel, Appendix II." *The Community of the Beloved Disciple*, New York: Paulist Press, 1979, pp. 183–198. Women's role as missionaries and leaders in these early years of the Church is expanded upon by Elizabeth Schüssler Fiorenza in *In Memory of Her: A Feminist Theological Reconstruction of Christian Origins*.

32 Elizabeth Schüssler Fiorenza, *In Memory of Her*, p. 478. See also Karen A. Barta, "On Being An Apostle." *The Bible Today*, May, (1995), pp. 153-159. Jesus was not structuring a society; did not live in an organized church and the Twelve were selected not as administrators but as eschatological judges of the renewed Israel (Mt 19:28; Lk 22:30). My purpose in including this observation here is not to downplay Peter's role among this first group of believers nor the need for authority. It is made in order that our patriarchal, hierarchical church structures not be presented to us as Jesus' divine wish for his church. They likely developed as expansion called for organization, and were probably modeled on the structures of Greco-Roman society which prevailed at the time.

33 St. John Chrysostom, "Homily III: Homilies on the Acts of the Apostles." *Nicene and Post-Nicene Fathers*, Volume II, p. 18. Such consideration by leadership indeed has some appeal for today. Many, myself included, despite our desire for inclusivity and gender equality in our church, would welcome, as a starting point, being listened to, and heard, full participants in the selection process of pastors and local bishops today.

34 St. John of Damascus, "The Ascension of Our Lord Jesus Christ." *The Life of the Blessed Virgin, The Theotokos*, Buona Vista, CA: Holy Apostles Convent and Dormition Skete, 1989, p. 407.

35 Carolyn Valone, "The Pentecost: Image and Experience in Late Sixteenth-Century Rome." *Sixteenth Century Journal*, XXIV/4, (1993): 804.

36 Ibid., p. 806.

37 Ibid., p. 817.

38 Francesco Panigarola, "Quotation from his Lenten sermons on the Holy Spirit delivered in St. Peter's in 1588," quoted in Valone, p. 818.

39 M. Étienne Faillon, *Vie de Monsieur Olier*, Paris: Poussielgue Frères, 1873, Vol. 3, p. 124.

40 Ibid., p. 73.

41 Ibid., p. 73.

42 Adriaen van der Werff, "The Pentecost." *The Bible in Art: The New Testament*, Richard Muhlberger, New York: Moore and Moore, Portland House, 1990, p. 146.

43 Acts 1:12-14 is part of the first reading of the Liturgy of the Word for the Masses, Our Lady of the Cenacle, Mary, Queen of the Apostles and Mary, Image of the Church II. The Mass, Our Lady of the Cenacle underlines her presence in the Cenacle as a mother, model of the Church at prayer, and model of virtue for all disciples. Her intercessory role is underlined in her role as Mother of Good Counsel. The Opening Prayer of the Mass, Mary Queen of the Apostles places Mary praying alone with the Apostles. The Preface, recalling Mary's visit to Elizabeth (Lk 1:39), points out that Mary was the first to proclaim Christ. The same Spirit which guided Mary to bring Jesus to John, made the Apostles fearless in preaching the Gospel to all nations. In Mary, Mother of Good Counsel and in Mary, Queen of the Apostles, Acts 2:1-4 is appended to Acts 1:12-14 to make up the first reading. The "all" which appears in the scriptures has been changed to read "the apostles all were together in one place." It would seem liberty was taken to ensure that those mentioned in 1:14 not be confused with the "all" in 2:1. One wonders what other liberties have been taken with the scripture texts in this Collection? *Collection of Masses of the Blessed Virgin Mary*, English Translation, Collegeville, MN: Order of St. Benedict, Inc., 1992, Lectionary, pp. 70, 72, 87, 100, 124; Sacramentary, pp. 83–85, 86–88, 230–232 and 133.

44 Pope John Paul II's use of this text in his Apostolic Letter on the Dignity of Women is discussed in endnote #53.

45 *Joel Reading Guide*. The Catholic Bible, New American Bible Study Edition, New York: Oxford University Press, 1995, pp. 280–282.

46 John A. Thompson, "Introduction to Joel." *The Interpreters' Bible*, Vol. 6, New York: Abingdon Press, 1956, p. 735. See also *Joel Reading Guide*, The Catholic Bible, New American Bible Study Edition, pp. 280–282. George Arthur Buttrick, ed., The Interpreters' Dictionary of the Bible, New York: Abingdon Press, 1962, pp. 926–929.

47 Geofrey E. Wood, "Book of Joel." *The Jerome Biblical Commentary*, Englewood, NJ: Prentice-Hall, 1990, p. 442.

48 Richard J. Dillon, Joseph A. Fitzmyer, S.J., "Acts of the Apostles." *The Jerome Biblical Commentary*, Englewood, NJ: Prentice-Hall, 1990, p. 173.

49 Irene Nowell, O.S.B. "The Coming of the Spirit in the Book of Joel." *The Bible Today* (March 1989), p. 90.

50 Colin Brown, ed., *Dictionary of New Testament Theology*, Devon, UK: The Paternoster Press, Vol. 2, 1976, p. 786.

51 Irene Nowell, *The Coming of the Spirit in the Book of Joel*, p. 92.

52 Robert P. Menzies, "Luke and the Spirit: A Reply to James Dunn." *Journal of Pentecostal Theology*, 4 (1994): 138.

53 Jaroslav Pelikan commenting on Joel's prophecy used in Peter's speech after Pentecost draws attention to the fact that in the text the masculine title *doulōs* and the feminine title *doulās* are used to describe God's male and female slaves. In the NT the feminine Greek word for slave, *doulē*, occurs only in Luke where Mary describes herself as the "slave of the Lord" (1:38; 1:48). The feminine *doulē* reappears in Acts 2:18 in its plural form *doulās*, referring to the female slaves of God, who like the men receive the power of God's Spirit to prophesy. For Pelikan, the history of the apostolic Church described in Acts beyond chapter 2 and its continuation through the ages, presents the fulfillment of Joel's prophecy, the promise for the male servants. He suggests that the place to look for the fulfillment of the promise for female slaves is Mary, who had identified herself at the Annunciation as "slave of the Lord." While he notes that Mary's behaviour at the Annunciation and her song the Magnificat do not convey a "passive," "quietistic" woman, he does not claim a visible place for her in Jesus' public ministry, neither in the foundation of nor in the public forum of the Church. Jaroslav Pelikan, *Mary Through the Centuries: Her Place in the History of Culture*, New Haven, CT: Yale University Press, 1996, p. 84. Pope John Paul II, in his discussion of Acts 2:18 in his Apostolic Letter on the Dignity and Vocation of Women, sees Mary, the Virgin Mother of God, as the fullest expression of women's feminine prophetic character (MD, V:16, VIII: 29, 30).

54 *Lumen Gentium* (Dogmatic Constitution on the Church) in Austin Flannery, OP, *The Conciliar and Post Conciliar Documents*, Vol. 1, LG, 56–59.

55 *For the Right Ordering and Development of Devotion to the Blessed Virgin* (Marialis Cultis), MC, 1974, Pauline Books and Media, 18. In this encyclical, Mary emerges clearly as a woman of faith, who experiences life with its ups and downs; a woman of strength who experienced poverty and suffering, flight and exile; as well as the woman who strengthened the disciples' faith in Jesus at Cana. Her mission of love from Nazareth to the house of Elizabeth (The Visitation), at Cana, and before her Son's suffering and death is underlined in relation to the Church's maternal concern for all people. She is presented as the perfect disciple of Christ, a model for men and women. MC, 28–39.

56 MC, 16–23.

57 MR, Part II, 26.

58 Susan Haskins, *Mary Magdalene*, Hammersmith, London: Harper Collins, 1993, p. 392. In addition to Haskins, see Elizabeth Schüssler Fiorenza, *But She Said: Feminist Practices of Biblical Interpretation*, Boston: Beacon Press, 1992, pp. 80–101; Barbara E. Reid, *Choosing the Better Part? Women in the Gospel of Luke*, Collegeville, MN: The Liturgical Press, 1996, pp. 124–134; 198–204.

59 Gregory the Great, "Homily XXXIII, PL LXXVI, col 1239" quoted in Susan Haskins, *Mary Magdalene*, 1993, pp. 96, 97.

60   Cardinal Pierre Bérulle, *Oeuvres Complètes*, Paris: Migne, 1856, p. 1111.

61   Elizabeth Moltmann-Wendell, *The Women Around Jesus*, New York: Crossroad, 1987, p. 68.

62   Pope John Paul II, in his message "To Pause in Wonder at the World's Reconciliation," May 18, 1997, continues to portray her as a converted sinner. He notes that Christ, putting on her lips the message of the resurrection, made her "in a way equal to the apostles. The witness of the women and of the apostles," he says, "the witness of the church, reaches not only Jerusalem and the hills of Galilee. It spreads to every corner of the world." *Osservatore Romano*, pp. 684–685.

63   Elizabeth A. Johnson, "Redeeming the Name of Christ." *Freeing Theology*, Catherine Mowry LaCugna, ed., San Francisco: Harper Collins, 1993, p. 126.

64   The memory of the leadership of women in the Church such as Phoebe, a deacon of the Church at Cenchrae (Rom 16:1-2), Junia whom Paul mentions as prominent among the apostles (Rom 3:7), Mary whom he says has worked very hard among them (Rom 3:6) could be celebrated as well.

65   MC, 35.

66   Elizabeth A. Johnson, C.S.J. "The Marian Tradition and the Reality of women." *Horizons*, 12/1 (1985): 132.

67   Gerald O'Collins, S.J. and Daniel Kenall, S.J. note that Pope Leo the Great, after the Council of Chalcedon, called her a "figure of the church." A century later, Pope Gregory the Great, referred to her as "another Eve" who announces not death but life (titles that are also ascribed to Mary.) Hippolitus of Rome referred to the women at the tomb as "apostles" which developed into Mary Magdalene often being called the "apostola apostolorum," apostle to the apostles. O'Collins and Kenall conclude that the gospels indicate the complementary roles of women, Peter, and the other disciples as witnesses to the risen Christ. Among the female recipients of the appearances, Mary Magdalene has the primary role. "Mary Magdalene as Major Witness to Jesus' Resurrection." *Theological Studies*, No. 48, (1987): 632, 646. According to Raymond E. Brown, S.S. the reporting of Jesus' appearance to Mary Magdalene is probably historical. "Roles of Women in the Fourth Gospel." *The Community of the Beloved Disciple*, New York/Ramsey: Paulist Press, 1979, p. 189.

68   Elizabeth Schüssler Fiorenza, *In Memory of Her*, p. 52.

Chapter 2

The Annunciation–Visitation: Mary's Vocation Is Revealed

1   Joseph A. Fitzmyer, S.J., "The Gospel According to Luke." *The Anchor Bible*, Garden City, NY: Doubleday, 1981, Vol. 28, p. 340. Luke in writing his infancy narrative makes his audience aware that Jesus entered the world in the midst of the political turmoil of the Roman occupation of Palestine. It also represents the heightened

hope of the Jewish people that "the coming of God into their midst would restore peace and justice. Political domination and social oppression, status based on power and privilege would end." Joel B. Green, *The Theology of the Gospel of Luke*, Cambridge, MA: Cambridge University Press, 1995, pp. 11–13. Scripture scholars point out that the early Christians' use of the title Son of God for Jesus referred to his human life lived in total obedience to his father. This title applied to Jesus as the second person of the Trinity is a later development in the church.

2   These points will be considered in depth in chapters 3 to 5.

3   Jacob Brever, ed., *Fundamentals of Judaism*, New York: Philip Fieldheim, Inc., 1969, p. 112.

4   Ibid., pp. 97–122.

5   Arthur E. Zannoni, "Jesus the Jew." *Catholic Update*, St. Anthony Messenger Press, November 1993: 2.

6   Marcel Dubois, "The Mother of Jesus: Reflection of a Christian Living in Israel." *The Sidic Review*, Vol. XX, No. 2 (August 1987): 7.

7   Bruce J. Malina, "Mother and Son." *Biblical Theology Bulletin*, Vol. 20 (Summer 1990): 54–64. This article considers Mary within the context of her Mediterranean society.

8   For further discussion of this fact see Joel B. Green, *The Theology of the Gospel of Luke*, Cambridge: Cambridge University Press, 1995. See also, Jane Schaberg, "Luke." *The Women's Bible Commentary*, Carol A. Newsom and Sharon H. Ringe, eds., Louisville, KY: Westminster/John Knox Press, 1992, pp. 275–292.

9   Matthew 1:18 is more explicit that the annunciation of Jesus' birth comes between these two stages: after Mary and Joseph are betrothed, but before they have come to live together." This point will be considered in Chapter 3.

   For further discussion of the law in Deuteronomy see Raymond E. Brown, S.S., *The Birth of the Messiah*, Garden City, NY: Doubleday, 1977, pp. 124–126.

10   Other texts that have a similar literary style include the call of Moses (Exod 3:1-12); call of Jeremiah (Jer 1:4-10); call of Isaiah (Is 6:1-8); call of Gideon (Judg 6:11-24). The latter text is often parallelled with the Annunciation.

11   There are five standard elements in the birth pattern: (1) the appearance of the angel; (2) fear by the one to whom the angel appears; (3) the message; (4) the objection (questioning); (5) reassurance (sign). See the birth announcements concerning Hagar with Ishmael (Gen 16:7, 8); Sarah's conception of Isaac (Gen 18:9-15); Samson's mother (Judg 13:1ff.); the announcement to Zechariah that Elizabeth would conceive a child (Luke 1:8-13). For discussion of the literary structure, see Raymond E. Brown, S.S., *The Birth of the Messiah*, pp.156, 292–296; and Ignace de la Potterie, S.J., *Mary in the Mystery of the Covenant*, Bertrand Buby, S.M., trans., New York: Alba House, 1992, pp. 10–13. The biblical vocation call pattern consists of 5 elements: (1) God significantly enters a human life; (2) God gives a mandate or a mission; (3) The person being called usually objects (question); (4) God makes creative use of this objection; (5) God reassures. *The*

Catholic Bible, Personal Study Edition, Jean Marie Hiesberger, ed., New American Bible, New York: Oxford University Press, 1995, p. 233.

12 Ignace de la Potterie, S.J., *Mary in the Mystery of the Covenant*, p. 10.

13 Ibid., pp. 14–17.

14 Barbara E. Reid, *Choosing the Better Part? Women in the Gospel of Luke*, Collegeville, MN: The Liturgical Press, 1996, p. 67.

15 Ignace de la Potterie S.J., *Mary in the Mystery of the Covenant*, pp. 17–20.

16 See Avital Wohlmann, "Mary of Nazareth: Why the Silence of Judaism?" *The Sidic Review*, Vol XX, No. E, (August 1987): 9-14.

17 Through the centuries interpretations of Mary as virgin and mother, the new Eve, have denigrated Eve and exalted Mary to other than human dimensions. Consequently, the full responsibility for sin has been placed on Eve's shoulders, leaving Adam unscathed. Women in a patriarchal church and society have suffered the fallout from this Eve/Mary parallel.

18 Donald Senior, C.P., "New Testament Images of Mary." *The Bible Today* (May 1986): 147, 148. Before Vatican II in the Catholic Church, emphasis on Mary's bodily virginity supported by a false body/spirit dualism fostered the superiority of virginity over marriage. This is not the message of the Annunciation.

19 Thomas Moore, *Care of the Soul*, New York: Harper Collins, 1992, p. 255.

20 See Raymond E. Brown S.S., *The Birth of the Messiah*, p. 314.

21 Mary is not the only one in the infancy narratives who receives the Spirit. Zechariah is promised that his child will be filled with the Holy Spirit before he is born (Luke 1:5, 41, 44). In the Visitation, Elizabeth is also filled with the Holy Spirit (Luke 1:41). Mary, filled with the Spirit, sings her Magnificat. When Mary and Joseph present Jesus in the temple, Simeon, filled with the Holy Spirit, prophesies about the child's and his mother's future (Luke 2:25-27). Later, Jesus will be led by the Spirit into the desert. Under the guidance of the Spirit, Jesus, reading from the prophet Isaiah in his village synagogue, will describe his ministry with the words, The Holy Spirit is upon me (Luke 4:18). In fact, all of Luke's gospel shows how the Spirit leads Jesus. It is the Spirit of Jesus which is communicated to his followers after the resurrection (Jn 20:22; Acts 1:8; 2:1-4), and guides the community which comes to be known as the Church. What the power of the Spirit throughout the Hebrew scriptures, in Mary, in the other players in the infancy narratives, in Jesus, in the community born at Pentecost (Acts 2:1) points to is the continued action of the Spirit in all generations. This underlines that life is movement. While fidelity to the past, to what has been considered tried and true cannot be sloughed off as unimportant, the scriptures point out that care must be taken not to stifle the action of the Spirit.

22 Johann G. Roten, S.M., "Memory and Mission: A Theological Reflection on Mary in the Paschal Mysteries." *Marian Studies*, XLII (1991): 132.

23 Ibid., p. 130.

24 Edward Schillebeeckx and Catharina Halkes, *Mary: Yesterday, Today, Tomorrow*, p. 68.

25 Theologically, this moment is described as the unborn John receiving the salvation that Jesus will offer to all humankind. The consecration of John in his mother's womb echoes that of Jeremiah (Jer 1:5).

26 Ibid., pp. 10, 11.

27 Raymond E. Brown S.S., *The Birth of the Messiah*, 1977, p. 333.

28 Johann G. Roten, S.M., "Memory and Mission: A Theological reflection on Mary in the Paschal Mysteries," p. 99.

29 Parallels can be shown between the Magnificat and what has come to be known as Miriam's hymn (Exod 15:1-18) and the Song of Hannah (1 Sam 2:1-10). All three songs are sung by women of courage who celebrate God's care, concern, justice, and mercy for those whom society looks down upon.

30 Matthew, unlike Luke, uses the expression "poor in spirit" and "the meek will possess the land" (Mt 5:3, 5). Both expressions are said to resonate with descriptions of the Qumran community, the Community of the Poor. Raymond E. Brown S.S., *The Birth of the Messiah*, p. 352.

31 The Magnificat, the Benedictus of Zechariah (Lk 1:67-79), the Gloria in Excelsis (Lk 2:13-14), and the Nunc Dimittis of Simeon (Lk 2:29-32) was probably a collection of Jewish hymns – four canticles, a collection which may have had its origin in the early post-Pentecostal community in Jerusalem. Raymond E. Brown, S.S., *An Adult Christ at Christmas*, Collegeville, MN: The Liturgical Press, 1978, p. 30. For a complete discussion of the composition of the canticles see Brown's *The Birth of the Messiah*, pp. 346–355.

32 Raymond E. Brown S.S., *The Birth of the Messiah*, pp. 350–355.

33 Ibid., p. 353.

34 Pope John Paul II, MR, 37.

35 Joel B. Green, "The Social Status of Mary in Luke 1,5–2,52." Biblica, Vol. 73:4 (1992): 468.

36 Barbara Reid, *Choosing the Better Part? Women in the Gospel of Luke*, pp. 84, 85.

37 Johannes B. Metz, *Poverty of Spirit*, New York: Paulist Press, 1968, p. 45.

38 Raymond E. Brown S.S., "The Annunciation to Mary, the Visitation, and the Magnificat (Luke 1:26-56)." *Worship*, 61, No. 3 (May 1988): 258.

39 Ibid., p. 259.

40 Johann G. Roten, S.M., "Memory and Mission: A Theological Reflection on Mary in the Paschal Mysteries," p. 19.

Chapter 3
Mary, Woman of Visitation

1   See Lorraine Caza, C.N.D., "Mission of Evangelization as Mystery of the Visitation." UISG Bulletin, 91(1993):27–39. I am grateful to Lorraine Caza for her article, which opened my heart to this deeper dimension of Luke's narrative of the Visitation.

2   All parts of the gospels that describe Jesus' teaching and interactions with individuals and with groups can be seen as visitations of God. Towards the end of his life, Jesus weeps over Jerusalem because it had failed to recognize God's time of visitation (Lk 19:44). Ibid., p. 30.

3   Luke has Mary and Joseph living in Nazareth. He needs the census to get them to Bethlehem for Jesus' birth. Matthew has the family living in a home in Bethlehem. He had to explain why they moved to Nazareth after their exile in Egypt, instead of returning to Bethlehem. For further discussion of these facts see Raymond E. Brown, S.S., *An Adult Christ at Christmas: Essays on the Three Biblical Stories in Matthew 1 and Luke 2*, Collegeville, MN: The Liturgical Press, 1978, p. 17, or Brown's *The Birth of the Messiah*, pp. 412–418.

4   Patricia Coon, "Journey to Bethlehem." Advent Reflection for Seniors, Montreal, Canada: (December, 1997).

5   Raymond E. Brown, S.S., *An Adult Christ at Christmas*, p. 19.

6   Joseph Fitzmeyer, S.J., "Luke." *The Anchor Bible*, Vol. 28, New York: Doubleday, 1981, p. 397.

7   Raymond E. Brown, S.S., *An Adult Christ at Christmas*, p. 24.

8   Following the birth of a girl, a woman was ceremoniously unclean for two weeks and her purification time was extended to sixty-six days, double the time required after the birth of a son (Lev 12:5). These attitudes towards women's menstruation and birth-giving, along with greater value being placed on the birth of sons than daughters, arose within a patriarchal society. Despite efforts and progress made in this century with regards to women's rights and equality, these attitudes continue to prevail in some cultures and religions. Prior to Vatican II, our baptismal liturgy included a prayer for the mother which emphasized her need for cleansing after the birth of her child.

9   This narrative seems to have been modelled on Hannah's presentation of her son Samuel in the temple (1 Sam 1–2).

10   Simeon's canticle, commonly known as the Nunc Dimittis, is one of four canticles in the Lucan Infancy narrative. See Chapter 2, endnote 31.

11   Raymond E. Brown, S.S., *An Adult Christ at Christmas*, p. 34.

12   Cf. Raymond E. Brown, S.S., *An Adult Christ at Christmas*, p. 35. Brown notes that Luke, at the beginning of Jesus' life, introduces a theme of opposition to Jesus and of persecution in the midst of normal Jewish ritual observance. This coupled with all that has transpired before makes it clear that acceptance – opposition is

the dialectic that will unfold in Jesus' life. By the time this gospel was written, this would have been experienced in Jesus' life and that of his followers. Brown, pp. 9, 26.

13 Anna's presence is said to foreshadow a later development of "consecrated widows whose duties included praying, fasting, visiting, and laying hands on the sick, making clothes, and doing good works. In fact Luke's gospel has more episodes about widows than any other." Barbara E. Reid, *Choosing the Better Part? Women in the Gospel of Luke*, pp. 92, 93.

14 Anna, as a woman prophet, enables us to look back and to look forward. She invites us to remember other First Testament women prophets, Miriam (Exod 15:20), Deborah (Judg 4-5), and Huldah (2 Kgs 22:14; 2 Chr 34:22). Her presence as a prophetess foreshadows the Pentecost event which is interpreted as the moment when God's servants and handmaids receive the gift of the Spirit and of prophesy (Acts 2:18). Unfortunately, while she follows two strong prophetic women, Mary and Elizabeth (Lk 1: 41, 46), Anna is the last woman mentioned as a prophet in Luke's gospel. From this moment on, woman will cry out in pain and in need and be attended to by Jesus. When they do speak they will be corrected (Lk 10:38-42; 11:27-28) or disbelieved (Lk 24:11). See Barbara E. Reid, *Choosing the Better Part?*, pp. 90–95.

15 J. Patrick Gaffney, S.M.M., "The Presentation ... Luke 2:21-40." *Queen*, Vol. XLVI, No. 3 (Sept.–Oct. 1995): 17.

16 See Chapter 1, p. 18.

17 Likely this requirement evolved into the Jewish religious ritual known as Bar Mitzvah which literally means a boy has become the son of the commandments, a man of duty.

18 Raymond Brown points out that based on the Greek, we must not interpret this reference to mean that Jesus is referring to the Temple as the house of God. *An Adult Christ at Christmas*, p. 47. Were the temple to be understood, it would contradict the fact that the Incarnation establishes in Jesus, God's presence among the people.

   Before Vatican II, the strong emphasis on adoration of Jesus before his presence kept in the tabernacle strongly suggested that God was to be found in the church that replaced the Jewish temple. This God can be controlled as much as the Jewish priests tried to control access to God in Jesus' time.

19 This story placed at the end of the Lucan infancy narrative poses difficulty for readers who forget that Jesus' identity announced to Mary at the Annunciation, affirmed by Elizabeth in the Visitation, announced by angels to the shepherds in the fields, grew out of post-resurrection faith in him. Forgetting this makes it difficult to remember that Mary had to grow in her understanding of who her son was and his mission.

20 Matthew's gospel was written from 70–90 CE; Mark's, 65–70 CE; Luke's, 70–90 CE; John's, 90–100 CE.

21 Adapted from Michael Trainor, ed., *St. Matthew: A Gospel for Searching People*, Ottawa: Novalis, 1994, pp. 8, 9, 15, 16.

22 Ibid., p. 13.

23 Stoning was considered the means of purging the evil of a woman found not to be a virgin when she was transferred to her husband's house. It would seem, "in a less severe legal system the command 'to purge this evil' could have been met by divorce than by stoning." Raymond E. Brown, S.S., et al., eds. Mary in the New Testament, Philadelphia: Fortress Press, 1978, footnote 174, p. 84.

24 Rosemary Luling Haughton, *Images for Change: The Transformation of Society*, Mahwah, NJ: Paulist Press, 1997, p. 144.

25 Elaine M. Wainwright, *Shall We Look for Another? A Feminist Reading of the Matthean Jesus*, Maryknoll, NY: Orbis Books, 1998, p. 63.

26 Ibid., pp. 63, 64.

27 Ibid., p. 65.

28 A grotto in the church of the Visitation in Ain Karim conveys the idea of a stone that, according to an ancient legend, concealed John the Baptist from Herod's persecution.

29 Raymond E. Brown S.S., *The Birth of the Messiah*, p. 183.

30 Elaine M. Wainwright, *Shall We Look for Another?*, p. 56.

31 Amy-Jill Levine, "Matthew." *Women's Bible Commentary*, p. 254.

32 Raymond E. Brown, S.S., *An Introduction to the New Testament*, New York: Doubleday, 1977, p. 174.

33 Elaine M. Wainwright, *Shall We Look for Another?*, p. 60.

34 Jerome Murphy O'Connor, O.P., *The Holy Land: An Oxford Archeological Guide from Earliest Times to 1700*, New York: Oxford University Press, 1998. Sepphoris (Zippori), pp. 412–418; Tiberias, pp. 455–463.

35 Ibid., p. 52.

36 Carol L. Myers, "Everyday Life: Women in the Period of the Hebrew Bible." *Women's Bible Commentary*, p. 246.

37 See Bruce J. Malina, "Mother and Son." *Biblical Theology Bulletin*, vol. 20, no. 2 (Summer, 1990): 54–64.

38 Albert Nolan, *Jesus Before Christianity*, Maryknoll, NY: Orbis Books, 1978, pp. 73–74.

39 Amy L. Wordelman, "Everyday Life: Women in the Period of the New Testament." *Women's Bible Commentary*, p. 396.

40 Bertrand Buby, S.M., *Mary of Galilee*, Vol. II, p. 51.

41 Archeology has uncovered the walls of homes in first-century Capernaum. The present Franciscan church is built above a structure which dates back to the first century. Discovery of pottery provides evidence that this structure was a home until the mid-first century. Egeria, the pilgrim who visited Capernaum between 381 and 384, noted "In Capernaum the house of the prince of the apostles has

been made into a church, with its original walls still standing. There is also the synagogue where the Lord cured a man possessed by the devil (Mk 1:23)." Jerome Murphy-O'Connor, *The Holy Land*, pp. 217–218.

42   Raymond E. Brown, S.S., *An Adult Christ at Christmas*, p. 34.

43   John Dominic Crossan, *The Birth of Christianity: Discovering What Happened in the Years Immediately After the Execution of Jesus*, San Francisco: Harper Collins, p. 324.

44   Some manuscripts read, Is this not the son of the carpenter and of Mary? See the footnote in the New Revised Standard Version of the Bible.

45   Anthony J. Saldini, *Matthew's Christian-Jewish Community*, Chicago: The University of Chicago Press, 1994, pp. 91–92.

46   Ibid., p. 94.

47   Ibid., p. 94.

48   Barbara E. Reid, *Choosing the Better Part? Women in the Gospel of Luke*, pp. 187, 188. For a discussion on Matthew's use of father see also Mary Rose D'Angelo, "'Abba' and 'Father': Imperial Theology and the Jesus Traditions," Journal of Biblical Literature, 111/4 (1992): 611–630.

49   Raymond E. Brown, S.S., et al., *Mary in the New Testament*, p. 170.

50   Raymond Brown suggests that this first and only mention of the brothers in Lk 8:21 and the association of them with the mother in terms of discipleship anticipates the presence of "Mary the mother of Jesus with his brothers in the believing community (Acts 1:14)." Brown, p. 170.

51   The implications for the church will be discussed in Chapter 6 and following.

52   For an in-depth analysis of interpretations of the wedding at Cana see The Mystery of the Wedding Feast in *Mary in the Mystery of the Covenant*, Ignace de la Potterie, S.J., Bertrand Buby, S.M., trans., New York: Alba House, 1972, pp. 157–208.

53   Aristide Serra, *Maria a Cana e sotto la Croce. Saggio di mariologia giovannea*, Rome, 1978, pp. 30–37 quoted in Ignace de la Potterie, *Mary in the Mystery of the Covenant*, pp. 190, 191.

54   MC, 57.

55   Ignace de la Potterie, *Mary in the Mystery of the Covenant*, p. 195.

56   Johann G. Roten, S.M. "Memory and Mission: A Theological Reflection on Mary," p. 100.

57   Ritva H. Williams, "The Mother of Jesus at Cana: A Social-Science Interpretation of John 2:1-12." *Catholic Biblical Quarterly*, 59 (1997): 682.

58   Jesus uses the term "woman" in addressing the Samaritan woman (Jn 4:41) and Mary Magdalene (Jn 20:15). These women are often seen as representing the community. In other words each of us can place ourselves within the story of the Samaritan woman. Any one of us can place ourselves in Mary Magdalene's place at the tomb and ask "where are we to find Jesus?" This point is also made of the "beloved" disciple. His being unnamed allows us to sit with Jesus at the Last Supper (Jn 13:1ff) and to stand at the foot of the cross (Jn 19:25). In Chapter 6

and following, we shall see how Mary's motherhood is transferred to the church, the community of equal disciples.

59 See Ignace de la Potterie, S.J., *Mary in the Mystery of the Covenant*, p. 228. Idem. Ignace de la Potterie, S.J., « Et a partir de cette heure, le Disciple l'acueille dans son intimité (Jn 19:27b). » *Marianum* XXII, No 124 (1980): 84–125.

60 Pope John Paul II, MR, 45.

61 Raymond E. Brown, S.S., *The Death of the Messiah*, vol. 2, New York: Doubleday, footnote 97, p. 1024.

62 Ibid., p. 1025.

63 Bertrand Buby, S.M., *Mary of Galilee*, Vol. I, p. 138.

64 For a reflection on the connection between this in-between time and our lives today see Marie Azzarello, C.N.D., "Mary and the Women Who Risked Following Jesus to and Beyond the Cross: A Paradigm for Today." *Grail: An Ecumenical Journal*, vol. 12, no. 2 (June 1996): 84–96. A French translation of this article, entitled "Un paradigme pour aujourd'hui: Marie est les femmes qui ont risqué du suivre Jésus jusqu'à et au delà de la Croix," appeared in Nouveau Dialogue, no. 108 (janvier–février 1996): 26–30.

65 Johann G. Roten, S.M., *Memory and Mission: A Theological Perspective*, p. 101.

Chapter 4
Becoming Disciples of Jesus

1 Normand Provencher, O.M.I., *Jesus of Nazareth*, Ottawa: Novalis, 1997, p. 36.

2 Ibid., p. 60.

3 Patrick Bearsley, S.M. "Mary the Perfect Disciple: A Paradigm for Mariology." *Theological Reflections*, 41 (1980): 483.

4 Ibid., p. 483.

5 John Paul II, MR, 20.

6 Mark and Matthew do not mention Mary after the encounter with Jesus during his public ministry. This "may be an indication that she did not figure prominently in the ecclesial communities and the traditions from which their Gospels sprang." Patrick J. Bearsley, S.M. "Mary the Perfect Disciple: A Paradigm for Mariology," p. 475.

7 The idea of "keeping events with concern" appears in Genesis 37:11. There Joseph relates his dream about the sun, the moon and the stars bowing down to him to his father and his brothers. While his brothers are jealous, his father keeps the matter in mind in order "to discover the hidden meaning behind marvellous events." Raymond E. Brown S.S., *An Adult Christ at Christmas*, p. 24.

8 Raymond E. Brown, S.S., *The Birth of the Messiah*, p. 406.

9 Raymond E. Brown, S.S., *An Adult Christ at Christmas*, p. 25.

10 Johann G. Roten, S.M., "Memory and Mission: A Theological Reflection on Mary," p. 115.

11 Bertrand Buby, S.M., *Mary the Faithful Disciple*, p. 23.

12 "Faith of Mary." *Dictionary of Mary*, New York: Catholic Book Publishing Company, 1985, p. 124.

13 John Paul II, MR, 14.

14 Johann G. Roten, S.M., "Memory and Mission: A Theological Reflection on Mary," p. 117.

15 Ibid., p. 115.

16 LG, 58.

17 John Paul II, MR, 25–28.

18 See Chapter 2.

19 This section is drawn from *Oeuvres Complètes du Cardinal Bérulle*, Paris: Antoine Estienne and Sebastien Huse (1644); reprinted Montsoult Seine and Oise: Maison de l'Instruction de l'Oratoire, (1960): Vol. 1, pp. 963, 964, 1103–1108.

20 Bérulle used the term "vie voyagère" to describe Jesus' life from his conception to his death and ascension. 'Journeying life' seems the most suitable translation.

21 Adapted from Mary Virginia Cotter, *The Writings of Marguerite Bourgeoys*, Montreal: 1976, p. 46. Cf. Gaston Cayron, Le Français Classique, *Lexique de la langue du dix-septième siècle*, Paris: Didier, 1948.

22 Jim Culliphor, "Musing from the Still Point." *Journeys: Exploring Jung's Psychology for the Contemporary Christian Pilgrimage*, Vol. 7, No. 1 (Winter, 1998): 2.

23 Ibid., p. 2.

24 Vicki Morgan, "Living out of the Centre." *Single Women Affirming Our Spiritual Journeys*, Mary O'Brien and Clare Christie, eds., Westport, CT: Bergin and Harvey, 1993, p. 173.

25 John Shea, "Giving Birth to Christ," *Church*, Vol. 6, No. 4 (Winter, 1990): 6.

26 Ibid., pp. 6–10.

27 Pope John Paul II, RM,11, 44.

28 George Wilson, S.J., "Authority with Credibility." *Human Development*, Vol. 12:41 (Winter, 1991): 29.

29 GS, 17.

30 EN, 20.

31 "The Spirit Source of Hope," adapted from Journey Through the Liturgical Year, *Living with Christ*, Ottawa: Novalis, August 1998.

32 Elizabeth A. Johnson, C.S.J., "The Marian Tradition and the Reality of Women," p. 132.

33 Gail Sheehy, *Passages: Predictable Crises of Adult Life*, New York: Dalton, 1976; *New Passages: Mapping Your Life Across Time*, New York: Random House, 1995.

34 Gerald O'Collins, *The Second Journey: Spiritual Awareness and the Mid-Life Crisis*, New York: Paulist Press, 1978.

35 Adapted from Johann G. Roten, S.M., "Re-readings in Marianist Spirituality." *The Promised Woman: Proceedings from the International Symposium on Marianist Spirituality*, Dayton, OH: 1992, p. 480.

36 Rosemary Haughton, *Images for Change:The Transformation of Society*, p. 141.

37 Clare Thompson, "Mary: The True Disciple." *Ecumenism*, No. 87 (September 1987), 32.

Chapter 5
Mary in the Circle of Disciples

1 For some time "Mary in the circle of disciples," "centre of unity," "woman of reconciliation" have been the phrases I have used to describe Luke's image of her among the disciples in the Upper Room and at Pentecost (Acts 1:14; 2:1-4). Elizabeth A. Johnson, C.S.J. used the expression "Mary in the Circle of Disciples" also in her article "Toward a Theology of Mary: Past, Present, Future" as the title for Part V. See *All Generations Shall Call Me Blessed*, Frances A. Eigo, O.S.A., ed. Villanova, PA: Villanova University Press, pp. 1–38.

2 See the discussion of Lk 8:19-21 in relation to Mk 3:31-35 and Mt 12:46-50 in Chapter 3.

3 Recent Church documents locate Mary in history and affirm her presence in the Upper Room and at Pentecost. LG, 59; MR, 26.

4 "The Blessed Virgin Mary, Mother of Reconciliation," and "The Blessed Virgin Mary, Mother of Consolation." *Collection of Masses of the Blessed Virgin Mary*. Collegeville, MN: The Liturgical Press, 1992, pp. 71, 277.

5 Robert A. Ludwig, *Reconstructing Catholicism for a New Generation*, New York: Crossroad, 1995, p. 72.

6 John's gospel, which places Mary standing at the foot of the cross with the beloved disciple and the women (Jn 19:25-30), affirms that Mary is a disciple of Jesus, a recipient of the Holy Spirit with the disciples gathered. Mary is at one with the Spirit-filled disciples, a disciple among disciples. Patrick J. Bearsley, S.M., "Mary The Perfect Disciple: A Paradigm for Mariology," pp. 490–91. John's gospel provides a second image of the conferring of the Spirit on the disciples on Easter day when they see the Risen Christ. 'The message is the same: the Spirit is not given to the twelve but to all the men and women disciples gathered together. As Jesus breathes on them they receive the Spirit along with the power to bind and to loose. In this first century context it refers to the communal discernment of whether or not to accept a candidate for baptism. Since this text is often used as a proof text for the power of the clergy to forgive sins, it is important to stress that the mission 'to bind and to loose' is given to the community of men and women disciples. Like Luke's description of Pentecost, John's narrative concerns

the bestowal of the Spirit on the whole infant church. As the Father has sent Jesus, so now he sends them." Homily Service (May 23, 1999): 51.

7   While the present structure of the Upper Room (Cenacle) is reminiscent of architecture of the fourteenth century, there is archeological and textual evidence for the existence of a second-century Christian building on Mount Zion. The fact that second-century Christians built on the site despite the obstacles which they would have encountered "betrays an attachment to the place which is explicable only in the terms of the importance the site had in the first century." Jerome Murphy-O'Connor, O.P., "The Cenacle: Topographical Setting for Acts 2:44-45." Vol 4, *The Book of Acts in Its Palestinian Setting*, Richard Bauckham, ed., Series, *The Book of Acts in Its First Century Setting*, p. 305. According to Karen Armstrong, non-Jewish Christians took over the Upper Room on Mount Zion which was outside the new town Hadrian began to construct after 135 CE. They called the Upper Room the "Mother of the churches" since this was where Christianity came into being. Karen Armstrong, *Jerusalem: One City, Three Faiths*, New York: Alfred A. Knopf, 1996, p. 170.

8   Given that it was nine o'clock in the morning, the crowds could have assembled for prayer at the Temple Mount. Given men's and women's acceptance of the message about Jesus, the disciples could have mingled with people in the Court of the Gentiles, or with Jews alone in the Court of the Women where men, women and children gathered.

9   Raymond E. Brown, S.S., *An Introduction to the New Testament*, p. 285. Brown notes that to be baptized in the name of Jesus likely meant that the one being baptized confessed who Jesus was: Jesus is Lord; Jesus is the Messiah (Christ); Jesus is the Son of God; Jesus is the Son of Man. Ibid., p. 286.

10   This equality in receiving the gift of the Spirit will prove true when the first Gentiles are baptized (Acts 10:44-48). Raymond Brown notes that this principle will need to be recalled when inevitably bickering arises over special roles in the Church (1 Cor 12). Ibid., p. 286.

11   The same may be said for the continued reporting in Acts of the spread of the Jesus movement in Jerusalem, throughout Judea, Samaria, and to the Gentiles, fulfilling Jesus' command to be his witnesses to the ends of the earth (Acts 1:8).

12   Archeologists have discovered several buildings south of the Temple Mount which contain a large number of rooms, ritual baths, and many cisterns. Scholars, based on these findings, have come to the conclusion that thousands came from the Diaspora to Jerusalem for Passover and the other pilgrimage feasts of Pentecost and Booths. These people in addition to rooming with relatives stayed in community centres built especially for them. This information helps us to envision the crowds which would have been in Jerusalem at Pentecost crowding relatives' homes, the inns, as well as Jerusalem's narrow streets, and markets. Wolfgang Reinhardt, "The Population Size of Jerusalem and the Numerical Growth of the Jerusalem Church," Series, Vol. 4, pp. 237–245.

13 Ibid. Demographic studies in latter years on ancient cities and archaeological discoveries in Jerusalem and first-century historians such as Josephus suggest that Jerusalem in Jesus' time and until the destruction of the Temple around 70 C.E. was a moderate urban centre which enjoyed great prosperity. This has led to the conclusion that first-century Jerusalem had more inhabitants than was usually assumed. Though an exact calculation of the population appears impossible at the present, these studies suggests that a figure of 60,000–120,000 inhabitants seems more realistic. The higher number is quite possible for the 30s of the first century. These studies contradict the lower figures of 30,000–55,000 inhabitants estimated by Joachim Jeremias in his book *Jerusalem in the Time of Jesus*, published in the 1960s.

14 Acts omission of any reference to the communities which formed beyond Jerusalem in the rest of Judea, and only a scant mention of "saints in Lydda and Joppa" (Acts 9:32, 41) suggests the monopoly that the community in Jerusalem played in those first years. F.F. Bruce, The Church of Jerusalem in the Acts of the Apostles." Bulletin of the John Ryland University Library, Vol. 67, No. 2, (Spring, 1985): 642. Raymond E. Brown, S.S. deals with the diversity evident in the seven churches after the death of the apostles. *The Churches the Apostles Left Behind*, New York/Ramsey: Paulist Press, 1984.

15 The connection between the description of the Pentecost event in Acts, the Spirit hovering over the water in Creation (Gen 1:1), and the covenant given to Moses at Sinai (Exod 19) was discussed in Chapter 1.

16 MR, 24.

17 The link between Mary receiving the Spirit at the Annunciation (Lk 1:35) and the community receiving the Spirit in Acts was underlined by Vatican II in the Constitution on the Church (LG, par. 59), and its Decree on the Missionary Activity of the Church (par. 4). Pope John Paul II emphasizes this as well in his encyclical letter Mother of the Redeemer, MR, 24.

18 Dimitri Sala, O.F.M., "Releasing the Power of the Spirit." *Emmanuel*, Vol. 105, No. 8, (Oct. 1999): 471.

19 See Chapter 3. The promise of the Annunciation rooted deeply within her heart must have enabled her to not lose hope during that critical period between the crucifixion, death, and resurrection of Jesus.

20 Beyond Pentecost the major speeches of Acts identified with Peter (Acts 3:12-26; 4:8-12; 5:29-32; 10:39-48) echo the same themes of the Magnificat found in Acts 2: 14-36.

21 The significance of the inclusion of Joel's prophecy in Peter's speech was discussed extensively in Chapter 1.

22 Robert A. Ludwig, *Reconstructing Catholicism for a New Generation*, New York: Crossroad, 1995, p. 73.

23 Bertrand Buby, S.M., "Mary, A Model of Ecclesia-Orans, In Acts 1:14," *Marian Studies*, Vol. XXXV (1984): 87–99.

24 LG, 63; MR, 26.

25 Authors since the second century have described Mary's teaching role in the foundational days of the Church. In the Middle Ages emphasis moved from her teaching new members of the community to her teaching the apostles alone. This narrow vision of her involvement in the community is found in the Basilica of St. Mary Major in Rome and in the church of St. Nizier in Troyes, France where paintings depict Mary teaching the Twelve alone. See Marie Azzarello, C.N.D., *Mary, Teacher of the Apostles, Builder of the Church*.

26 MR, 27.

27 Ibid., 26; LG, 63. Pope John Paul II describes Mary as being among all believers "like a mirror" in which are reflected the mighty works of God. MR, 25.

Chapter 6
Mary and the Jerusalem Community: Life in Visitation

1 Elizabeth A. Johnson, *Consider Jesus: Waves of Renewal in Christology*, New York: Crossroad, 1990, p. 6.

2 All speeches follow the same style. Luke may have shaped them from memories of an early apostolic preaching style. Raymond E. Brown, S.S., *An Introduction to the New Testament*, p. 319.

3 Later Paul's proclamation of the word has the same effect (12:24; 13:43; 14:1).

4 Scripture scholars agree that the present gospels arose out of different Christian communities in the late first century. The literary structure of the gospels shows that they did not just repeat the oral tradition but interpreted it in relation to the existing circumstances and problems which different communities faced.

5 David A. Fiensy, "The Composition of the Jerusalem Church," *The Book of Acts in Its Palestinian Setting*, Richard Bauckman, ed., vol. 4, Grand Rapids, MI: Eerdmans, 1995, pp. 213–236.

In this article Fiensy provides a detailed description of first-century Jerusalem. In discussing the spread of the Jesus movement I have made use of his descriptions of Jerusalem's population mix.

6 The interaction between Jesus and the disciples going home to Emmaus is often presented to Christians today as a model for storytelling – how the process of evangelization takes place.

7 Eugene La Verdiere, *The Eucharist in the New Testament and the Early Church*, Collegeville, MN: The Liturgical Press, 1996, p. 103.

8 Ibid., p. 104.

9 Ibid, p.103. Paul, during his own mission, will remind members of the Corinthian community that "you show that you are a letter of Christ written not with ink but with the Spirit of the living God, not on tablets of stones but on tablets of human hearts" (2 Cor 3:2).

10 Later during the Council of Jerusalem the theological differences concerning attitudes towards the Mosaic law and circumcision which are evident in the community at this time become clear (Acts 15).

11 What is most strange about this account is that after Stephen's death the persecution forced many within the new movement to leave Jerusalem with the notable exception of the apostles (Acts 8:1). Later we find a Christian community in Jerusalem without any suggestion of a return (Acts 9:26). According to David L. Barr it is possible that the Greek-speaking Jews having lived in the Diaspora did not see the place of the Temple, the law, and ritual purity in the same way as those who had resided in Jerusalem all their lives. The story in Acts suggests that the more orthodox Hebrew element of the community was unaffected by the persecution. It is possible that only the Hellenists and their sympathizers were under attack. A later meeting between Paul and James the leader in Jerusalem suggests that some members of the Jerusalem church remained strong orthodox Jews (Acts 21:17ff.). David L. Barr, *Introduction to the New Testament*, pp. 318–319.

12 Eamon Caroll, "Mary in the Apostolic Church – Work in Progress." One in Christ, *25th Anniversary of the Decree on Ecumenism*, ESBVM, Liverpool Congress (1989): 374.

13 Cf. Albert Nolan, *Jesus Before Christianity*, p. 165.

14 Roman occupation had contributed to the ever growing gap between wealthy members of their society and the majority who were impoverished. Oppressive religious laws determined who was righteous in God's eyes, who was pure, and who was not; which persons and what things were clean or unclean. Patriarchy, which structured society and religious practices, privileged men over women, children, and slaves. These political, social, and religious structures created sharp distinctions and boundaries among themselves, and segregated these first Jewish believers from their Gentile neighbours. Robert A. Ludwig, *Reconstructing Catholicism for a New Generation*, New York: Crossroad, 1995, p. 66.

15 Jerome H. Neyrey, "The Symbolic Universe of Luke-Acts." *The Social World of Luke-Acts*, Jerome H. Neyrey, ed., Peabody, MA: Hendrickson Publishers, 1991, p. 207.

16 Albert Nolan, *Jesus Before Christianity*, p. 165.

17 John Dominic Crossan, The Birth of Christianity, San Francisco: Harper, 1998, p. 472.

18 Ibid., p. 472.

19 Brian Capper maintains that the community of goods is a historically verifiable aspect of the life of the earliest Jerusalem community. "The Palestinian Context of Community of Goods." *The Book of Acts in Its First Century Setting* Series, Richard A. Bauckman, ed., vol. 4, Grand Rapids, MI: Eerdmans, 1995 p. 354.

20 Marianne Race, Laurie Brink, *In This Place: Reflections on the Land of the Gospels for the Liturgical Year*, Collegeville, MN: The Liturgical Press, 1998, pp. 185–186.

21 Elizabeth A. Johnson, C.S.J., *Consider Jesus*, p. 55.

22 John H. Ashworth, M.H.M., "Hospitality in Luke-Acts." *The Bible Today*, Vol. 35, No. 5, (Sept–Oct, 1997): 302.

23 The miracles of the multiplication of the loaves and fishes probably reminded the first disciples of a similar story in the Hebrew scriptures (2 Kings 4:42-44). Elisha tells a man who brought food from his first crop to give it to the people. The man, like the disciples later, expresses his concern that so little food could feed so many people. To his surprise, there is food left.

24 Luke gives no indication regarding the composition of the Jerusalem community. David A. Fiensey notes that although the sources, especially the book of Acts, give only hints about the make-up of the Jerusalem church, the indications are that nearly all levels of society were represented. The church seems to have been a microcosm of the city. Upper Zion housed the wealthy: the Temple and the lay nobility. The lower City housed the lower class who were likely the poorer priests, the small merchants like the bakers, and the craftsmen such as the weavers and day labourers. On the margins of the society were the slaves and the destitute: the beggars, some lame, some blind, some terribly ill. These lived on the outskirts of the city with or without a residence. Further this city had a substantial element of Greek-speaking Jews. David A. Fiensey, "The Composition of the Jerusalem Church," pp. 213–236. See also Sean Freyne, *The World of the New Testament*, Vol. 2, Wilmington, DE.: Michael Glazier, 1985.

25 Halvor Moxnes, "Patron-Client Relationships and the New Community in Luke-Acts." *The Social World of Luke-Acts*, Jerome H. Neyrey, ed. Peabody, MA: Hendrickson Publishers, 1991, p. 265.

26 Robert A. Ludwig, *Reconstructing Catholicism*, p. 107.

27 This assembly has become known as the Council of Jerusalem which took place in 50 CE. It was the first church council.

28 James H. Neyrey, "The Symbolic Universe of Luke-Acts," p. 297.

29 John Ashworth, M.H.M., "Hospitality in Luke-Acts." *The Bible Today*, Vol. 35, No. 5, (Sept.–Oct., 1997): 302.

30 John Dominic Crossan, *The Birth of Christianity*, p. 307.

31 "Here the Christian paradox confronts us. The paradox, of course, is that the one who performs the action is thereby cleansed, even more than the one who has been 'washed.' And, for the author of John, this mystery is the key to eternal life. Thus, Jesus tells his disciples, 'If you understand this, blessed are you if you do it'" (13:17). Barbara E. Bowe, R.S.C.J. "John 13 and Christian Service," *The Bible Today*, Vol. 32, No. 4 (July 1994): 227.

32 Halvor Moxnes, "Patron-Client Relations and the New Community in Luke-Acts," p. 261.

33 Ibid., p. 261.

34 Evidence of women in leadership roles in the new community was discussed fully in Chapter 1. It suffices here to say again that they played an important role as apostles, teachers, missionary co-workers with Paul, founders and leaders

of house churches, prophets etc. For further reading, see *Women of Spirit: Female Leadership in the Jewish and Christian Traditions*, Rosemary Ruether and Eleanor McLaughlin, eds., New York: Simon & Schuster, 1979, pp. 30–57. Fran Ferder and John Heagle, *Partnership: Women and Men in Ministry*, Notre Dame, IN: Ave Maria Press, 1989, pp. 81–95. Thomas F. O'Meara, O.P., *Theology of Ministry*, New York/Mahwah, NJ: Paulist Press, 1999, pp. 71–72.

35   Laurie Brink, Marianne Race, *In This Place: Reflections on the Land of the Gospels for the Liturgical Year*, pp. 185, 186.

36   Carolyn Osiek, R.S.C.J. "Road" would be a more literal translation of the Greek word odos. "Bible Terms Today: The Way (*odos*), Sect (*Haeresis*), Christian (*Christianoi*)." *The Bible Today*, Vol 24, No 2 (March 1986): 85.

37   Barbara E. Bowe, R.S.C. J., "The Birth of the Church." *The Bible Today*, Vol 37, No 5 (September 1999): 291.

38   Rt. Rev. Alan Clark, D.D., "The Holy Spirit and Mary." *Mary's Place in Christian Dialogue*, Wilton, CT: Morehouse–Barlow, 1982, p. 83.

39   Paul expresses the unity of believers and their need for each other in the analogy that they are members of the body of Christ (1 Cor 12:12ff.).

40   See Chapter 1.

41   Thomas F. O'Meara, O.P., *Theology of Ministry*, p. 52.

42   Ibid., p. 48.

43   Sean Freyne, *The World of the New Testament*, pp. 138–140.

44   Egalitarian communities had no identifiable places of assembly for at least 200 years. Unlike Judaism and pagan cults there was no identifiable priesthood. John G. Gager, *Kingdom and Community: The Social World of Early Christianity*, Englewood Cliffs, NJ: Prentice-Hall, 1975, p. 130.

45   Some years after his conversion, Paul is astonished at the divisions which have arisen in the Corinthian community. He affirms that each person not the place is the locus of the presence of the Spirit. "Do you not know," he says, "that you are God's temple and that God's Spirit dwells in you?" (1 Cor 3:16). The point is that had they remembered this, divisions would not have been allowed to take root in the community.

46   John H. Elliot, "Temple versus Household in Luke-Acts: A Contrast in Social Institutions." *The Social World of Luke-Acts: Models of Interpretation*, Jerome H. Neyrey ed., Peabody, MA: Hendrickson Publishers, 1991, p. 231.

47   Daniel K. Falk, "Jewish Prayer and Literature in the Early Church." *The Book of Acts in Its Palestinian Setting*, Richard Bauckham, ed., *The Book of Acts in Its First Century Setting* Series, vol. 4, 1995, p. 299.

48   Stephen on the other hand declared that God never desired a permanently fixed dwelling-place like the Temple, that a movable shrine was more suitable for a pilgrim people (Acts 7:44-50). F.F. Bruce, *The Church in Jerusalem*, p. 647.

49   Eugene La Verdiere, *The Eucharist in the New Testament and the Early Church*, p. 104.

50   Ibid., p. 104.

51   Carol Francis Jegen, B.V.M., "Mary and the Church of the Future." *All Generations Shall Call Me Blessed*, Francis A. Eigo, ed., Villanova, PA: Villanova University Press, 1994, p. 185.

52   Ibid., p. 185.

53   Bertrand Buby, S.M., "Mary, A Model of Ecclesia-Orans, In Acts 1:14," p. 89.

54   Ibid., p. 90.

55   In a community where men and women were baptized equally there was no discussion about Gentile women not having to observe Jewish menstrual and childbirth purity regulations. One hopes these were rejected as well.

Chapter 7
Mary and the Transformation of the Church

1   Acts 1:12-14; 2:1ff. The Church as a "community of equal disciples" roots us in the Pentecost experience where the Spirit empowers Mary and the men and women disciples equally without distinction. In Acts 6:2, the Church is called a "community of disciples. " This same description of the Church is found in John 20:19-23 where the Spirit is given to the disciples gathered. Pope John Paul II in his encyclical Redeemer of Man describes the Church as "the community of disciples, each of whom is called in a different way to follow the one way who is Christ." RM, 21. Avery Dulles suggests that the model of church as a community of disciples makes disciples "feel at home in a Church that must always find its way in a rapidly changing and fluid situation, a pilgrim Church still distant from its goal." Avery Dulles, S.J., *Models of the Church*, Revised Edition, New York: Doubleday, 1987, p. 223.

2   Cf. chapters 6, 7. The Second Vatican Council concluded The Constitution on the Church with a chapter on Mary entitled "The Role of the Blessed Virgin Mary, Mother of God, in the Mystery of Christ and the Church." In so doing, the Council placed Mary clearly among the people of God, at the centre of the Church, "the pre-eminent and singular member in the community of believers." The Council underlined that Mary at all times, and in all place represents what the Church is to be. LG, 53, 63. Pope John Paul II discusses Mary's active presence at the centre of the pilgrim Church in his encyclical *Mother of the Redeemer*. MR, 25-37.

3   LG, 56–58. Cf. chapters 2 to 6.

4   Cf. LG, 59; 63; 68; MC, 28; MR, 6; Eucharistic Prayers II and III.

5   Cf. MC, 56. Earlier, reflecting on Mary's faith journey as a model for our own I referred to Pope Paul VI's description of her as "our sister in faith, who fully shared our lot." Cf. chapters 2–5.

6   See chapters 2 and 4.

7   Patrick J. Bearsley, S.M., "Mary the Perfect Disciple: A Paradigm for Mariology," p. 491. Cf. Acts 1:14; 2:1ff.; Jn 19:25.

8   Pope Paul VI on November 21, 1964, in his address following the acceptance of The Constitution on the Church at the Second Vatican Council claimed that Mary was "the archetype of the Church." AAS 56 (1964): 1014–1018.

Archetypes are original patterns or models. They stand before us as examples for imitation. So the Church in every generation should resemble Mary as it lives and acts in Jesus' name.

9   The expression "community of equal disciples" refers to the universal church and the local Churches. The Church in relation to the dioceses around the world becomes a Community of Communities of disciples where unity in diversity is operative. Each local parish community of disciples would, in turn, be a community of communities. The understanding here is that disciples belong to small faith communities.

10   See endnote 1 above. Cf. Chapter 5. Patrick Bearsly, S.M. also claims Mary as the paradigm of the church as a community of disciples minus any reference to equality among women and men. See "Mary, the Perfect Disciple: A Paradigm for Mariology," p. 491.

11   Edward Schillebeeckx and Catherine Halkes, *Mary Yesterday, Today and Tomorrow*, New York: Crossroad, 1993, p. 68.

12   Roy S. Anderson, *The Soul of Ministry*, Louisville, KY, Westminster/John Knox Press, 1997, p. 134. Cf. Chapter 7, part 3.

13   Dimitri Sala, "Releasing the Power of the Spirit," p. 471.

14   Ibid., p. 471.

15   Ibid., p. 471.

16   Thomas O'Meara, *Theology of Ministry*, p. 146.

17   Dimitri Sala, O.F.M., "Releasing the Power of the Spirit," p. 471.

18   Johann Metz claims that the church's crisis today is due to a deficit in discipleship and to difficulties in adapting to Jesus. He cautions the church against a church of discipleship which is split into two parts: either relegated to the realm of private-religious spirituality or to a purely social-political dimension of action. For him a mysticism of discipleship will always incorporate both elements. The disciple who follows Jesus knows that, like him, intimacy with God, response to God's love should be at the source of all actions. Johann B. Metz, "For a Renewed Church Before a New Council: A Concept in Four Theses." *Toward Vatican III: The Work That Needs to Be Done*, David Tracy with Hans Kung, Johann B. Metz, eds., New York: Concilium, The Seabury Press, 1978, pp. 139–140.

19   Ladislas Orsy, in his article "New Era of Participation in Church Life" comments that in the early Christian communities baptism was considered the greatest of the sacraments. The newly baptized were granted the highest honours and given special places in the gatherings of the community. Later the balance shifted. Baptism became commonplace, and orders emerged as conferring the highest

dignity. This emphasis led gradually to a conception that the church consisted principally of the clergy. All the others had a passive role to play. Ladislas Orsy, "New Era of Participation in Church Life." *Origins* 17 (28 April 1988): p. 799. In the early church, candidates supported by the community entered into a step-by-step process toward full membership in the church. The reinstatement of the Rite of Initiation of Catechumens is an effort to regain what was lost with the introduction of baptism upon request following the conversion of Emperor Constantine in 313. Without playing God, it would seem that infant baptism only makes sense if parents are committed disciples of Jesus.

20 Cf. Chapter 4. Today the sacrament of baptism is often spoken of as "the ordination of the laity which authorizes them to participate in Christ's ministry in and for the world." Barbara Schwahn, "Towards an Ecumenical Theology of the 'People of God.'" *A Letter from Christ to the World: An Exploration of the Role of the Laity in the Church Today*, Nicholas Apostola, ed., Geneva: WCC Publications, 1998, p. 49.

"The beauty of the symbolic meaning of ordination is that it honours the truth that each person is capable of making deeply significant contributions to the lives of others, not just through their professions but through the quality of the persons they become." Carolyn Myss, *Anatomy of the Spirit*, New York: Three Rivers Press, 1996, pp. 238, 239.

21 The Church as a community of disciples recognizes that children learn to be disciples of Jesus first at home, in the domestic church. LG, 11. Each person is a valued member of the community at whatever stage of life they are.

22 Pope John Paul II, *The Spirit: Giver of Life and Love, A Catechesis on the Creed*, Volume III, Boston, MA: Pauline Media and Books, 1988, p.11.

23 Cf. LG, 32.

24 LG, chapter 5, 39–42. cf. LG, 32.

25 Cf. LG, 4, 12. The Second Vatican Council classified these gifts as hierarchical and charismatic. In commenting on the gifts of members, the Council pointed out that "these gifts were not only extraordinary 'like speaking in tongues' but also simple gifts" lived out by disciples in daily life. Teaching children how to pray, communicating faith to children, being a healing, consoling presence to others, giving encouragement, promoting peace and justice are just a few simple gifts though most would agree that how they are concretized can be well described as "extraordinary" happenings in people's lives. The Council's recognition that disciples can receive gifts of the Spirit independently of the sacraments and the ministries of the Church is of singular importance.

26 LG, 12.

27 Roy Anderson, *The Soul of Ministry*, p. 134.

28 The recognition that all are called to ministry through baptism requires new language to distinguish the nature of different commitments that arise out of baptism. For disciples called to embrace a vowed life in community, terms such

as "Consecrated life, " "religious life" no longer give a clear idea of the nature of this commitment since all disciples are anointed in baptism, all consecrated to God in baptism, all called to holiness.

29 Avery Dulles, *Models of the Church*, p. 233.

30 Werner Schwartz, "Baptism, Ecclesiology and Vocation." Letter from Christ to the World: An Exploration of the Role of the Laity in the Church Today, Nicholas Apostola, ed. Geneva: WCC Publications, 1998, p. 90.

Ron Rolheiser, O.M.I., in an article entitled "Praying for Pentecost in Exile," suggests that tendencies that militate against disciples of Jesus living gospel values to the full are continuous watching of television game shows, sitcoms, sporting events etc. Not that these in themselves are bad, but that they numb us to the larger issues crying out for justice in the world. *The Catholic Register* (June 18, 2001): 19.

31 Godlind Bilke, "Formation of the Laos." *A Letter from Christ to the World: An Exploration of the Role of the Laity in the Church Today*, Nicholas Apostola, ed, Geneva: WCC Publications, 1998, pp. 70, 71.

32 Jerome Murphy-O'Connor, "Eucharist and Community in First Corinthians." Worship Vol. 50 (September 1976): 378.

33 LG, 13.

34 Richard R. Gaillardetz, "Church as Communion Universal and Local." *Church*, Vol. 13, no. 3 (Fall 1997): 8.

35 See chapters 5 and 6; cf. Marianne Race, Laurie Brink, *In This Place: Reflections on the Land of the Gospels for the Liturgical Cycles*, pp. 185, 186.

36 Roy S. Anderson, *The Soul of Ministry*, p. 134.

37 Joan Patricia Back, "Baptism, Ecclesiology and Vocation." *Letter from Christ to the World: An Exploration of the Role of the Laity in the Church Today*, Nicholas Apostola, ed. Geneva: WCC Publications, 1998, p. 102.

38 Johann B. Metz, "For a New Church: A Concept in Four Theses." *Toward Vatican III: The Work That Needs to Be Done*, David Tracy, Hans Kung, Johann B. Metz, eds. New York: Concilium, The Seabury Press, 1978, p. 139.

39 Parish and Diocesan Councils, Diocesan Synods and Committees are some avenues of participation presently available in the church. Participation in a community of equal disciples involves disciples' involvement in the total life of the church. See endnotes 41 and 43 below.

40 Cf. chapters 5 and 6.

41 Ladislas Orsy, "New Era of Participation in Church Life." *Origins* 17 (28 April 1988): 797–799. Orsy notes that "two shifts in the life of the church contributed to the loss of this practice. One was the shift in emphasis from the sacrament of baptism to that of orders; the other, the process of centralization which developed after the Reformation." p. 799. The Second Vatican Council in chapter 2 of the Constitution on the Church noted that all belong to the Church by equal right (LG, 9). Participation logically follows. As noted in Chapters 2 and 4 of the

Constitution on the Church all the faithful share in the apostolic work of the Church. Through their baptism and confirmation all are commissioned to that apostolate by the Lord himself (LG, 12, 30, 31).

42　Robert A. Ludwig, *Reconstructing Catholicism*, p. 124. Ludwig notes that the diversity of gifts and ministries is causing a crisis in the church not because the gifts aren't needed but because so much has been put into the primacy of priestly ministry that frustration abounds, especially in women, who generally speaking are not allowed to speak in church today.

43　According to Ladislas Orsy participation is not a democracy where decisions are based on a tally of 50% +1. This is not a pastor using a parish council for consultation only. Neither is it a bishop using a diocesan pastoral council or synod in this way, nor members of councils at any level insisting that a pastor or bishop must not disregard a proposition of the council or the synod. Rather, the process towards being of one mind and heart is radically different and requires prayerful discernment. "New Era of Participation in Church Life," p. 799.

44　LG, 10.

45　LG, chapters 2 and 4.

46　LG, 9.

47　LG, 10.

48　Daniel Cere, "Priests, Prophets, and Kings: Towards a High Doctrine of the Lay Vocation." *The Rambler*, Montreal: Newman Institute of Catholic Studies, 1999, p. 8.

49　Cf. LG, 56–59, 61. The Council described Mary as an associate of Christ. Pope John Paul II discusses this title given to Mary in his encyclical Mother of the Redeemer, MR, 39.

　　Through the centuries popes and theologians have written extensively on Mary as the model priest. At the beginning of the 20th century, all devotion to Mary as priest was banned. See John Wijngaards, "The Priesthood of Mary." *The Tablet*, vol. 253, 4 (December, 1999): 1638–1640. See also John Samaha, S.M., "Mary's priestly dimension." *The Month* (May 2000): 184–189. Both authors provide an historical overview of the development of this devotion. In his article, Samaha discusses Mary's priestly role as an associate of Christ.

50　Cf. chapter 2. Rethinking our own call to be "servants of God, a servant church" will be considered in Chapter 8.

51　Daniel Cere, PhD., "Priests, Prophets, and Kings." p. 10.

52　LG, 10. Cf. Acts 2:42, 47; Rom 12:1; 1 Pt 2:4,5.

53　LG, 10 quoting from encyclical letters of Popes Pius XI and XII. Guerric of Igny in the twelfth century noted that "the priest does not consecrate alone; nor does he offer alone: the whole assembly of believers consecrates and offers Jesus to God." Sermo 5, PL 85, 87 quoted by J.M.R. Tillard, O.P. in "Recognition of ministries: What is the real question?" *One in Christ* (1985–1): 33.

The Catechism of the Catholic Church in speaking of celebrants of "liturgy" notes that it is "the whole community, the Body of Christ united with its Head, that celebrates." (No. 1140)

54 LG, 61; MR, 39.

55 LG, 62.

56 LG, 56; 61. Cf. MR, 39.

57 LG, 10, 12. Cf. 1 Pt 3:15.

58 MR, 35-37.

59 Dimitri Sala, "Releasing the Power of the Spirit," p. 466.

60 Cf. LG, 36-38.

61 Cf. LG, 31.

62 "The distinction between clergy and lay is an unfortunate historical development in Christianity. It led to a double-standard of discipleship: those who were really called to follow Christ, to represent him, and to embody his ministry and mission; and the merely baptized, who are totally dependent on those who represent and embody Christ to broker their salvation. No such distinction can be found in the New Testament. Ordination is a community designation of ministry function and a celebration of the ordained's charism. It is a further specification of one's baptismal commitment. But it is not becoming 'more than' or 'higher than' or 'over' other members in the community." Robert A. Ludwig, *Reconstructing Catholicism*, p. 125. According to Thomas O'Meara, this movement to distinguish between clergy and laity had begun by the third century. "Ministry became priesthood and was grafted on to canonical position." Thomas O'Meara, *Theology of Ministry*, p. 47.

63 The call of the individual disciple to live like Mary, bringing Jesus into the world was discussed in Chapter 4, part II.

64 LG, 1, 37, 38. Cf. Joan Patricia Back, "Baptism, Ecclesiology and Vocation: A Catholic Perspective," *A Letter from Christ to the World*, p. 102.

Chapter 8
The Annunciation–Visitation Motif in the Life of the Church

1 Chapter 8 considers the church, a community of equal disciples in the local church (parish), a microcosm of the universal church where unity in diversity is operative.

2 The responsibility of hearing the word of God and putting it into practice belongs to the whole community, not just the individual disciple. This is in keeping with the vision of Vatican II that the word of God emerges within the whole Church. All the faithful must be learners and teachers. GS, 44,62. Cf. chapters 4 and 6.

3   Cf. LG, 35; DV, 8; GS, 4.

Pope John Paul II in speaking about the relationship between Mary's prayerful, pondering heart in relation to Jesus notes that the church is committed to preserve the word of God, investigate its richness with discernment and prayer to bear witness to Christ before all humankind. MR, 43.

4   "Lord" as a title for Jesus is rarely used today. When applied to God, it suggests that God is male, or can be best visualized as male. This, of course, is not true. Until God can be addressed in more inclusive language, this title will be avoided by many Christians when speaking about God. Cf. *The Collegeville Pastoral Dictionary of Biblical Theology*, pp. 564–567.

5   Ibid., pp. 933–936.

6   Cf. Richard Bergeron, "The Kerygma to Non-Practicing Persons," Lecture given at the University of Montreal, Canada, 1992.

7   Elizabeth A. Johnson, C.S.J., *Consider Jesus*, p. 6.

8   Sean Freyne, *The World of the New Testament*, p. 183.

9   Raymond Brown notes that "the Paraclete (Spirit) preserves the past without corruption because all is received from Jesus and gives no new revelation. Yet, the Paraclete is a living teacher who does not just repeat a tradition from a dead past. Dwelling in the heart of each Christian, the Spirit will contemporize it in each period and in each place, thus enabling Christians to face the things to come. Raymond E. Brown, S.S., *The Churches the Apostles Left Behind*, pp. 107, 108. "For Mark: Jesus is the suffering Messiah. For Matthew: he is the new Moses, teacher of the new law. For Luke: Jesus, filled with the Holy Spirit, is saviour of all. For John: Jesus is the Word of God made flesh. For Paul: Jesus is the crucified and risen Christ. These varied statements about Jesus showed their concern to express who Jesus was in language that was meaningful to each community with its differing needs and problems to be addressed." Elizabeth A. Johnson, C.S.J., *Consider Jesus*, p. 6.

10 GS, 44, 62; DV, 8. Cf. Lk 1:39-59; Acts 2:11.

11 Charles Kannengieser, "A Call to Conversion." *Unity: A Publication of Benedict Labre House of Hospitality*, Vol. 36, No. 3 (Spring, 1993): 6.

12 Pope John Paul II, "God gradually reveals his fatherhood." General Audience, Wednesday, January 13, 1999, *L'Osservatore Romano*, No. 3 (January 20, 1999): 11.

13 Ibid., p. 11.

14 Elizabeth A. Johnson in her book *Consider Jesus* points out the need for rephrasing doctrines about Jesus' nature as God and man in terminology of our day. Drawing on the reflections of theologians such as Edward Schillebeeckx she proposes that the idea that Jesus is the Word of God might be better expressed by describing him as the parable of God. He did not just tell parables but he is the story that God is telling the world (pp. 62, 63).

Johnson also suggests that Jesus Christ, Liberator, evokes a new image of God, who is on the side of the oppressed with the aim to free them. In naming Jesus

"Liberator" Johnson says we are "committing ourselves personally and as church to enter with Christ into the struggle for justice." (Consider Jesus, pp. 93, 94.) Leonardo Boff picks up this same theme. "Perhaps," he says, "a suitable description of Jesus would be Liberator of a consciousness oppressed by sin and all alienations and Liberator of the sad human condition in its relationships with the world, the other, and God." Leonardo Boff, *Jesus Christ Liberator, A Critical Christology for Our Times*, Maryknoll, NY: Orbis, 1981, p. 240.

15   As important as the ministry of preaching is in the life of a priest, "such one-way communication does not maintain the community's faith. The dilemmas faced today are problems of the entire community, requiring communal reflection on the implications of their faith in relation to present circumstances." Michael Warren, "Speaking and Learning in the Local Church: A Look at the Material Conditions." *Worship*, Vol. 69, No. 1 (January 1995): 50.

16   Pierre Babin, O.M.I., in a talk given to the Canadian Conference of Catholic Bishops pointed out that faith must be presented in terms of goods – salvation, healing – rather than in terms of truth. He noted that faith built on the awakening of the inner self (the spiritual) will remain strong. Faith based solely on catechetical teaching will waver. "To evangelize," he said, "is to make friends and invite them to the wedding feast (Mt 22:14)." Pierre Babin, O.M.I., "The Church and Social Communications." Address to the Canadian Conference of Catholic Bishops, Ottawa, 1999.

17   LG, 5.

18   Cf. Chapter 6.

19   Cf. Chapter 6.

20   Rom 10:9-18. Cf. chapters 4 and 6.

21   Pope Paul VI, *Evangelization in the Modern World*, EN, 46.

22   LG, 64, 65; The Council notes that all who join in the Church's apostolic mission should be animated with the same motherly love as Mary. Cf. MR, 40. Pope John Paul, elaborating on Mary's motherhood, notes that Mary brings to the Upper Room at Pentecost the "new motherhood" which became her part at the foot of the cross. This motherhood remains hers but on Pentecost it is transferred from her as a "model" to the whole Church. LE, 21.

23   Cf. chapters 4 and 6.

24   Cf. Acts 9:2; 22:4

25   MR, 35.

26   Ibid., 37.

27   Johann Roten, S.M., "The 'Merciless' Magnificat." *The Mary Page*, Meditations, www.udayton.edu/mary/meditations.

28   Cf. Acts 2:37; 3:19; Lk 2: 34-35.

29   Cf. Chapter 6.

30   Viz., scientists engaged in the evolution of technology; medical researchers discovering new medicines to help heal illnesses; people's growing sense of

responsibility for the environment; the movement to solidarity and reconciliation among people in South Africa; women in war torn countries, such as Palestine and Israel, on opposite sides of the political divide uniting their efforts to bond together to seek peace for their people; caregivers for the elderly, for people with AIDS; people dying of cancer in palliative care units.

Pope John Paul II also notes the emerging gifts of laity, the rise of new faith communities in the Church, a deepening Christian unity, reconciliation with our Orthodox sisters and brothers, dialogue with other religions, and with contemporary culture as signs of the Spirit at work. Pope John Paul II, "Apostolic Letter in Preparation for the Jubilee Year 2000," 46.

31 Cf. Chapter 6.

32 Cf. Chapter 7.

33 GS, 1.

34 Johannes B. Metz, "For a Renewed Church Before a New Council: A Concept in Four Theses," p. 141.

35 I have chosen to express the "basileia" of God, usually translated as "kingdom" by the term "kindom" used by many theologians today to offset the patriarchal, hierarchical structure implicit in the word kingdom. Jesus' outreach to people, communicating the love, tenderness, compassion, mercy, justice of God was relational. He was about wholeness and inclusion. The word "kingdom" highlights rank, differences, and inequality. For further reading, see Diarmid O'Murchu, *Religion in Exile*, New York: Crossroad Publishing Company, 2000, pp. 121–124.

36 Johann B. Metz, "For a Renewed Church Before a New Council," p. 141.

37 Cf. Chapter 8, "Sharing the Story of Jesus Today."

Pope Paul VI in his encyclical *On Evangelization in the Modern World* makes it clear that evangelization, sharing the good news about Jesus, cannot be separated from the struggle for justice, development, peace, and liberation for all people in the world. EN, 31. Today, we are aware that beyond these concerns, evangelization, the good news about Jesus, cannot be separated from justice for planet earth.

In its document on the Pastoral Constitution of the Church in the Modern World, the Council acknowledged that the Church has much to learn from the world's accomplishments. In this way, the church will enter into dialogue with the world to find solutions to modern-day problems. GS, 3, 92.

38 In recent years, the refusal by some consumers in Western countries to buy products made by Nike and Liz Claiborne, companies that were identified as exploiting workers in Third World countries, led these companies to make changes in their policies.

39 Cf. Chapter 6.

40 Sometime ago I happened on these words of an Aboriginal Australian Woman but I do not know their source. She is quoted as saying, "If you have come to help me, you are wasting your time; if you have come because your liberation is

bound up with mine, come let us work together." In my opinion her message is applicable to any ministry.

41 MR, 37.

42 Rosemary Radforth Reuther, *Sexism and God-Talk*, pp. 154–157.

43 Cf. GS, 46; Augusta Neal, S.N.D. de Namur, "The Magnificat and the Economy." *Sisters Today*, Vol. 56, No. 3 (November 1984): 133.

44 This observation was made in 1987 by the World Commission on Environment and Development, Our Common Futures, Oxford, England, Oxford University Press, p. 4 quoted in *Cry of the Earth, Cry of the Poor*, The Social Affairs Committee, Assemblée des évéques du Québec, Message May 1, 2001. Recently community workers on both sides of the continent made the same observation in commenting on the protests in which they were involved in Seattle, Washington (November, 2000) and at the Summit of the Americas (April, 2001) Quebec City, Canada. *The Gazette*, Montreal, Canada (June 13, 2001): 1

45 *Cry of the Earth, Cry of the Poor*, p. 2.

46 Pope John Paul II, "Respect for Human Rights: The Secret of True Peace." Message for the Celebration of the World Day of Peace, January 1, 1999. The United Nations designated the year 2000 as an "international year of the culture of peace." In its Manifesto 2000, the United Nations called the world community to respect the life and dignity of each human being; to practice nonviolence; share time and material resources so as to put an end to exclusion, injustice and oppression; defend freedom of expression and cultural diversity; give preference always to listening and dialogue; contribute to the development of community in order to create new forms of solidarity. Situations worldwide show that a culture of peace requires long term good will on the part of all people, governments and corporations.

47 Elise Boulding, "Peace Culture: The Problem of Managing Human Difference." *Cross Currents*, Winter (1998/99): 446. Boulding notes that by contrast, the holy war culture is a male-warrior construct based on the exercise of power. This culture typically demands the subjection of women, children, and the weak to men. This social structure of patriarchy continues to mold generations of the major religious traditions - Hinduism, Buddhism, Judaism, Christianity, Islam.

48 Ibid., p. 457.

49 "Fostering of Peace and Establishment of a Community of Nations." GS, 77–93.

50 Cf. "The Blessed Virgin Mary, Queen of Peace." *Collection of Masses of the Blessed Virgin Mary*, pp. 289–291.

51 Recent brain research shows that the right brain specializes in intuition, musical, relational and spacial capacities and the left brain is linguistic and mathematical thinking. Both men and women possess these. Rosemary Radford Ruether, *Sexism and God-Talk*, p. 11.

52   Throughout this book I have maintained that Mary as the archetype of Christian discipleship holds together the inner-outer life of discipleship for women and men. Earlier I noted the impact that Hans Urs von Balthasar's identification of the Marian Principle has had on the thinking of Pope John Paul II. Mary in this theology is subject to the authority of Peter. She is kept as the model of the interior life of men and women called to be the bride of her Son. The purpose of the Church represented in its maleness by Peter and his successors is to educate its members to such a womanly role. This theology relegates Mary to the inner realm, the private sphere of life and prevents women from being full and equal partners in the church. "This dualistic thinking also supports a secular culture that divides the symbolically feminine religious world of the intimate self linked to church, family, friends and school, described as the spirituality of interiority, from the symbolically masculine techno-scientific world of mass society, with its centralized and bureaucratized heavy institutions, implicitly described as the non-spirituality of exteriority." Cf. Joe Holland, "As cultural world turns, spirit is turning, too." *National Catholic Reporter* (October 28, 1989): 10. Maria Riley, O.P. notes that the most critical issue in Catholic social theology is the understanding of human nature. She notes that references to women in the documents always carry a rider (the women's role in accordance with their nature, women's proper role) but they never speak of men this way. "All Issues Are Women's Issues." Scarboro Mission, (January, 1996): 8.

53   Cf. Elizabeth A. Johnson, C.S.J., "The Maleness of Christ." *The Power of Naming: A Concilium Reader in Feminist Liberation Theology*, Maryknoll, NY: Orbis, 1996, pp. 312–314. In Chapter 7, I discussed the equality of men and women that arises from baptism where all are clothed with Christ (Gal 3:28).

54   Roy S. Anderson, *The Soul of Ministry*, p. 143.

55   Rosemary Radford Ruether, *Sexism and God-Talk*, p. 191–192.

56   Roy S. Anderson, *The Soul of Ministry*, p. 201.

57   Cf. Robert K. Greenleaf, *Servant Leadership: A Journey into the Nature of Legitimate Power and Greatness*, New York/Mahwah: Paulist Press, 1991, p. 239.

58   Ladislas Orsy points out that the historical evidence of lay persons participating in decision-making processes in the church is overwhelming. Like participation in the church, this is not a new fad. He notes that some earlier ecumenical councils permitted lay persons to be voting members. "Surely," he writes, "this was not a doctrinal deviation. It seems to follow that lay people could be voting members of synods or councils." "Lay Persons in Church Governance? A Disputed Question." America (April 6, 1996): 10–13.

59   Cf. Werner Schwartz, "Baptism, Ecclesiology and Vocation," p. 95.

60   Ibid., p. 89.

61   See "Servant." *The Collegeville Pastoral Dictionary of Biblical Theology*, Caroll Stuhlmueller, ed., Collegeville, MN: The Liturgical Press, 1996, p. 899.

62 Cf. Chapter 2. For Paul, being a "servant of God" leads to disciples' freedom as God's sons and daughters, heirs with Christ, who filled with the Spirit of Jesus in our hearts cry Abba! Father! (Gal 4:6-7).

63 Ellen M. Leonard, C.S.J., "Footwashing: A Pattern for Discipleship." Talk given at the Newman Chapel, University of Toronto, (April 1, 1997): 10. Leonard shows how the notion of servant in imitation of Jesus served also to keep black people in bondage. In Chapter 2, I pointed out how Mary as "servant of the Lord" was misused to keep women in a subservient relationship with their husbands and with the church represented in the clergy. But "in the Liturgy, 'servant' is our common vocation in faith as well as the communion signified and celebrated in the Eucharist." *The Collegeville Pastoral Dictionary*, p. 900.

64 Cf. Chapter 7.

65 David S. Young, *Servant Leadership for Church Renewal*, p. 39. In Chapter 1 I pointed out that women and men were called by God to be both "servants and apostles" in the world (Rom 1:1; 16:1-2; 1 Cor 3:5). Unfortunately, the understanding of ministry in the church moved from the service of disciples to one another to become the privilege and responsibility of the clergy (bishops, priests, and deacons) creating two distinct groups in the church, the clergy who ministered and the laity who were ministered to. See Chapter 7.

66 GS, 3, 92. Cf. Mk 10:45; Mt 20:28; Lk 22:27.

67 Ellen M. Leonard, C.S.J., "Footwashing: A Pattern for Disicpleship," p. 13. Two thousand years of history have shown that the equality among women and men as "servants of God," so evident at Pentecost and in the primitive church, was soon lost as the hierarchical clerical structure took root.

68 David S. Young, *Servant Leadership for Church Renewal*, p. 135.

69 Barbara E. Bowe, R.S.C.J., "John 13 and Christian Service." *The Bible Today* (July 1994): 227.

70 Cf. H. W. Beyer, "Diakone" in G. Kittel, *Theological Dictionary of the New Testament*, Vol. 2, Grand Rapids, MI: Eerdmans, 1964, p. 92.

71 The discussion on the Magnificat has focused mainly on the larger issues facing the church in the world. The Magnificat also finds expression in the outreach of the community to help parents stand by and support pregnant teenagers, children carried away by drugs and alcohol; support of adults who care for elderly parents; husbands or wives whose spouses and/or children are ill; as well as comforting the dying; extending shelter to the homeless; providing food, drink, and clothing for those in need; visiting the sick, the dying, the lonely, prisoners; to name a few areas where the community can and does lend a hand.

72 We need only remember martyrs of recent years such as Archbishop Romero, Ita Ford M.M., Maura Clarke M.M., Dorothy Kazel O.S.U., Jean Donovan, the six Jesuits, their housekeeper, and her daughter who were murdered in El Salvador and the countless heros and heroines around the world who have dared to speak

out against the injustices their people experienced at the hands of ruthless government powers.

73   This interpretation is of recent origin. In earlier years, the image of the woman clothed with the sun (Rev 12:1-2) was applied to Mary. This woman, whose son is snatched up to heaven and who is pursued by the dragon into the wilderness, was seen to represent the new Israel, the Christian Church. *The Collegeville Pastoral Dictionary*, p. 595.

74   Andrew M. Britz, O.S.B., "Are We Willing to Sing Alleluia in Today's World?" *Catholic New Times* (9 May 1999): 3. He points out that "a church that is better at pointing out sin than it is at enabling its members to dream that great dream, at freeing them to discover the reign of God in each new age and culture, is missing the heart of its calling."

75   Ron Lewinski, "The Church in the New Millennium." *Modern Liturgy* (November 1997): 9.

76   Ibid., p. 12.

77   Pope John Paul II, *Called and Gifted for the Third Millennium*, 43.

78   Pope John Paul II, Apostolic Letter "Lay Members of Christ's Faithful People," CL, 4.

79   William Farley quoted in *The Spirituality of Work: Business People*, William Droel, Chicago, IL: ACTA Publications, p. 59.

80   Ibid., p. 1.

Chapter 9
The Ongoing Transformation of Adult Disciples

1   Cf. chapters 4, 5, 6. The same can be said for all disciples in the gospels, be they the women of Luke 8, the Twelve, Mary Magdalene at the tomb of Jesus, the disciples on the road to Emmaus in the post-resurrection accounts in the gospels of their meetings with Jesus.

2   Today, small dynamic faith-sharing communities of disciples exist in the church around the world offering support and encouragement to women and men struggling to live their faith in cultures that are becoming more and more adverse to the values of peace, justice, and mercy that the gospel offers. Cf. Lay Members of Christ's Faithful, CL, 26. Small faith-sharing groups can provide a response to many Christians yearning for spirituality, places where they can share their stories, honour their faith experience, struggles, and doubts that the sterility and anonymity of large church gatherings cannot be sensitive to except in a very general way. These small groups are possibly a response to today's yearning for spirituality that is leading many Christians to New Age groups. These faith groups could incorporate Yoga and Tai Chi as a means of creating inner space essential to listening deeply to God's Word. The community will also be faced with creating circles of faith for different age groups. How to respect those who do not wish

to take part and not make them feel like second class citizens will be an ongoing challenge.

3   Avery Dulles notes that many deprived of such contacts see the church as an impersonal, hierarchical institution set over against them not mutual support and stimulation. Avery Dulles, *Models of the Church*, p. 218. A community of disciples will need to find creative ways of reaching out to many in the community whose work schedules, young children, age, or sickness prevent them from taking part in faith communities. Nurturing the domestic church so young families may share faith and reflect on the gospel at home while following the calendar of the church year could be of great help. With careful preparation, the celebration of the Eucharist could include time for reflection, and disciples sharing with one another and with the community ways the gospel of the day touches their lives. I saw this happen in a church in Tegucigalpa, Honduras. But then these men and women didn't seem to have their eyes on a clock, expecting to be out of the church in one hour. In some areas of Europe, basic communities take their turn to prepare the homily out of their reflection on the Sunday's gospel, then invite the whole community gathered to enter into dialogue on the gospel.

4   Avery Dulles, S.J., *A Church to Believe In*, p. 32.

5   Josep M. Rovira Belloso, "Discernment of Spirits: Who Is Capable of Discerning?" *Concilium*, New York: The Seabury Press, 1979, pp. 91, 92.

6   My closest experience of a local church being transformed into parishes that were becoming structured as a community of communities took place during the Renew Program in the English-speaking parishes of the Archdiocese of Montreal, Canada in the late 80s, early 90s, and in the months that followed its completion. Unfortunately, the process halted when a diocesan synod took precedence. The present merging of parishes and the sale of church properties in Montreal and other cities in North America now in process run the risk of creating even larger, impersonal parishes.

7   The Church as "communion" connects well with Paul's imagery of the church as the body of Christ. "In Rom. 12; and 1 Cor. 12 the main point is the mutual union, mutual concern, and mutual dependence of the members of the local community." Avery Dulles, *Models of the Church*, Expanded Edition, New York: Image Books/Doubleday, 1987, p. 50.

8   Walter Kasper, *Theology and Church*, New York: Crossroad, 1989, p. 152.

9   Cf. CL, 24.

10 LG, 11.

11 LG, 50.

12 Elizabeth A. Johnson, C.S.J., "Toward a Theology of Mary," p. 29. Cf. Chapter 8.

13 GS, 92; 56:1.

14 Conflict was part of the Jerusalem community as disagreements arose concerning the distribution of food to Greek widows (Acts 6:1ff); the struggle over Peter

eating unclean food with Gentiles (Acts 11:2); and the conflict over whether or not Gentile men converts should be subjected to circumcision (Acts 15). See Chapter 7.

15 One could say that this characteristic is evident in Mary and Elizabeth at the Visitation. These women had come to a profound reconciliation in their personal lives about who they were and their worth. Both rejected the view of women that rose from a patriarchal society and religion that diminished their worth and their value. Both women saw themselves in God's eyes, trusting unconditionally in God's presence and love in their lives.

16 Cf. Chapter 5.

17 John Shea, "Forgiveness and Reconciliation." *Called to Be Christian: Grounding Spirituality in Sacrament, Community and Scripture*, Chicago, IL: Acta Publications, 1998, Audio Tape 3.

18 My emphasis here is on the behaviour of a community of equal disciples that follows Jesus in Mary's footsteps. An ideal to be hoped for. But a major conflict, one of many that Christians face today, arises from different visions of the church. This is not only a North American phenomenon. Those who support a community of equal disciples in various parts of the world are faced constantly with a seemingly entrenched hierarchical structure. Efforts and suggestions that a change in the present way the church is structured would enhance not diminish communal life in the church and its presence in the world are often stifled with the argument that the church is not a democracy. Those who carry the vision of the church as a community of equal disciples are suffering. Yet, disciples who seek a community of equal disciples know that those for whom the status quo works also suffer. The ideal would be for people of both visions to enter into prayerful dialogue. Unfortunately, the will to enter into the demands of such a process seems to be lacking on both sides.

19 GS, 28. Cf. Lk 6:37-38; Mt 7:1-11; 14:10-12.

20 Bernard J. Cooke, "We Have the Power." *Religion Teacher's Journal* (April–May 1987): 2:28.

21 Certainly, in these times, we can take courage from the efforts made at reconciliation in South Africa as it tried to rise above Apartheid; in Rwanda from mass genocide; in North America between aboriginal people and their white oppressors. In the church we can take heart from Pope John Paul's confession of past sins on the part of the church against the people of Israel, the dignity of women and the unity of the human race, and of sins related to the fundamental rights of the human person, made public on the First Sunday of Lent 2000. More recently we can take courage from his confession of sins against the Orthodox Church, and his visit to the Ummayed mosque in Damascus, May 2001. Both efforts of Pope John Paul have opened the door to much needed reconciliation between and among peoples, a reconciliation that must take root in all our hearts. Cf. GS no. 28.

22 LG, 68.

23 Cf. chapters 4, 6.

24 LG, 58, 63, 65; MR, 25, 28, 42.

25 Jean-Marie Tillard, O.P., points out that the Greek word for bishop signifies his responsibility to ensure that the great grace of God's visit made in Jesus Christ is kept visible in and through the Christian community. See his book *Je crois en dépit de tout*, Paris: Les Éditions du Cerf, 2001, p. 27.

26 See "Letter to All God's People." *A Letter from Christ to the World*, Nicholas Apostola, ed., Geneva: WCC Publications, 1998, pp. 143–145.

27 Robert A. Ludwig, *Reconstructing Catholicism*, p. 203.

28 Cf. Chapter 4.

29 Walter Kasper, *Theology and Church*, New York: Crossroad, 1989, p. 157.

30 In this sense, what is happening in the church is part of the major thresholds people throughout the world are facing as the world enters a new age of consciousness unknown in the history of humankind brought on by the technological revolution.

31 LG, 1, 2. This same message has been repeated again and again in the various encyclicals, apostolic letters of the recent popes and reports following the many synods held since Vatican II.

Conclusion

1 See Chapter 8, endnote 22.

2 Pope Paul VI, Discourse given to the College of Bishops, November 21/64, AAS 56 (1964), 1015.

3 LG, 63; MR, 43. Cf. Herbert Richardson, "Mother of the Church." *The Current* 5 (1965): 48–61.

4 Ibid., p. 51. Adapted in the context of Church, a community of equal disciples.

5 Elizabeth A. Johnson, C.S.J., "Toward a Theology of Mary," pp. 28–29.

6 St. Augustine, in a Sermon on Mary, noted that through her God, in becoming human in Jesus, overturned the pyramid, placing God at the base, taking onto God everything and everyone. God becoming one with us in Jesus affirmed the sacredness of all humanity and creation was affirmed. St. Augustine, *Sermons on Mary*, No. 72, 189, 3(PL 38, 1006). Cf. Jn 1:14; Phil 2:6.

7 See Johannes B. Metz, "For a Renewed Church Before a Council: A Concept in Four Theses," pp. 142–143.

8 Raymond Brown, S.S., *The Churches the Apostles Left Behind*, pp. 40–41.

Reflection Questions for Individuals or Small Groups

These questions are offered to help you integrate the material in each chapter. As such, they do not cover all possibilities for reflection. They are presented knowing that the reader's personal reflection on the content chapter-by-chapter is the most important.

If these questions are used in small faith-sharing groups, I suggest that the format already used in many Christian communities be followed:

- Invitation to pause and enter more deeply into the presence of God
- Reading of the question aloud (a section of a chapter could also be read)
- Time for reflection
- Invitation to group sharing
- Invitation to act that flows from the sharing
- Closing prayer giving thanks to God: for each other, for faith and insights shared, challenges met, desires expressed, commitments taken.

Whatever way you choose to use these questions, may your reflection lead you deeper into living life from the centre of your being, mindful that attentive listening to the spirit evident in Mary and the disciples in the Upper Room must inhabit our hearts.

Chapter 1

1. A major portion of Chapter 1 focuses on the impact that scriptural silence about Mary and the women disciples' presence and active involvement in the community after Pentecost has had on the life of the Church. How does this resonate with your experience?

2. How do you receive the suggestion that the Church needs a renewed image of discipleship that can speak to the reality of men and women trying to live out their commitment as disciples of Jesus in today's continually evolving complex world?

3. What has been your experience of Mary, the mother of Jesus, within your Christian tradition?

4. What significance does Mary have for you at this point in your life?

5. How do you receive the suggestion that we look for a renewed image of discipleship for Christian women and men and for the church as a community of equal disciples in the biblical memory of Mary, the mother of Jesus?

Chapter 2

1. Reread the Annunciation story, putting your name in place of Mary's. What did you experience as you did this? How did you feel? What was your response?

2. What is your experience of being loved personally, favoured by God? How do you name God's love for you?

3. When in your life have you lived in faith, trusting that "nothing is impossible with God"?

4. Identify moments of Annunciation in your life:
   - joy-filled moments
   - pain-filled moments
   - leaps of faith

5. When have you been called, like Mary, to move beyond social expectations, outside the status quo? What did it feel like for you?

6. Ponder the Visitation from Elizabeth's side – a woman pregnant after years of barrenness.

There are moments in life, whether we have given birth to a child or not, when we all feel barren. What have been those moments in your life? How did you feel? How did you ride out the time?

7. Like Mary and Elizabeth in the Annunciation–Visitation, we carry things unborn in our hearts. We have ideas, hopes, and dreams that we long to bring to birth.

What are your ideas, your hopes, your dreams?

What would waiting patiently as they take shape in you, are readied for birth, be like for you? How would you recognize when the time has come to give birth?

8. Reread prayerfully the section on the Magnificat.

What challenges does the Magnificat bring into your life at this time?

Creative Writing

Ponder a picture of the Annunciation. Write a dialogue between you and Mary about her experience.

- Use your dominant hand to ask her questions.

- Use your non-dominant hand to write what you hear Mary say to you.

Mary stayed with Elizabeth for three months.

Write a dialogue between Elizabeth, an older, experienced pregnant woman, and Mary, a pregnant teenager. Both women carried promises of hope for their children, for themselves.

Chapter 3

1. This chapter points out that Mary, following the Annunciation, was evangelized through the events of her life with Jesus, leading her deeper and deeper into the mystery of her vocation as his mother. How do you receive this?

2. Identify moments in your life when "just doing your duty" brought about an unexpected experience of God for you.

3. All the figures in the infancy narratives show us what it means to walk in faith. With whom do you most identify at this time in your life?

4. Take the time to look over a recent day or week in your life.

Name the persons that stand out for you. Identify the events.
What impact did they have on you?
What joys and challenges did you meet?
How were they moments of God's visitation for you?

5. What difference would approaching life as visitation make in your life?

6. How would it affect your relationships at home, at work, in your neighbourhood, your parish? How would it affect the way you play?

Mary During Jesus' Public Ministry

1. Mark, Matthew, and Luke all include a narrative in their gospels describing Mary's encounter with her son during his public ministry and his rejection in his own hometown.

a) Which account are you more comfortable with? Why?

b) How do you receive the position taken in this chapter that Mary was confronted with major choices in her life as her vocation as Jesus' mother unfolded?

2. Looking at Mary at the wedding in Cana in light of the society in which she lived provides a different reading of this text than the one to which we are usually accustomed. How did you receive this interpretation of the text?

3. Choose other areas in this chapter that you would like to reflect on personally. What points, if any, could your faith sharing group consider together?

Chapter 4

1. Read and reflect daily on a few verses of Luke's travel account of Jesus' journey to Jerusalem (Lk 9:51–19:27). How is Jesus calling you to be his disciple today?

2. As disciples of Jesus we are called, like Mary, to listen to God's word and do it. How does that translate into your daily life?

3. Our faith journey as Christians began with our Baptism.

Take a sheet of paper, draw a line, and mark off periods in your life: e.g., childhood, adolescence, early adulthood, middle years, senior years.

Identify circumstances, events, joys, crises, moments of clarity, and times of darkness that have played a significant role in your faith journey.

   - What was your experience of God in these times?

Choose a word, phrase, or verse from scripture that best describes your relationship with God at this time.

   - How do you share your faith in God with others?

4. Reflect on the Magnificat.

   - Who are the poor and oppressed people around you?

   - Perhaps you are already trying to help them bring about change in their circumstances. If not, what steps can you take to help them bring about change in their lives?

5. Biblical justice is about being in right relationship with God, self and neighbour.

   - What does this mean for you?

   - How do you address systemic injustice if it is present in your workplace, in your neighbourhood, or in government policy?

6. Write your own Magnificat.

Chapter 5

1. How do you receive the suggestion that hidden in Acts 1:14 are Mary and the disciples' stories of coming to faith in the risen Jesus?

2. What can we learn as church today from the reflections on Mary as a woman of reconciliation?

3. What hope do the parallels Luke draws between Mary in the Annunciation–Visitation and the community of equal disciples, the Church born at Pentecost, offer to Christians living as disciples of Jesus being church in the world today?

Chapter 6

1. Take time to reflect on each section of Chapter 6.

   a) What is new for you in this reflection?

   b) What do you feel calls for further reflection and discussion?

2. Stephen in his speech before his death resists a permanent dwelling place for God (Acts 7:48-60). What does this mean for you?

3. Peter hears God say to him that nothing is profane or unclean (Acts 10:15).

What does the call for an inclusive table mean to us as church today?

4. Jesus calls us to wash one another's feet (Jn13:1-10). What barriers among people hinder the giving to and receiving from one another that this action implies?

Chapter 7

Chapter 7 proposes that Mary, as the archetype of Christian discipleship for women and men, holds the key to the transformation of the church into communities of equal disciples.

1. What excites you about this proposal?

2. What steps would your parish need to implement to become a community of equal disciples who follow Jesus in imitation of Mary?

3. Reflect on Mary as a model for Christians to live their priestly, prophetic, royal mission in Jesus' name. What impact might this have on your life? On the life of your parish?

4. How would you promote this vision of church without alienating those who prefer a certain anonymity in relation to church practice?

Chapter 8

1. Today, many Christians recognize the need for new language to express the significance of God and Jesus in their lives so that Jesus' message in the gospels can be life-giving for others.

   a) Do you share this concern?

   b) What steps are being taken in your parish and your diocese to bring this about?

   c) Do you agree with Pierre Babin's statement that "faith must be presented in terms of goods – salvation, healing rather than in terms of truths because faith based on the awakening of the inner self will endure. Faith based solely on catechetical teaching will waver."

2. Identify threads of the Magnificat that are evident in the life of your parish.

3. What steps can your parish take to make a "culture of peace" an integral part of its life?

4. How do you receive the idea that the church as a community of equal disciples following in Mary's footsteps will be a church of solidarity, a church of the poor, a church of hospitality?

5. Reflect on the section on servant leaders in the Christian community, and the section related to reclaiming our identity as "servants of God," a "servant church" in the world.

What challenges are present for you?

Chapter 9

1. Creating Upper Rooms, sacred places to assist the ongoing transformation of adult disciples links with the discussion on the call of each disciple to live life from the centre (Chapter 4).

What value do you see in forming such groups in your parish, if none exist?

2. In what way would your parish's attentiveness to the relational life of the Trinity and the principles that govern the universe – individuality, differentiation and communion – help build communion among members?

3. How do you receive the emphasis in this chapter on the communal face of sin and the need for disciples to be a community of forgiveness and reconciliation?

4. In a church of discipleship, contemplation and action cannot be separated. In what way can celebrations of the Eucharist and the sacraments foster this dimension of Christian discipleship?

5. Mary's life in visitation honours that God visits in and through life's circumstances, creation, the universe in which we live. The visitation underlines that life is a process and that major thresholds occur along life's journey.

 How would a "journey spirituality" inspired by Mary, presented to disciples in Chapter 3, and here for the church, help members to identify the faith journey of their church (parish) together?

6. This book proposes that Mary is a guide for the transformation of discipleship and church into a community of equal disciples.

    a) What appeal does this approach have for you?

    b) What thresholds would your parish and the church need to cross for this to become reality?

Bibliography

Abbott, Walter M., ed. *The Documents of Vatican II*. New York: Guild Press, 1996.

———. "Reconciliation as Widening the Circle." *New Theology Review* 12 (1999): 77–80.

Anderson, Roy S. *The Soul of Ministry: Forming Leaders for God's People*. Westminster: John Knox Press, 1997.

Arbuckle, Gerald A. *Earthing the Gospel*. Maryknoll, NY: Orbis Books, 1990.

Armstrong, Karen. *Jerusalem: One City, Three Faiths*. New York: Alfred A. Knopf, 1996.

Asa, Leland F. *The Psychology of Religious Commitment and Development*. New York: University Press of America, 1995.

Ashworth, John. "Hospitality in Luke-Acts." *The Bible Today* (September-October 1997): 300–305.

Augustine, St. *Sermons on Mary*. In *Patrologia: Series Latina*, ed. J.P. Migne, 72A, 189, 3 (Pl38, 1006). Paris, 1865.

Avron, Robert. *The Jewish Jesus*. Maryknoll, NY: Orbis Books, 1971.

Azzarello, Marie, CND. *Reflection on Instruction in the Writings of Marguerite Bourgeoys and Her Contemporaries: Implications for Today*. Montreal: Congregation of Notre Dame, 1993.

———. *Mary, Teacher of the Apostles, Builder of the Church: An Historical Overview*. Unpublished research available for review at the Marguerite Bourgeoys Centre, Montreal (1993).

———. "Mary and the Women Who Risked Following Jesus to and beyond the Cross: A Paradigm for Today." *Grail* (June 1996): 84–96.

Babin, Pierre, OMI. *The Church and Social Communications*. Address to the Plenary Assembly of the Canadian Conference of Catholic Bishops. (Ottawa: October 18, 1999).

Back, Joan P. "Baptism, Ecclesiology and Vocation: A Catholic Perspective." In *A Letter from Christ to the World: An Exploration of the Role of the Laity in the Church Today*, ed. Nicholas Apostola, 98–103. Geneva: WCC Publications, 1998.

Barr, David L. *Reading the New Testament as Story: The Three Worlds of the Text*. 2d ed. Belmont, CA: Wadsworth, 1995.

Barrose, Thomas. "The Johannine Relationship of Love to Faith." In *A Companion to John: Readings in Johannine Theology*, ed. Michael. J. Taylor. New York: Alba House, 1977.

Barta, Karen A. "On Being an Apostle." *The Bible Today* (May 1995): 153–159.

Baskin, Judith R., ed. *Jewish Women in Historical Perspective*. Detroit, MI: Wayne State University Press, 1991.

Bearsley, Patrick, SM. "Mary, the Perfect Disciple: A Paradigm for Mariology." *Theological Studies* 41 (1980): 461–504.

Beattie, Tina. *Rediscovering Mary: Insights from the Gospels*. Liguori, MO: Triumph, 1995.

Bergeron, Richard. "The Kerygma to Non-Practising Persons." Lecture given at the University of Montreal (January 1992).

de Bérulle, Cardinal. *Ouevres Completes du Cardinal Bérulle*. 2 vols. Paris: Antoine Estienne & Sebastien Huse, 1644; reprinted Montsoult Seine & Oise, Maison de l'Instruction de l'Oratoire, 1960.

Bilgalke, Godlind. "Formation of the Laos." *A Letter from Christ to the World: An Exploration of the Role of the Laity in the Church Today*, ed. Nicholas Apostola, 58–71. Geneva: WCC Publications, 1998.

Boff, Leonardo. *Jesus Christ, Liberator: A Critical Theology for Our Time*. Maryknoll, NY: Orbis Books, 1981.

Boulding, Elise. "Peace Culture: The Problem of Managing Differences." *Cross Currents* (Winter 1989/99): 445–457.

Bowe, Barbara E. "John 13 and Christian Service." *The Bible Today* (July 1994): 223–227.

———. "The Birth of the Church." *The Bible Today* (September 1999): 288–293.

Branick, Vincent P., SM. *Mary, the Spirit and the Church*. New York/Mahwah, NJ: Paulist Press, 1980.

Brennan, Patrick. "Priesthood of the Faithful: Re-Imaging the Parish." Address to the Convention "Call to Action." Audio tape (November 3–5, 1995).

Brever, Jacob, ed. *Fundamentals of Judaism*. New York: Philip Fieldheim, 1969.

Britz, Andrew M., OSB. "Are We Willing to Sing Alleluia in Today's World?" *Catholic New Times* (May 9, 1999): 3.

Brown, Colin, ed. *Dictionary of New Testament Theology*. Exeter, UK: The Paternoster Press, 1976.

Brown, Raymond E., SS. *The Gospel According to John*, Volume I (I-XII). Garden City, NY: Doubleday, 1966.

———. "Roles of Women in the Fourth Gospel." *Theological Studies* (December 1975): 688–699.

———. *The Birth of the Messiah*. Garden City, NY: Doubleday, 1977.

———. *An Adult Christ at Christmas*. Collegeville, MN: The Liturgical Press, 1978.

———. *The Community of the Beloved Disciple*. New York: Paulist Press, 1979.

———. *The Gospel According to John*, Volume II (XIII-XXI). Garden City, NY: Doubleday, 1979.

———. *A Coming Christ in Advent*. Collegeville, MN: The Liturgical Press, 1988.

———. "The Annunciation to Mary, the Visitation, and the Magnificat." *Worship* (May 1988): 249–259.

———. *A Risen Christ at Eastertime*. Collegeville, MN: The Liturgical Press, 1991.

———. *A One and Coming Spirit at Pentecost*. Collegeville, MN: The Liturgical Press, 1994.

———. *The Death of the Messiah*, Vols. I and II. New York: Doubleday, 1994.

———. "The Acts of the Apostles." In *An Introduction to the New Testament*, 279–332. New York: Doubleday, 1997.

Brown, Raymond E., SS. et al., eds. *Mary in the New Testament*. Philadelphia: Fortress Press, 1978.

Bruce, F.F. "The Church of Jerusalem in the Acts of the Apostles." *Bulletin of the John Ryland University Library* (Spring 1985).

———. *The Book of Acts*. Rev. ed. Grand Rapids, MI: Eerdmans, 1998.

Buby, Bertrand, SM. "The Biblical Prayer of Mary (Luke 2:19; 51)." *Review for Religious* (1980/4): 577–581.

———. "The Commitment of Faith and Love in the Fourth Gospel." *Review for Religious* (1981/4): 561–567.

———. *Mary the Faithful Disciple*. New York/Mahwah, NJ: Paulist Press, 1985.

———. "Mary, Faithful Disciple." *Emmanuel* (May 1993): 214–221.

———. *Mary of Galilee, Volume I: Mary in the New Testament*. New York: Alba House, 1994.

———. *Mary of Galilee, Volume II: Woman of Israel, Daughter of Zion*. New York: Alba House, 1995.

———. *Mary of Galilee, Volume III: The Marian Heritage of the Early Church*. New York: Alba House, 1997.

Burton, Christie. "Christ in Ten Thousand Places." *Cistercian Studies* (2000): 113–123.

Callahan, Sidney. "Person and Gender: Quelle Différence." *Church* (Summer 1990): 5–9.

Called and Gifted for the Third Millennium. Reflection of the U.S. Catholic Bishops on the Thirtieth Anniversary of the Laity and the Fifteenth Anniversary of Called and Gifted. 1995.

Capper, Brian. "The Palestinian Context of Community of Goods." In *The Book of Acts in Its Palestinian Setting*, ed. Richard Bauckham, vol. 4, 341–350. Grand Rapids, MI: Eerdmans, 1995.

Carr, Anne. "Mary in the Mystery of the Church: Vatican Council II." In *Mary According to Women*, ed. Carol Frances Jegen, 5–29. Kansas City, MO: Leaven Press, 1985.

———. "Mary: Model of Faith." In *Mary, Woman of Nazareth*, ed. Doris Donnelly, 7–24. New York/Mahwah, NJ: Paulist Press, 1989.

Cere, Daniel. "Rouse Yourself: Newman's High Doctrine of the Laity." *The Newman Rambler* (Summer 2000): 13–32.

———. "Religion in the Market Place." *The Newman Rambler* (Winter 2000): 8–10.

———. "Priests, Prophets, and Kings: Towards a 'High' Doctrine of the Lay Vocation." *The Newman Rambler* (Winter 2001): 1–21.

Champagne, Claude. "The New Evangelization of John Paul II." *Canadian Religious Conference Bulletin* (Fall 1993): 10–11.

Chrysostom, John, St. "Homily IV, Homilies on the Acts of the Apostles." *Nicene and Post-Nicene Fathers*. Vol. II. Peabody, MA.: Hendrickson, 1994.

———. "Homily LXXIII, on Matthew 23:14." *Nicene and Post-Nicene Fathers*. Vol. X. Peabody, MA.: Hendrickson, 1994.

Clark, Rt. Rev. Alan. "The Holy Spirit and Mary." In *Mary's Place in Christian Dialogue*, ed. Alberic Stacpoole, 79–88. Wilton, CT: Morehouse-Barlow, 1982.

Cobb, John B., Jr. "Globalization with a human face." *The Christian Century* (November 3, 1999): 1054–1056.

Cohen, Harold. "Mary at Cana and on Calvary." In *Mary, the Spirit and the Church*, ed. Vincent P. Branick. New York/Mahwah: Paulist Press, 1980.

Collection of Masses of the Blessed Virgin Mary, Vols. I and II. Collegeville, MN: The Liturgical Press, 1992.

Conn, Joann Wolski. "A Discipleship of Equals: Past, Present, Future." *Horizons* 2 (1987): 231–261.

Cooke, Bernard J. "We have the power." *Religion Teacher's Journal* (April/May 1987): 28.

Craney, Titus, SA. *Is Mary Relevant? Commentary on Chapter 8 of* Lumen Gentium. New York: Exposition Press, 1970.

Crossan, John Dominic. *The Birth of Christianity*. San Francisco: Harper, 1998.

Crouzel, H., SJ. *Marie, modèle du spirituel et de l'apôtre selon Origène*. Études Mariales: Mariologie et Oecumenism. Église Orthodox: Doctrine Mariale et Influence Sur L'Occident, Paris: P. Lethielleux, 1962.

Cry of the Earth, Cry of the Poor. Document published by The Social Affairs Committee, Assemblé des Éveques du Québec (May 1, 2000).

Culliphor, Jim. "Musing from the Still Point." *Journey: Exploring Jung's Psychology for the Contemporary Christian's Pilgrimage* (Winter 1998): 2.

Cuneen, Sally. *Mother Church*. New York/Mahwah, NJ: Paulist Press, 1991.

———. *In Search of Mary*. New York: Ballantine, 1996.

Damascus, John, St. "The Ascension of Our Lord Jesus Christ." In *The Life of the Blessed Virgin, The* Theotokos, 407. Buona Vista, CA: Holy Angels Convent and Dormition Skete, 1989.

D'Angelo, Mary Rose. "'Abba' and 'Father': Imperial Theology and the Jesus Tradition." *Journal of Biblical Literature* (1992): 611–630.

Darr, Katheryn Pfisterer. *Far More Precious than Jewels: Perspectives on Biblical Women*. Louisville: Westminster/John Knox Press, 1991.

De Fiores and Salvatore Meo, eds. *Nuovo Dizionario di Mariologie*. Milan: Edizio Pauline, 1985.

De Gido, Sandra, OSM. "The Sacrament of Baptism: Celebrating the Embrace of God." *Catholic Update* Cincinnati: St. Anthony Messenger Press.

Deiss, Lucien. *Joseph, Mary, Jesus*. Collegeville, MN: The Liturgical Press, 1996.

Dewey, Joanna. "The Gospel of Mark." In *Searching the Scripture: A Feminist Commentary*, ed. Elizabeth Schüssler Fiorenza, 470–509. New York: Crossroad, 1994.

Dictionary of Mary. New York: Catholic Book, 1985.

Dillon, Richard J. "Acts of the Apostles." In *The New Jerome Biblical Commentary*, ed. Raymond E. Brown, SS, et al., 722–767. Englewood Cliffs, NJ: Prentice-Hall, 1990.

Dodd, Christine, *Called to Mission: A Workbook for the Decade of Evangelization*. Collegeville, MN: The Liturgical Press, 1991.

Donnelly, Doris, ed. *Mary, Woman of Nazareth*. New York/Mahwah, NJ: Paulist Press, 1989.

Doohan, Leonard. *Luke: The Perennial Spirituality*. Santa Fe, NM: Bear & Co., 1982.

Doyle, Denis M. "Communion Ecclesiology and the Silencing of Boff." *America* (September 12, 1992): 139–143.

———. *Communion Ecclesiology*. Maryknoll, NY: Orbis Books, 2000.

Droel, William. *Report of Business People in the Spirituality of Work*. Chicago, IL: Acta, 1991.

Droel, William and Gregory F. Augustine Pierce. "Ministry Goes to Work." *Church* (Fall 1993): 13–16.

Dubois, Marcel. "The Mother of Jesus: Reflections of a Christian Living in Israel." *The Sidic Review* (August 1987): 4–8.

Dulles, Avery, SJ. *A Church to Believe in: Discipleship and the Dynamics of Freedom*. New York: Crossroad, 1982.

———. *Models of the Church*. Rev. ed. New York: Doubleday, 1987.

———. "The Papacy for a Global Church." *America* (July 15, 2000): 6–11.

"Eckhart." In *The Wisdom of the Christian Mystics*, ed. Timothy Freake, 28. Boston: Journey Editions, 1998.

Elliott, John H. "Temple Versus Households in Luke-Acts: A Contrast in Social Institutions." In *The Social World of Luke-Acts*, ed. Jerome H. Neyrey, 2–240. Peabody, MA: Hendrickson, 1991.

Erst, Anna Marie. *Shauvot*. Chicago: The National Institute for Catholic Jewish Education.

"The Eucharist and Freedom." Document of the Pontifical Committee for International Eucharistic Congresses. *The Pope Speaks* (November 13, 1996): 97–117.

Falk, Daniel K. "Jewish Prayer and Literature in the Early Church." In *The Book of Acts in Its Palestinian Setting*, ed. Richard Bauckham, vol. 4, 267–301. Grand Rapids, MI: Eerdmans, 1995.

Ferder, Fran and John Heagle. *Partnership: Women and Men in Ministry*. Notre Dame, IN.: Ave Maria Press, 1989.

Fiensy, David A. "The Composition of the Jerusalem Church." In *The Book of Acts in Its Palestinian Setting*, ed. Richard Bauckham, vol. 4, 213–236. Grand Rapids, MI: Eerdmans, 1995.

Fiorenza, Elizabeth Schüssler. *In Memory of Her: A Feminist Theological Reconstruction of Christian Origins*. New York: Crossroad, 1985.

———. *But She Said: Feminist Practices of Biblical Interpretation*. Boston: Beacon Press, 1992.

———. "Feminist Hermeneutics." In *The Anchor Bible Dictionary*, ed. David Noel Freedman, 782–791. New York: Doubleday, 1992.

———. *Discipleship of Equals*. New York: Crossroad, 1993.

Fitzmyer, Joseph A., SJ. *Luke the Theologian: Aspects of His Teaching*. New York: Paulist Press, 1989.

Flannery, Austin P., ed. *Vatican Council II: The Conciliar and Post Conciliar Documents*. 2 vols. Grand Rapids, MI: Eerdmans, 1975 and 1984.

Gabrielle, Edward. "To Pray as Jesus Taught." *Emmanuel* (December 1996): 592–598.

Gaffney, J. Patrick, SMM. "The Presentation: Luke 2: 21-40." *The Queen* (September-October 1995): 16–17.

———. "Mary in the Gospel of John: The Marriage Feast of Cana." *The Queen* (May-June 1996): 16–17.

———. "The Mother of Jesus Was There (John 2:1)." *The Queen* (November-December 1996): 16–17.

Gager, John G. *Kingdom and Community: The Social World of Early Christianity.* Englewood Cliffs, NJ: Prentice-Hall, 1975.

Gaillardetz, Richard R. "Church as Communion: Universal and Local." *Church* (Fall 1997): 5–10.

Galilea, Segundo. *The Beatitudes: To Evangelize as Jesus Did.* Maryknoll, NY: Orbis Books, 1984.

Gaventa, Beverly Roberts. *Mary: Glimpses of the Mother of Jesus.* Columbia, SC: University of South Carolina Press, 1995.

Gebara, Ivone and M. Bingemar. *Mary: Mother of God, Mother of the Poor.* Maryknoll, NY: Orbis Books, 1989.

Graef, Hilda. *Mary: A History of Doctrine and Devotion.* 2 vols. London: Sheed and Ward, 1963 and 1965.

Granfield, Patrick, OSB. "The Concept of the Church as Communion." *Origins* (April 22, 2000): 754–758.

Grassi, J. "The Role of Jesus' Mother in John's Gospel: A Reappraisal." *CBQ* (1986): 67–80.

Green, Joel B. *The Theology of the Gospel of Luke.* New York: Cambridge University Press, 1985.

———. "The Social Status of Mary in Luke 1:5—2:52: A Plea for Methodological Integration." *Biblica* 73:4 (1992): 457–471.

Greenleaf, Robert K. *Servant Leadership: A Journey into the Nature of Legitimate Power and Greatness.* New York/Mahwah, NJ: Paulist Press, 1991.

Gubler, Marie-Louise. "Luke's Portrait of Mary." *Theology Digest* (Spring 1989): 19–24.

Hackenworth, Quentin, SM. *The Grain of Wheat: Dynamics of Spiritual Growth.* Dayton, OH: Center for Marianist Studies, 1997.

Haughton, Rosemary Luling. *Images for Change: The Transformation of Society.* Mahwah, NJ: Paulist Press, 1997.

Heft, James L., SM. "Marian Themes in the Writings of Hans Urs Von Balthasar." *Marian Studies* (1980): 45–65.

Hines, Mary E. "Mary and the Prophetic Mission of the Church." *Journal of Ecumenical Studies* (Spring 1991): 281–298.

———. "Community for Liberation." In *Freeing Theology*, ed. Catherine Mowry LaCugna, 161–184. San Francisco: Harper, 1993.

Hogan, William F. "Eucharistic Community of Disciples." *Review for Religious* (November–December 1985): 829–833.

———. "Mary and Our Reconciliation in Christ." *Review for Religious* (May–June 1987): 321–330.

Holland, Joe. "As Cultural World Turns, Spirit Is Turning Too." *National Catholic Reporter* (October 28, 1989): 10–11.

Hoppe, Leslie J., OFM. "Visitation of God." In *The Collegeville Pastoral Dictionary of Biblical Theology*, ed. Carroll Stuhlmueller, CP, 1048–1049. Collegeville, MN: The Liturgical Press, 1996.

Huffington, Ariana. *The Fourth Instinct: The Call of the Soul*. New York: Simon and Shuster, 1994.

Hultgren, Arland J. "Matthew's Infancy Narrative and the Nativity of the Emerging Community." *Horizons in Biblical Theology* (December 1997): 91–105.

Jegen, Carol Frances, BVM. "Mary, Mother of a Renewing Church." *The Bible Today* (May 1986): 153–157.

———. "Mary and the Church of the Future." In *All Generations Shall Call Me Blessed*, ed. Frances A. Eigo, 175–199. Villanova, PA: Villanova University Press, 1994.

Jeremias, Joachim. *Jerusalem in the Times of Jesus*. London: SCM Press, 1969.

John Paul II. "Offer Forgiveness, Receive Peace." *The Pope Speaks* (December 8, 1986): 169–173.

———. *Tertio Millennio Adveniente*. (Apostolic Letter as the Third Millennium Draws Near). *Origins*, 46 (November 24, 1994): 401, 403–416.

———. *Ut Unum Sint*. (That All May Be One). *Origins* 4 (June 8, 1995): 49, 5–72.

———. *The Spirit, Giver of Life and Love: A Catechesis on the Creed*. Volume III. Boston: Pauline Books and Media, 1996.

———. "Respect for Human Rights: The Secret of True Peace." *Vatican* (December 8, 1998): 1–8.

———. "God Gradually Reveals His Fatherhood." *L'osservatore Romano* (January 20, 1999): 11.

——— *Theotókos: Woman, Mother, Disciple*. Boston: Pauline Books and Media, 2000.

Johnson, Elizabeth, CSJ. "The Marian Tradition and the Reality of Women." *Horizons* 12/1 (1985): 116–135.

———. "Reconstructing a Theology of Mary." In *Mary, Woman of Nazareth*, ed. Doris Donnelly, 69–91. New York/Mahwah, NJ: Paulist Press, 1989.

———. "Toward a Theology of Mary: Past, Present, Future." In *All Generations Shall Call Me Blessed*, ed. Frances A. Eigo, 1–38. Villanova, PA: Villanova University Press, 1994.

———. "God Poured Out: Recovering the Spirit." *Praying* (May-June 1994): 4–8, 41.

———. *Consider Jesus: Waves of Renewal in Christology*. New York: Crossroad, 1995.

———. "The Maleness of Christ." In *The Power of Naming*, ed. Elizabeth Schüssler Fiorenza, 307–315. Maryknoll, NY: Orbis Books, 1996.

———. "A Community of Holy People in a Sacred World: Rethinking the Communion of Saints." *New Theology Review* (May 1999): 5–16.

Kannengieser, Charles. "Call to Conversion." *Unity*, a publication of Benedict Labre House (Spring 1993): 5–7.

Karris, Robert J., OFM. *Invitation to Luke: A Commentary on the Gospel of Luke*. Garden City, NY: Image Books, 1977.

———. "Women and Discipleship in Luke." *The Bible Today* (November 1997): 351–355.

———. "Mary's Magnificat." *The Bible Today* (May 2001): 145–149.

Kasper, Walter. *Theology and Church*. New York: Crossroad, 1989.

———. "On the Church." *The Tablet* (June 23, 2001): 927–929.

Keenan, John P. *The Gospel of Mark: A Mahayana Reading*. Maryknoll, NY: Orbis Books, 1995.

Keller, Helga Melza. "Mary Magdalene Re-Discovered." *Theology Digest* (Fall 2000): 237–243.

King, Karen L. "Canonization and Marginalization: Mary of Magdala." *Concilium* 3 (1998): 29–36.

Kittel, G. "Diakone." In *Theological Dictionary of the New Testament*. Vol. 2, 81–93. Grand Rapids, MI: Eerdmans, 1964.

Kraemer, Ross Shepard. *Her Share of the Blessings*. New York: Oxford University Press, 1992.

Küng, Hans. *That the World May Believe*. New York: Sheed and Ward, 1963.

———. *Structures of the Church*. New York: Nelson, 1964.

———. *The Church in Anguish: Has the Vatican Betrayed Vatican II?* San Francisco: Harper and Row, 1987.

———. *Refounding the Church Today*. New York: Crossroad, 1990.

Küng, Hans and Jürgen Moltman, eds. *Mary in the Churches*. New York: Seabury, 1983.

Lathman, Don. *Being Unmistakably Christian at Work*. Trowbridge, Wiltshire: The Cromwell Press, 2000.

Laurentin, René. "Mary, Model of the Charismatic as seen in Acts 1–2, Luke 1–2, John." In *Mary, The Spirit and the Church*, ed. Vincent P. Branick, SM, 28–43. New York: Paulist Press, 1980.

La Verdiere, Eugene, SSS. "His Mother Mary." *Emmanuel* (May 1987): 191–197.

———. "The Annunciation to Mary: A Story of Faith." *Emmanuel* Part I (November-December 1995); Part II: The Greeting (January-February 1996); Part IV: The Question (May 1996).

———. *The Eucharist in the New Testament and the Early Church*. Collegeville, MN: The Liturgical Press, 1996.

Leckey, Dolores. "*Christifideles Laici*: An Unfinished Four-Act Play." *Church* (Spring 1990): 11–18.

Lee, Bernard, SM. "Let the Brothers of Mary Call No Man Father." In *The Promised Woman*, ed. Lawrence J. Cada, SM, 421–435. Dayton, OH: North American Centre for Marianist Studies, 1995.

Leonard, Ellen M., CSJ. "Footwashing: A Pattern for Discipleship." Talk given at the Newman Chapel, University of Toronto (April 1, 1997): 1–15. Available from the Canadian Religious Conference, Ottawa.

Lewinski, Ron. "The Church in the New Millennium." *Modern Liturgy* (November 1997): 9–14.

Lieu, Judith M. "The Mother of the Son in the Fourth Gospel." *Journal of Biblical Literature* 117/1 (1988): 61–67.

Ludwig, Robert A. *Reconstructing Catholicism for a New Generation*. New York: Crossroad, 1995.

Malina, Bruce. *The New Testament World: Christian Origins and Cultural Anthropology*. Atlanta: John Knox Press, 1986.

———. "Mother and Son." *Biblical Theology Bulletin* (Summer 1990): 54–64.

———. *Windows on the World of Jesus*. Louisville: Westminster/John Knox Press, 1993.

———. *The Social World of Jesus of the Gospels*. London/New York: Routledge, 1996.

Malone, Mary T. "Mary, Advocate of Justice." In *All Generations Shall Call Me Blessed*, ed. Frances A. Eigo, 86–105. Villanova, PA: Villanova University Press, 1994.

Martin, Clarice J. "The Acts of the Apostles." In *Searching the Scriptures*, ed. Elizabeth Schüssler Fiorenza, 763–799. New York: Crossroad, 1994.

Martin, James. "Living a Spiritual Life in the Corporate World." *America* (July 1-8, 2000): 16–19.

Martin, Troy W. "Assessing the Johannine Epithet 'the Mother of Jesus.'" *The Catholic Biblical Quarterly* (January 1998): 63–73.

McBride, Alfred. *The Gospel of the Holy Spirit: A Commentary on the Acts of the Apostles*. New York: Hawthorne, 1975.

Meier, John P. "The Circle of the Twelve: Did It Exist during Jesus' Time?" *Journal of Biblical Literature* 116/4 (1997): 635–672.

Metz, Johanne B. *Poverty of Spirit*. New York: Paulist Press, 1968.

———. "For a Renewed Church before a New Council: A Concept in Four Theses." In *Towards Vatican III: The Work that Needs to Be Done*, eds. David Tracy with Hans Küng and Johanne B. Metz, 137–145. New York: Seabury, 1978.

Moore, Thomas. *Care of the Soul*. New York: Harper Collins, 1992.

Morgan, Vicki. "Living Out of the Centre." In *Single Women Affirming Our Spiritual Journeys*, eds. Mary O'Brien and Clare Christie, 163–173. Westport, CT: Bergin and Harvey, 1993.

Morwood, Michael. *Tomorrow's Catholic: Understanding God and Jesus in a New Millennium*. Mystic, CT: Twentythird Publications, 1997.

Moxnes, Halvor. "Patron-Client Relations and the Community in Luke-Acts." In *The Social World of Luke-Acts*, ed. Jerome H. Neyrey, 241–304. Peabody, MA: Hendrikson, 1991.

Mowery, Robert L. "From Lord to Father in Matthew 1–7." *Catholic Biblical Quarterly* (October 1997): 642–656.

Murnion, Philip J. "The Pastor and the Community of Disciples." *Momentum* (February-March 1994): 7–10.

Myss, Carolyn. *Anatomy of the Spirit*. New York: Three Rivers Press, 1996.

Nicum, Curt. "A Note on Acts 1:14." *Novum Testamentum* (April 1994): 196–199.

Nolan, Albert. *Jesus before Christianity*. Maryknoll, NY: Orbis Books, 1978.

Nolan, Mary Kay, OP. "The Magnificat, Canticle of a Liberated People: A Hermeneutical Study of Luke 1:46-55, Investigating the World behind the Text by Interpretive Inquiry." Doctoral dissertation presented at the IMRI (Pontifical Theological Faculty Marianum), 1995.

———. *Mary's Song: Living Her Timeless Prayer*. Notre Dame, IN: Ave Maria Press, 2001.

Nowell, Irene, OSB. "The Coming of the Spirit in the Book of Joel." *The Bible Today* (March 1989): 87–92.

———. *Women in the Old Testament*. Collegeville, MN: The Liturgical Press, 1997.

O'Collins, Gerald. *The Second Journey: Spiritual Awareness and the Mid-Life Crisis*. New York: Paulist Press, 1978.

O'Connor, Jerome Murphy, OP. "Eucharist and Community in First Corinthians." *Worship*, Part I (September 1976): 370–385; Part II (January 1977): 56–59.

————."The Cenacle and Community: The Background of Acts." In *Scripture and Other Artifacts: Essays on the Bible and Archeology in Honor of Philip J. King*, eds. Michael D. Coogan et al., 296–310. Westminster: John Knox Press, 1994.

————."The Cenacle: Topographical Setting for Acts 2:44-45." In *The Book of Acts in Its Palestinian Setting*, ed. Richard Bauckham, 303–321. Grand Rapids, MI: Eerdmans, 1995.

O'Day, Gail."Acts." In *The Women's Bible Commentary*, eds. Carol A. Newsom and Sharon H. Ringe, 305–312. Westminster: John Knox Press, 1992.

O'Meara, Thomas, OP. *Theology of Ministry*. Mahwah, NJ: Paulist Press, 1999.

O'Murchu, Diarmid. *Religion in Exile*. New York: Crossroad, 2000.

O'Neill, Aquin. "The Mystery of Being Human Together." In *Freeing Theology*, ed. Catherine Mowry LaCugna, 139–160. San Francisco: Harper, 1993.

Orsy, Ladislas. "New Era of Participation in Church Life." *Origins* (April 28, 1988): 796–800.

————."Lay Persons in Church Governance: A Disputed Question." *America* (April 6, 1996): 10–13.

————. "The Papacy for an Ecumenical Age: A Response to Avery Dulles." *America* (October 21, 2000): 9-15.

Osiek, Carolyn, RSCJ."Women in the Church." *The Bible Today* (July 1994): 228–233.

————. "Bible Terms Today: *The Way* (Odos); *Sect* (Hairesis); *Christian* (Christianoi)." *The Bible Today* (March 1996): 72–76.

Pagels, Elaine. *The Gnostic Gospels*. New York: Vintage, 1981.

Palmer, Darryl W. "The Literary Background of Acts 1:1-44." *New Testament Studies* 3 (1987): 427–435.

Paul VI. General Audience, November 21, 1964. *AAS* 56 (1964): 1015.

de la Potterie, Ignace, SJ. *Mary in the Mystery of the Covenant*, trans. Bertrand Buby, SM. New York: Alba House, 1992.

Pottmeyer, Hermann J. "Primacy in Communion." *America* (June 3-10, 2000): 15–18.

Prévost, Jean-Pierre. *Mother of Jesus*. Ottawa: Novalis, 1988.

Primeau, Patrick, SM. "Marian Community and Ministry." *Review for Religious* (July-August 1992): 601–603.

Provencher, Norman, OMI. *Jesus of Nazareth*. Ottawa: Novalis, 1997.

Race, Marianne and Laurie Brink. *In This Place: Reflections on the Land of the Gospels for the Liturgical Cycles*. Collegeville, MN: The Liturgical Press, 1998.

Rahner, Karl and Wilhelm Thüsing. *A New Christology*. New York: Seabury, 1980.

Reid, Barbara E. *Choosing the Better Part: Women in the Gospel of Luke.* Collegeville, MN: The Liturgical Press, 1996.

Reif, Stefan. *Judaism and Hebrew Prayer: New Perspectives on Jewish Liturgical History.* New York: Cambridge University Press, 1993.

Reimes, Ivone Richter. *Women in the Acts of the Apostles, A Feminist Liberation Perspective.* Minneapolis: Fortress Press, 1995.

Reinhardt, Wolfgang. "The Population Size of Jerusalem and the Numerical Growth of the Jerusalem Church." In *The Book of Acts in Its Palestinian Setting*, ed. Richard Bauckham, 237–265. Grand Rapids, MI: Eerdmans, 1995.

Richard, Lucien, OMI. "On Evangelization, Culture, and Spirituality: A Post-Vatican II Perspective." *The Catholic World* (March/April 1991): 61–66.

Richardson, Herbert. "Mother of the Church." *The Current* 5 (1965): 48–61.

Ricci, Carla. *Mary Magdalene and Many Others.* Minneapolis: Fortress Press, 1994.

Riley, Maria, OP. "All Issues Are Women's Issues." *Scarboro Mission* (January 1996): 4–8.

———. "Solidarity: A Spirituality for Our Times." *Center Focus* (November 1999): 4, 5.

Roten, Johann G., SM. "Memory and Mission: A Theological Reflection on Mary in the Paschal Mysteries." *Marian Studies* XLII (1991): 73–132.

———. "Re-Reading in Marianist Spirituality." In *The Promised Woman*, ed. Lawrence J. Cada, SM, 461–483. Dayton, OH: North American Centre for Marianist Studies, 1995.

———. The "Merciless" Magnificat. *The Mary Page*, Meditations. www.udayton.edu/mary/meditations.

Ruether, Rosemary Radford. Mary: *The Feminine Face of the Church.* Philadelphia, PA: The Westminster Press, 1977.

———. *Sexism and God-Talk: Toward a Feminist Theology.* Boston: Beacon Press, 1983.

Ryan, Claude. "Christians in Public Life." *The Newman Rambler* (Winter 2001): 23–1.

Sala, Dimitri. "Releasing the Power of the Spirit." *Emmanuel* (October 1999): 460–471.

Saldarni, Anthony J. *Matthew's Christian-Jewish Community.* Chicago: The University of Chicago Press, 1994.

Samaha, John, SM. "Mary's Priestly Dimension." *The Month* (May 2000): 184–189.

Schaberg, Jane. "Luke." In *The Women's Bible Commentary*, eds. Carol A. Newsom and Sharon H. Ringe, 275–292. Westminster: John Knox Press, 1992.

Schaeffer, Janet, OP. "Called to Discipleship: Sacraments Are about Sending Us Forth." *The Catechist* (January 1999): 32–34.

Schillebeecks, Edward and Catherine Halkes. *Mary: Yesterday, Today and Tomorrow.* New York: Crossroad, 1993.

Schmidt, Alvin J. *Veiled and Silenced: How Culture Shaped Sexist Theology.* Macon, GA: Mercer University Press, 1989.

Schneiders, Sandra M., IHM. "The Foot Washing (John 13:1-20): An Experiment in Hermeneutics." *Catholic Biblical Quarterly* 43 (1981): 76–92.

———. "Women in the Fourth Gospel and the Role of Women in the Contemporary Church." *Biblical Theology Bulletin* (April 1982): 35–45.

Schwahn, Barbara. "Towards an Ecumenical Theology of the People of God." In *A Letter from Christ to the World: An Exploration of the Role of the Laity in the Church Today,* ed. Nicholas Apostola, 47–57. Geneva: WCC Publications, 1998.

Schwartz, Werner. "Baptism, Ecclesiology and Vocation." In *A Letter from Christ to the World: An Exploration of the Role of the Laity in the Church Today,* ed. Nicholas Apostola, 85–97. Geneva: WCC Publications, 1998.

Senior, Donald, CP. "New Testament Images of Mary." *The Bible Today* (May 1986): 143–152.

Senior, Donald, CP and Carol Stuhlmeuller. *The Biblical Foundations for Mission.* Maryknoll, NY: Orbis Books, 1983.

Shea, John. "Giving Birth to Christ." *Church* (Winter 1990): 5–10.

———. "The Process of Adult Conversion." *Grounding Spirituality in Sacrament, Community and Scripture.* Tape II. Audio Retreat, Chicago, IL: Acta, 1998.

Sheehy, Gail. *Passages: Predictable Crises of Adult Life.* New York: Dalton, 1976.

———. *New Passages: Mapping Your Life across Time.* New York: Random House, 1995.

Spears, Larry C. "Creating Caring Leadership for the 21st Century." *The Not-For-Profit CEO* (July 1998): 1–3.

Stuhlmueller, Carroll, CP, ed. *The Collegeville Pastoral Dictionary of Biblical Theology.* Collegeville, MN: The Liturgical Press, 1991.

Suenens, Leon Josef Cardinal. "The Relations that Exists between the Holy Spirit and Mary." In *Mary's Place in Christian Dialogue,* ed. Alberic Stacpoole, OSB, 69–78. Connecticut: Morehouse-Barlow, 1982.

Sweetland, Dennis M. "Following Jesus: Discipleship in Luke-Acts." In *New View on Luke-Acts,* ed. Carl Richard, 109–114. Collegeville, MN: The Liturgical Press, 1990.

Sweetster, Thomas P., SJ. "A Parish for Tomorrow." *Human Development* (Spring 2001): 25–29.

Tataryn, Myroslaw. "The Holy Spirit in the Eastern Christian Tradition." *The Canadian Catholic Review* (December 1998): 32–39.

Tetlow, Elizabeth M. *Women and Ministry in the New Testament: The Status of Women in Greek, Roman and Jewish Society.* New York/Ramsey: Paulist Press, 1980.

Thompson, Clare. "Mary: The True Disciple." *Ecumenism* (September 1987): 31–33.

Thurian, Max. *Mary: Mother of the Lord, Figure of the Church.* London: The Faith Press, 1963.

Thurston, Anne. *Knowing Her Place.* New York/Mahwah, NJ: Paulist Press, 1998.

Tillard, Jean-Marie, OP. "Recognition of Ministries: What Is the Real Question?" *One in Christ* (1985): 31–39.

———. *Je crois en dépit de tout.* Paris: Les Éditions du Cerf, 2001.

Trainor, Michael, ed. *St. Matthew: A Gospel for Searching People.* Ottawa: Novalis, 1994.

Valone, Carolyn. "The Pentecost Image and Experience in Late Sixteenth-Century Rome." *Sixteenth Century Journal* XXIV/4 (1993): 801–827.

Van der Horst, Peter. "Hellenistic Parallels to the Acts of the Apostles 2:1–47." *Journal for the Study of the New Testament* 25 (1985): 49–60.

Vanier, Jean. *Community and Growth: Our Pilgrimage Together.* Toronto: Griffin House, 1979.

Voss, Gerhard. "Marian Spirituality: Reactions to *Redemptoris Mater.*" *Theology Digest* (Spring 1988): 14–15.

Wainwright, Elaine M. *Shall We Look for Another? A Feminist Reading of the Matthean Jesus.* Maryknoll, NY: Orbis Books, 1998.

Warren, Michael. "Speaking and Learning in the Local Church: A Look at the Material Conditions." *Worship* (January 1995): 28–50.

Welker, Michael. *God the Spirit.* Minneapolis: Fortress Press, 1994.

Wijngaards, John. "The Priesthood of Mary." *The Tablet* (December 1999): 1638–1640.

Wilkinson, John. *Egeria's Travels.* Newly translated with supporting documents and notes. London: SPCK, 1971.

———. *Jerusalem as Jesus Knew It: Archaeology as Evidence.* London: Thames and Hudson, 1978.

Williams, Ritva H. "The Mother of Jesus at Cana. A Social-Science Interpretation of John 2:1–12." *The Catholic Biblical Quarterly* 59 (1997): 679–692.

Wilmes, Hedwig Meyer. "The Diversity of Ministries in a Post-Modern Church." In *The Non-Ordination of Women and the Politics of Power,* eds. Elizabeth Schüssler Fiorenza and Hermann Häring, 69–85. Maryknoll, NY: Orbis Books, 1999.

Wilson, George, SJ. "Authority with Credibility." *Human Development* (Winter 1991): 25–30.

Winter, Miriam Therese, MMS. "Buried Treasures: Rediscovering Women's Roles in the Bible." *US Catholic* (June 1993): 6–13.

Witherington, Ben. "The Anti-Feminist Tendencies in the Western Text of the New Testament." *Journal of Biblical Literature* (March 1984): 82–84.

Wohlmann, Avital. "Mary of Nazareth: Why the Silence of Judaism?" *The Sidic Review* 2 (1987): 9–14.

Wordleman, Amy L. "Everyday Life: Women in the Period of the New Testament." In *The Woman's Bible Commentary*, eds. Carol A. Newsom and Sharon H. Ringe, 390–396. Westminster: John Knox Press, 1992.

Young, David S. *Servant Leadership for Church Renewal*. Scottdale, PA: Herald Press, 1999.

Zehnle, R. F. *Peter's Pentecost Discourse: Acts 2 and 3*. Nashville: Abingdon, 1971.